CONTEMPORARY MEGAPROJECTS

Contemporary Megaprojects

Organization, Vision, and
Resistance in the 21st Century

Edited by
Seth Schindler, Simin Fadaee
and Dan Brockington

berghahn
NEW YORK · OXFORD
www.berghahnbooks.com

Published in 2021 by
Berghahn Books
www.berghahnbooks.com

© 2021 Berghahn Books

Originally published as a special issue of *Environment & Society*:
Volume 10, issue 1 (2019)

Library of Congress Cataloging-in-Publication Data

Names: Schindler, Seth, editor. | Fadaee, Simin, editor. | Brockington, Dan, editor.
Title: Contemporary megaprojects : organization, vision, and resistance in the
21st century / edited by Seth Schindler, Simin Fadaee and Dan Brockington.
Other titles: Environment and society.
Description: New York : Berghahn Books, 2021. | "Originally published as a
special issue of Environment & society: volume 10, issue 1 (2019)"—Verso. |
Includes bibliographical references and index.
Identifiers: LCCN 2021006685 | ISBN 9781800731516 (hardback) | ISBN
9781800731523 (paperback) | ISBN 9781800731530 (ebook)
Subjects: LCSH: Project management—Social aspects. | Engineering—
Management—Social aspects. | Economic development projects.
Classification: LCC HD69.P75 C6475 2021 | DDC 658.4/04—dc23
LC record available at https://lccn.loc.gov/2021006685

British Library Cataloguing in Publication Data

A catalogue record for this book is available from the British Library

ISBN 978-1-80073-151-6 hardback
ISBN 978-1-80073-152-3 paperback
ISBN 978-1-80073-153-0 ebook

Contents

Illustrations, Tables, and Figures

---■---

Illustrations

Tables

Figures

INTRODUCTION

Contemporary Megaprojects
An Introduction

Seth Schindler, Simin Fadaee, and Dan Brockington

The Chinese Government announced the Belt and Road Initiative in 2013, and since then, more than 130 countries have embraced its vision of a Sinocentric expansion of global production and trade networks. Chinese President Xi Jinping highlighted the Belt and Road Initiative's unprecedented scale and scope when he hailed it as the "project of the century" (Dunford and Liu 2019). The Belt and Road Initiative is a mega megaproject—a meta mega project if you will—combining multiple initiatives that are emblematic of contemporary megaprojects. It strikes a chord with other massive-scale infrastructure initiatives geared toward continental integration such as the Greater Mekong Subregion, the Lamu Port–South Sudan–Ethiopia Transport Corridor, and the Initiative for the Integration of the Regional Infrastructure of South America.

The chapters in this volume suggest megaprojects are once again on the political agenda but this renewed enthusiasm for megaprojects is not simply a rehash of high-modernist planning. In contrast to their mid-20th century counterparts, contemporary megaprojects are often decentralized and pursued by a range of stakeholders who leverage cutting-edge technology to 'see' complex systems as legible and singular phenomena. They are unprecedented in their ambition and they have the potential to reconfigure long-standing relationships that have animated social and ecological systems. The chapters in this volume explore the novel features of contemporary megaprojects, show how the proponents of contemporary megaprojects aspire to technologically enabled omnipresence, and document the resistance that megaprojects have provoked.

Contemporary megaprojects are not necessarily large-scale infrastructure developments comprised of brick and mortar. The cover image was taken in 2010 in Laos, and the barren vista that extends to the horizon presages the construction of what Miles Kenney-Lazar and Noboru Ishikawa (chapter four) refer to as a "mega-plantation." The production of mega-plantations across Southeast Asia is decentralized, yet the constituent components cohere into the regional proliferation of monoculture agro-industrial landscapes. The emptiness of this landscape is jarring, absent of infrastructure save a single road that stretches into an unending vista that appears devoid of life. Yet it is this emptiness which denotes the complete reworking of this place. The decentralized pursuit of the transformation of this landscape fundamentally alters long-standing ecologies, biodiversity, and social relations and it is an order of magnitude greater than earlier modes of plantation and industrial agriculture. It constitutes an "operational landscape" (Brenner and Katsikis 2020) whose integration with global value chains necessitates the production and standardization of expansive territories (Schindler and Kanai 2019; Mezzadra and Neilson 2019; Arboleda 2020).

The decentralized nature of many contemporary megaprojects also separates them from high modernist schemes that imbued states and planners with omnipotence to "see" and manipulate their environments (Scott 1998). The centralized nature of planning in the postwar era imposed limits on what could be envisioned and undertaken. Indeed, the ambition of planners was blunted by their inability to exercise power on the ground, and/or fiscal and political constraints imposed by central government authorities. With the neoliberal turn in the 1980s, planners were disempowered, and in many countries, the envisioning of megaprojects was limited to those that could at least be partially funded by the private sector. Contemporary megaprojects are often envisioned or encouraged by states whose assertiveness has been reaffirmed, but a host of non-state actors play an integral role in their realization. This diffused authority, action, and responsibility allows for (1) projects of unprecedented scale and scope to be envisioned and undertaken, and (2) entirely new ways of "seeing" territory and populations.

Given that the scope, complexity, and organization of megaprojects have changed, it is helpful to distinguish axes of difference. We identify three, two of which are shown in Figure 0.1.

The horizontal axis captures the fact that megaprojects are not just things that change landscapes and infrastructure. They cannot only be measured in tons of concrete or earth moved. Megaprojects are imagined before they come to exist—and many only exist as figments of imagination, or as fragments of larger visions. And yet the prospect of a megaproject can have material effects for decades. As projects progress, they may move further to the left of the axis. They become more material—but not always. Some aspirational projects (space exploration and the colonization of Mars) will be animated by grandiose ambitions by necessity, whatever their realization. Other projects, because they are more decentralized (again, mega-plantations are a good example), are less imagined and unfold incrementally in real time.

The vertical axis captures the extent to which particular projects are centrally organized or diffusely planned. Megaprojects have traditionally been understood as singular discrete undertakings distinguished by their cost and complexity. It is only for that reason that they can so often be delayed and go over budget (Flyvbjerg 2014). But these days, with so many participants, there may not be a single timetable, or indeed a single budget to exceed. In this volume, we include decentralized projects purposefully undertaken by a myriad of actors, sometimes with little or no coordination, whose influence is cumulative and has the potential to fundamentally transform longstanding relationships that have animated social and ecological systems. To return to the mega-plantation example, the actors involved pursue a shared set of objectives and employ a singular body of expertise.

Figure 0.1. Axes of Difference in Contemporary Megaprojects

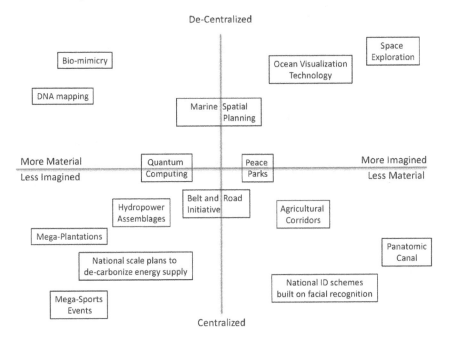

Their myriad and quotidian actions result in the regularization of agro-industrial production whose far-reaching impacts and the expansiveness of its landscapes constitute a megaproject despite the absence of centralized coordination. Note that some large diffuse projects, such as mapping the human genome, which was a large-scale exercise undertaken across many different units, can look more centralized and controlled as we zoom in on particular parts of the enterprise. Furthermore, the extent of centralized control is not fixed and can change over time.

Taken together, these axes allowed us to map the megaprojects referred to in this collection, as well as others with which we are familiar. Admittedly, plotting this chart required a considerable amount of subjectivity and the precise location of particular megaprojects is indeed debatable. The chart nevertheless demonstrates the fact that the nature of megaprojects has changed. The bottom left-hand corner—material changes brought about by central planning—has typically been the space for megaprojects, but contemporary megaprojects are more pervasive, ambitious, and decentralized than their antecedents. We encourage the reader to consider diffuse imagined projects that fall into the upper-right quadrant, which, even if they are never realized, may transform our societies and environments.

The final axis, not shown on this graph, is that of scale. Megaprojects can vary from the molecular (quantum computing, CERN) to the planetary and beyond (space exploration). They can cover vast areas and be concerned with the smallest entities. The point here is that "mega" can mean vast in scope in traditional human terms, as well as intensely intimate and intricate. The common denominator to both is that they have transformative potential and will still absorb hundreds of millions of dollars and many years of labor time. We have not portrayed scale in this diagram as it would become hard to read, but it is easy to envisage it forming a third axis.

The chapters focus on particular megaprojects, and we have organized them in a way that juxtaposes various types and highlights their variegated nature. We begin with the imaginative. Ashley Carse and David Kneas's premise is that many megaprojects do not actually happen. In many cases they never break ground; or, if they do, construction may be stalled or never completed. And yet, the authors demonstrate that these projects are significant, and can reshape politics, landscapes and social experiences. Nevertheless, Carse and Kneas contend that academics have insufficiently incorporated the unbuilt and imagined into their theories of why and how infrastructure matters. They suggest a crucial way of understanding incomplete megaprojects is through "timescapes" (following Bear), in which different understandings and experiences of time coalesce into "time-knots" (following Chakrabarty). The authors offer a series of heuristic devices with which to examine the time-knots of unbuilt and unfinished infrastructures: "shadow histories, present absence, suspended presents, nostalgic futures, and zombies." "Shadow histories"—the histories of things that did not happen, such as the Trans-Saharan Railway, the Panatomic Canal (to have been constructed by detonating two hundred large nuclear warheads), or Atlantropa (the project to dam, and drain, the Mediterranean Sea)—offer insights into the contingencies of the present. "Nostalgic futures" point to the remembered promises and aspirations that once accompanied a project. "Present absence" refers to the consequences of failed, incomplete, or withdrawn projects. "Suspended presents" capture the transformations of daily life associated with experiences of delay, from hope to disillusionment. The Kaeng Suea Ten Dam in Thailand, for example, has threatened the eviction of communities for nearly four decades, yet it remains a vision. The "zombie" heuristic, on the other hand, draws attention to putative projects that, while never quite suspending daily life by their imminence, also never quite go away.

The subsequent chapter moves across the framework to focus on decentralized megaproject whose objectives are increasingly realized. Veronica Davidov shows how biomimicry serves as an inspirational source for the optimization of technologies such as robotics and industrial design. Nature is thus constructed as an abundant mega-resource. However, biomimicry as an "epistemic object" does not entail a homogenous field. Rather, it coheres in a variety of ways in different disciplines. For example, it can be regarded as a philosophical object, it can be debated ethically, or it can be understood as a design praxis and method. Moreover, there are several practices—such as particular strands of geo-engineering and the practice of trophic rewilding—that might not officially be categorized as biomimetic but would fall within the scope of biomimicry and should be explored within the field to underline its potentials and implications. Davidov suggests the most fruitful way of engaging with biomimicry is to situate it within broader social, political, and economic contexts in order to understand its epistemic and economic merits and the challenges it poses. Multiple ethnographies of biomimetic projects would enable such critical encounter.

Mega sporting events have long been touted as transformative and John Lauermann shows how they have become increasingly contested and controversial. There is a growing cleavage between the proponents and opponents of these events. Claims made by proponents of mega-events that emphasize their long-term benefits are increasingly met by skepticism and protests. Lauermann traces and compares the scholarly literature on these two fronts of urban politics. Advocates of these mega-events argue that after a few weeks of elite use of urban space, the infrastructure can be used by ordinary residents, or they emphasize the potential of these projects beyond obvious goals such as the possibility of influencing other institutional platforms or programs. However, as Lauermann demonstrates, the recent surge of protests and resistance against these events challenges this narrative. These mobilizations are temporary political campaigns, referred to as "fast activism," and have been increasingly successful in forcing cities to cancel bids.

The emergence and development of monoculture agro-industrial plantations across Southeast Asia is the subject of chapter four. Kenney-Lazar and Ishikawa demonstrate how these projects have led to displacement and replacement of human and nonhuman communities. Although the ideological driver of these projects dates back to the colonial period, they explore the more recent emergence and origins of "mega-plantations." The proliferation of mega-plantations has led to widespread displacement and dispossession, and they have been accompanied by far-reaching environmental impacts such as deforestation, forest fires, and air pollution. Despite diversification of political strategies and increased numbers of strikes, protests, and multiple forms of everyday resistance by different groups of people, the expansion of land incorporated into mega-plantation continues for the foreseeable future.

We switch from mega-plantations to another type of operational landscape in chapter five, in which Serena Stein and Marc Kalina interrogate agricultural growth corridors. They are meant to foster rural development in the Global South, and the authors show how they are imagined and experienced on an everyday basis. Many "corridors" are rooted in colonial history and developmental trajectories of the mid-twentieth century, yet they have proliferated across the Global South in the past decade. These megaprojects combine infrastructure investment with agribusiness across borders and regions and mostly emerged in Africa after the 2008 crisis of food, fuel, and finance. Their proponents anticipate that through the integration of smallholder farmers to national, regional, and international production networks, these corridors reduce poverty and provide food security. However, as research has shown, they disrupt smallholder farmers' operations and their access to food. They also inhibit access to shared resources such as water and land. Hence, these projects have been fiercely contested by various civil society groups and social movements. The authors encourage future research to attend to processes of becoming and the ways people experience them on the ground.

Hydropower projects should be understood instead as global assemblages with specific relations to networks of power rather than a singular infrastructure project according to Grant Gutierrez, Sarah Kelly, Joshua Cousins and Christopher Sneddon. They suggest understanding different forms of engagement and the significance ascribed to hydropower projects by various actors is a more meaningful way of understanding these projects. For most of their history, large hydropower projects have been embedded in hegemonic modernist and nationalist projects and were considered one of the most important pathways to modernization. However, their long-term negative social and ecological impacts provoked contestation and conflict locally and transnationally. These movements set the stage for the emergence of one of the first grassroots ecological movements in the Global South, and an alliance of transnational anti-dam groups have recently popularized the slogan "water is life" to emphasize the interlinkage between water and power. In its latest phase, small and decentralized hydropower projects are initiated in the name of support for renewable energy, greenhouse gas emissions, and economic development despite opposition of scientists and activists.

The expansion of hydropower capacity is not the only megaproject in the field of water management and governance. Luke Fairbanks, Noëlle Boucquey, Lisa Campbell, and Sarah Wise show how new marine spatial planning (MSP) projects are being implemented with the intention of governing and regulating oceans worldwide. MSP focuses on combining and managing traditionally disconnected individual sectors such as fishing and shipping through an overarching system of governance. The authors highlight four key elements of MSP: planning discourse, ocean economies, online data, and new networks of ocean actors. The integration of multiple sectors across these four fields purportedly contributes to socioecological harmony and broader goals of sustainable development. The authors question these claims through an analysis of one MSP initiative in the United

States and they urge researchers to apply relational theory and political ecology in future analyses that examine the implications of MSP megaprojects.

As noted above, the aspiration to "see" everything in an expansive totalizing vision is not new, but technological advancements are changing and expanding the field of "vision." Stephanie Ratté narrates the novel ways in which a range of actors are leveraging cutting-edge technology to render oceans knowable and measurable. She shows this is a highly decentralized project undertaken by actors whose objectives are occasionally in conflict. For example, the transformation of oceans from a vast unknown wilderness to a legible and catalogued space is a goal pursued by those hoping to exploit this frontier's resources, as well as by conservationists. Ratté argues that one consequence of transforming this unknown frontier into a singular topographical space is that humans—and their impacts on maritime ecosystems—are obscured.

The book moves from oceanic depths to the final frontier in the last chapter. Micha Rahder focuses on imaginaries of outer space, which fuel renewed interest in space exploration. Fears of environmental and sociopolitical catastrophes have, in recent decades, informed two interconnected imaginaries. The first, which this chapter refers to as Earth 2.0, envisions an improved human future, while ecocentric imaginaries decenter humans as the prime agents of change. They go beyond human timescales and focus on evolutionary ecologies that defy human exceptionalism and their mastery on/of the planet. According to Rahder, Earth 2.0 motivates investments, focuses on the present and, in most cases, ignores the inherent inequalities linked with such an imaginary. In contrast, eco-centric imaginaries focus on interrelations and commonalities and do not aim at reasserting domination or control on Earth. The author suggests both approaches should become more sensitive to politics related to the particularity of their imaginaries.

When taken together, the chapters demonstrate several trends. First, contemporary megaprojects are bankrolled by new sources of finance. We began this introduction with a discussion of the Belt and Road Initiative, and China is one emergent source of megaproject finance. After the 2008 financial crisis, China "combined huge government spending with a spectacular loosening of monetary policy" and "for the first time in the modern era, it was the movement of the Chinese economy that carried the world economy" (Tooze 2018: 249, 251). The US Department of the Treasury embarked on an equally deliberate fiscal stimulus package meant to calm investors and bolster markets. The result has been a decade of cheap capital that has often been funneled into megaprojects.

While capital may become more expensive in the future, there seems to be a durable appetite for megaprojects among a diverse group of financiers and investors. There are hard economic drivers behind this trend. As Sarah Bracking (2016) has argued, megaprojects provide a means by which the "great predators" of capitalism extract huge revenues from states. These they derive both from the construction of things and from the contracts to run and maintain them, which provide revenue streams that can then be financialized. As Ashwin Desai (2016) put it (writing of the World Cup in South Africa): "Global finance capital . . . thrives in a world of large-scale investment in mega-projects, mega-events, and the short-term investment, long-term debt, and creative financing associated with them" (cited in Bracking 2016: 94). The economic gains fuel the establishment of a social field in which megaprojects are highly valued. Just as high modernism had its priests and practitioners who operated in a rather rarefied and insular field, megaproject planning is validated within an emergent social field animated by global networks of professionals who contribute to the production of a body of knowledge and activate finance for undertakings that can only be described with superlatives.

All this is contested, and resistance to megaprojects takes many forms. The most obvious example is the collective resistance against the construction or intervention of a particular megaproject, but this is difficult when megaprojects are diffuse. Quite simply, villagers in Laos may block a single mega-plantation, but they are unlikely to hold back the unrelenting tide of agro-industrial production that threatens to sweep away everything before it. Thus, another form of resistance that is less visible but just as important is the undermining of the epistemic justification for the constituent components of decentralized megaprojects. Alternatively, opponents of megaprojects may undermine megaprojects by embracing the discourse and modes of analysis employed by their proponents. Although all types of resistance come with risks and trade-offs such as community disempowerment and creation of social divisions; continuous resistance over time can lead to formation of long-lasting networks of people affected by these projects

Finally, the articles in this collection raise a series of questions that can be taken up in future research on megaprojects. First, what are the objects upon which proponents of megaproject seek to act? While social engineering was typically among the objectives of high modernist projects, it has not been emphasized by the articles in this volume. That is not to say people are not impacted by megaprojects. Rather, the "improvement" of "deviant" or "abnormal" target populations (Li 2007) is not an explicit goal of megaproject proponents. Instead, megaprojects seem to target scales and places that are far removed from everyday life, such as the molecular and the seabed. The transformation of territory seems to be an overriding priority of many contemporary megaprojects, one result of which, according to their proponents, is the improvement of the well-being of local residents. To take Stein and Kalina's analysis of growth corridors as an example, they are not meant to act directly on target populations; rather, local farmers will supposedly benefit, as transportation infrastructure will afford them improved access to markets. Thus, the megaproject provides peasants with the opportunity to act entrepreneurially, but there is no attempt to act on them directly and transform them into entrepreneurs. Ultimately, contemporary megaprojects make individuals responsible for their own "improvement."

Second, how do the diffused networks of actors that undertake megaprojects "see" the spaces, people, and landscapes upon which they act? One theme that emerged in this volume was the recent technological advancements to seeing people and things as data. The codification of vast amounts of information into ones and zeros can itself be a megaproject, and at other times, it enables megaprojects. Just as Shoshana Zuboff (2015) argued that the aggregation of a vast amount of data has allowed for human experience to be reduced to more measurable behavior, technological advancements in a range of fields allow for entirely new modes of grappling with what Timothy Morton (2013) refers to as 'hyperobjects'. The contributions in this volume demonstrate that a host of actors are applying recently developed technologies in attempts to render legible the incomprehensible vastness of oceans and outer space. Thus, there is a desire to smash epistemological as well as ontological boundaries, which may indeed be a fundamental human trait, but contemporary ways of seeing and knowing are driven by aspirations of technologically enabled omnipresence.

Will contemporary megaprojects totalize experience and catalogue all existing relationships among people and things? It seems inevitable that certain places, people, and things will be excluded. How will people remain illegible, and will this be though their own volition? And how do these modes of seeing and knowing activate new relationships and behavior? These are the questions that are raised by the chapters in this volume.

SETH SCHINDLER is Senior Lecturer in Urban Development and Transformation in the Global Development Institute at the University of Manchester. He previously coordinated the MA in Global Studies at Humboldt University of Berlin. His research is focused on deindustrialization in developing countries and large-scale urban transformation initiatives that integrate cities intro transnational urban systems.

SIMIN FADAEE is Senior Lecturer in Sociology at the University of Manchester. Her research focuses broadly on issues of political sociology, social movements and activism, environmentalism and environmental politics. She is the author of *Social Movements in Iran: Environmentalism and Civil Society* (Routledge 2012) and the editor of *Understanding Southern Social Movements* (Routledge 2016). She is a co-editor of the journal *Sociology* and serves as a board member of the Research Committee on Social Classes and Social Movements (RC47) of the International Sociological Association (ISA).

DAN BROCKINGTON is Professor of Development Studies and co-director of the Sheffield Institute of International Development at the University of Sheffield. His research covers the social impacts of conservation policy, natural resource management, the relationships between capitalism and conservation, media and celebrity in development, large N studies of NGO networks, irrigation development, development data and long term livelihood change in East Africa. His books include *Fortress Conservation, Nature Unbound* (with Rosaleen Duffy and Jim Igoe), *Celebrity Advocacy and International Development, Celebrity and the Environment*, and he has recently published (with Peter Billie Larson) *The Anthropology of Conservation NGOs*.

REFERENCES

Arboleda, Martín. 2020. *Planetary Mine: Territories of Extraction under Late Capitalism*. London: Verso.

Bracking, Sarah. 2016. *The Financialisation of Power: How Financiers Rule Africa*. London: Routledge.

Brenner, Neil, and Nikos Katsikis. 2020. "Operational Landscapes: Hinterlands of the Capitalocene." *Architectural Design* 90 (1): 22-31.

Desai, Ashwin. 2016. "Between Madiba Magic and Spectacular Capitalism: The FIFA World Cup in South Africa." In *Mega-Events and Globalization: Capital and Spectacle in a Changing World Order*, ed. Richard Gruneau and John Horne, 81–94. London: Routledge.

Dunford, Michael, and Weidong Liu. 2019. "Chinese Perspectives on the Belt and Road Initiative." *Cambridge Journal of Regions, Economy and Society* 12 (1): 145–167.

Flyvbjerg, Bent. 2014. "What You Should Know about Megaprojects and Why: An Overview." *Project Management Journal* 45 (2): 6–19.

Li, Tania M. 2007. *The Will to Improve: Governmentality, Development, and the Practice of Politics*. Durham, NC: Duke University Press.

Mezzadra, Sandro and Brett Neilson. 2019. *The Politics of Operations: Excavating Contemporary Capitalism*. Durham: Duke University Press.

Morton, Timothy. 2013. *Hyperobjects: Philosophy and Ecology after the End of the World*. Minneapolis: University of Minnesota Press.

Schindler, Seth and J. Miguel Kanai. 2019. "Getting the Territory Right: Infrastructure-Led Development and the Re-Emergence of Spatial Planning Strategies." *Regional Studies*. Early View: https://doi.org/10.1080/00343404.2019.1661984

Scott, James C. 1998. *Seeing Like a State: How Certain Schemes to Improve the Human Condition Have Failed*. New Haven, CT: Yale University Press.

Tooze, Adam. 2018. *Crashed: How a Decade of Financial Crises Changed the World*. London: Allen Lane.

Zuboff, Shoshana. 2015. "Big Other: Surveillance Capitalism and the Prospects of an Information Civilization." *Journal of Information Technology* 30: 75–89.

CHAPTER 1

Unbuilt and Unfinished
The Temporalities of Infrastructure

Ashley Carse and David Kneas

The study of infrastructure can illuminate a variety of social phenomena. The state is theorized through roads (Guldi 2012; Harvey and Knox 2015). Research on water pipes and water meters sheds new light on governance and citizenship (Anand 2017; Millington 2018; Von Schnitzler 2016). Railroad histories reveal changing experiences of time and space (Bear 2007; Schivelbusch 2014). Studies of industrial disasters illuminate the promises and paradoxes of modern environmental movements as responses to corporate power (Fortun 2001; Kirsch 2014). Analyses of ports, containers, and logistics provide insights about the rise of economic globalization (Levinson 2006) and the spatial organization of capitalism (Cowen 2014).

The infrastructure projects that concern scholars are often considered complete, or, if not, their materialization is assumed to be imminent. And yet, many—if not most—of the dams, roads, railroads, ports, airports, and pipelines generally classified as infrastructure exist in states aptly characterized as unbuilt or unfinished. Planned, blocked, delayed, or abandoned, such projects are ubiquitous—the norm, rather than the exception. This article engages a growing body of literature across the social sciences and humanities that troubles the linear, stagewise development timelines of planning imaginaries (e.g., plan, budget, procure, construct, complete). As we will show, unbuilt and unfinished infrastructures can become the axes of social worlds and sites where temporalities are knotted and reworked in unpredictable ways.

Scholars tend to use the unbuilt or unfinished project as a foil that reveals the assumptions implicit in a field of inquiry, thus providing an opportunity to reorient or reframe the conversation. What, for example, might be learned about social and political integration if we focus on the long-term incompletion of the Pan-American Highway at the Darién Gap (Ficek 2016; Miller 2014), rather than the completion of the US transcontinental railroad? What might be revealed about the impacts of infrastructure-driven displacement (Gellert and Lynch 2003) if we compare the massive resettlement efforts associated with the Aswan and Three Gorges dams with the anxious experiences of communities who have waited decades to be resettled by Thailand's (unbuilt) Kaeng Sue Ten Dam (Kirchherr et al. 2018)? How does urban theory look different when infrastructural improvisation and unfinishedness in African cities (Baumgardt 2017; Mbembe and Roitman 1995; Simone 2004) is treated as the norm rather than exception (Furlong 2014)? How does understanding of mega-events like the Olympics or the World Cup shift if we analyze the effects of bids that failed alongside those that won (Lauermann 2016)?

Unbuilt and unfinished infrastructures are hiding in plain sight. We make no claims to discovery here. If anything, we emphasize that this is a widespread phenomenon. Budgets evaporate, political winds shift, markets fluctuate, protests gain traction, and paradigms fall out of fashion. The history of international development is littered with the wreckage of failed projects (Scott 1998). Archives overflow with unrealized plans and drawings of unbuilt structures, prompting scholars to meditate on their meaning (Harbison 2001; Lehmann 2016) and stage public exhibitions (Goldin and Lubell 2013, 2016). And yet, reading across fields, we are struck by the gap between the obviousness of the unfinished as an empirical phenomenon and its aura of theoretical novelty. One possible explanation is that scholars often deploy the unfinished project to reorient conversations in their own fields. Anthropologists and geographers rethink social experiences of space and place (Peyton 2017; Yarrow 2017). Science and technology studies (STS) scholars reimagine technological failure and success (Latour 1996; Rankin 2017). Historians reconsider historiographical assumptions and interpretive norms (Keiner forthcoming; Miller 2014). These are all important concerns, but the cumulative effect is siloed conversations.

Even if unfinishedness is, in some sense, a normal state of affairs, it seems particularly salient to understand in the early twenty-first century. China's Belt and Road Initiative is the exemplar of a multitrillion-dollar infrastructure boom in which transportation, communication, and energy systems are developed at unprecedented scale and expense (Flyvbjerg 2014). However, we should not accept the project timelines presented by funders, builders, and boosters at face value. In the case of the Belt and Road Initiative, such timelines may not square with the realities on the ground (Landry 2018)—a disjuncture that illustrates a broader phenomenon. Bent Flyvbjerg's "iron law of megaprojects" posits that they are "over budget, over time, over and over again" (2014: 11) because of receding implementation horizons, cost overruns, and political backlashes. Moreover, the presentation of the construction boom as universal elides the fact that, even as new infrastructures are planned and built, many others are falling apart. Disinvestment and deferred maintenance are the order of the day in places where neoliberal reforms like fiscal austerity and privatization "splinter" infrastructure (Graham and Marvin 2001) and aging systems are a matter of national concern (ASCE 2017).

Our interest in the unbuilt and unfinished emerged, unexpectedly, from a similar experience conducting fieldwork on prospective mining in Ecuador (David Kneas) and environmental management in Panama (Ashley Carse). For Ecuadorians living in the liminal space between the departure of one mining company and arrival of another, the prominent temporal orientation was not anticipation but aftermath (Kneas 2018). Characterized by a sense of relief and reconciliation, subject positions associated with the resource conflict began to fade, a process of unbecoming that challenges linear trajectories of resource extraction and identity formation. Meanwhile, for residents of a rural Panamanian community, the permanently unfinished status of the only access road became a useful object for making sense of changing relationships with other people and places over time (Carse 2014: 185–204). Scholars observe that rural people may describe poverty in terms of access to infrastructure, particularly roads (Porter 2002), but the assumption that roads are finished—or "arrive"—in a community at a single identifiable moment in time does not square with widespread experiences of road advance and retreat. In discussing these fieldwork experiences, we realized how beneficial it might be to put our research and writing into conversation with scholarship on infrastructure and temporality.

The goal of this article is to bring literatures on unbuilt and unfinished infrastructures into dialogue and develop a set of conceptual tools, or heuristics, for conducting research and analysis on the theme. An obvious way to conceptualize unfinishedness would be to take the temporal assumptions of infrastructure planning for granted. We call this "project time" (Karasti et al. 2010)—a linear succession of phases or stages oriented toward meeting pre-defined objectives. (Imagine the stylized project timelines presented in project documents.) Seen through this temporal frame, we seem to know in advance what an unbuilt or unfinished infrastructure is: a project stalled at some identifiable point (or stage) along a timeline with a defined end point.

The multidisciplinary literature on the unbuilt and unfinished, by contrast, prompts us to think pluralistically about infrastructure and time. It draws our attention to how multiple temporalities can coalesce as planners, builders, politicians, potential users, and opponents negotiate with a project and each another. In this sense, infrastructures, whether unbuilt or unfinished, are sites where temporalities emerge in dialectical relation. For us, following Dipesh Chakrabarty (2000), the point is not to resolve the resulting tensions—to untie what he calls time-knots—but to approach them as sites for inquiry. Also useful here is the anthropologist Laura Bear's "timescapes" heuristic, which focuses analysis on how the dominant time maps of capitalist modernity—linear, homogeneous, and focused on short-term accumulation (e.g., our "project time")—articulate with "other practices of time" (2016: 489). By working through multiple, often entangled forms of temporal reckoning, experience, and practice, the researcher can elucidate important sociomaterial relationships and processes that a narrow focus on project time would obscure, while not losing sight of its potency as a social and political force.

The remainder of this article is organized in two parts. The first develops a general theoretical framework for understanding unbuilt and unfinished infrastructures. The second presents a typology of heuristics for analyzing infrastructure and temporality: shadow histories, present absences, suspended presents, nostalgic futures, and zombies. These are not mutually exclusive categories but rather a collection of analytical lenses that make different temporal configurations visible, prompting novel research questions and methodological approaches.

What (and When) is an Unfinished Infrastructure?

Scholars approach the unbuilt and unfinished from variety of theoretical perspectives and explore a range of projects, from policy and urban planning to art and literature. To narrow our scope, we focus on anthropology, architecture, geography, history, and STS. As we reviewed the literature, we observed that most of the work that engages the theme explicitly was published in the past decade. Why now? Insomuch as concepts emerge as heuristics that counter established ways of thinking (Dove 2000), we might interpret growing interest in unfinishedness as a symptom of postmodern anxiety about narratives of progress and historical inevitability. It also reflects social scientific "turns" related to ontology, materiality, and post-humanism (Jensen et al. 2017) that have con-gealed around infrastructure (Larkin 2013). In public and scholarly discourse alike, the concern with infrastructure coincides with its decoupling from progress narratives, both in terms of the material deterioration of twentieth-century networks and the faded promise of unbuilt futures (Harvey et al. 2017b; Howe et al. 2015). Like interest in ruins (Gordillo 2014; Johnson 2013; Stoler 2013; Yarrow 2017), scholarship on the unbuilt and unfinished grapples with materials and time—with what was, what might be, and what might have been.

The word infrastructure is complex, with multiple and contested meanings that have changed over time (Carse 2017). Here, we conceptualize infrastructure as a material as-semblage built to support a higher-order project that is at once embedded in and consti-tutive of social relations (Carse 2012; Edwards 2003; Star 1999; Star and Ruhleder 1996). Anthropologists and geographers have begun to engage with the temporal dimensions of infrastructure (Anand et al. 2018; Barry 2017; Hetherington 2014, 2019). This is a longstanding concern in the history of technology, where, to cite one influential example, a body of work traces the development of large sociotechnical systems (Hughes 1983, 1987; Mayntz and Hughes 1988; Summerton 1994). If, as this literature emphasizes, technical systems change *in time*—that is, develop through "stages" and, later, begin to "age"—then they also alter social experiences of time. For example, railroad companies played an instrumental role in replacing the myriad "local times" that were once defined

Illustration 1.1. The Chinchero International Airport is an unfinished megaproject in a town near Cusco, Peru. The planned site is visible below in the undeveloped *pampa* beyond the city center. First proposed in the 1970s, it has been repeatedly postponed because of planning issues, political conflicts, and corruption. Although the airport—imagined as a tourist gateway to Machu Picchu— is unbuilt, residents acted as if it would arrive (Delgado 2018). Some invested in land or taxis in hopes of future profits; others were "simply preparing mentally" for changes expected to accompany the airport (61) (Delgado 2018, image reprinted with permission).

astronomically with standardized time zones in order to facilitate scheduling and reduce the risk of accidents (Koselleck 2004; Schivelbusch 2014; Thompson 1967).

For Susan Leigh Star, the important question is not *what* is an infrastructure, but *when* (Star and Ruhleder 1996). For her, an artifact *becomes* infrastructure for someone, within a set of relationships, and for a particular activity. In this sense, infrastructure is not simply a class of artifacts associated with pre-determined sectors like energy, water, transportation, and communication, but a process of making and maintaining relationships. Thus, those who take this approach emphasize "infrastructuring" (Blok et al. 2016; Donovan 2015; Pipek and Wulf 2009) or infrastructural work (Bowker 1994; Carse 2014), the organizational techniques that create the conditions for achieving a higher-order objective. If infrastructure is processual, as this work suggests, then one might conclude that finishedness is illusory—that everything is unfinished.

The negative prefix "un-" implies that finished is an achievable state. Is it? For Gilles Deleuze and Felix Guattari (Deleuze 1995; Deleuze and Guattari 1987), and many inspired by their work, becoming is the nature of reality itself. In a volume inspired by this line of thought, *Unfinished*, João Biehl and Peter Locke (2017: x) advocate for unfinishedness, understood as "both precondition and product of becoming," as an orienting analytic for ethnographic research and writing (see also Biehl 2013). If we extend this ontological position to infrastructure and society, there seems to be little reason to hold onto unfinishedness as a categorical distinction. Even the surface of a freshly paved road is immediately being destroyed by weather, tires, hooves, and plant life (Carse 2019). This means that, without maintenance, the fate of the human built world is to fall apart (Weisman 2007). And yet, the position that everything is unfinished, while philosophically compelling, also threatens to elide the lived importance of those cultural meanings and practices that are oriented toward, and assume, the possibility of finishedness.

For the literary scholar James Ramsey Wallen (2015), "unfinished" is a "logical monstrosity," because the term tells us neither how a given work came to be unfinished (death, abandonment, arson) nor how unfinished it is (a single stanza written or a near-complete magnum opus). The same can be said of infrastructure. "Unfinished" conflates a range of project narratives and statuses: proposed, planned, funded, underway, delayed, failed, abandoned, and so on. Yet, as Matthew Harle (2019: 11) argues, the word remains useful because it draws attention to the dialectical relationship between the project and the conjectural image of its finished form. Moreover, Wallen (2015) posits that the unfinished literary work is not a type of text but rather a label that influences interpretive practices. Within this genre, there is an expectation of an ending or resolution of the preceding material. Insomuch as infrastructure narratives constitute a genre of their own, it has been framed by the dominant assumptions and norms of engineering, economics, and planning, including a set of expectations about the (ideal) ending.

Our inclination as historically oriented ethnographers is to theorize from actor categories and empirical situations rather than philosophical first principles. While acknowledging the conceptual slipperiness of unfinishedness, we argue that the sense of an ending is a useful "fiction" that allows people to make sense of the world and their place in it (Kermode 1967). By the same token, the experience of living with an ending deferred also plays an important role in the dreams and dramas that surround infrastructures. For centuries, technologies have been treated as measures of symbolically loaded ideas of like "civilization" or "development" that imply linear change in a positive direction (Adas 1989). It is precisely the promissory quality of these narratives that makes infrastructure so potent in public life (Hetherington 2017). When it comes to infrastructure, the possibility of finishedness (as an idea or ideal) shapes how people think about, talk about, and act with regard to projects and other actors. Approached pragmatically, then, finishedness becomes real not as an a priori principle but in its effects.

Illustration 1.2: Atlantropa, an unbuilt oceanic dam that would have closed off the Mediterranean Sea at the Strait of Gibraltar and connected Europe to Africa, was designed in the late 1920s by the German architect Herman Sörgel. The project, a radical response to a comprehensive sense of political and environmental crisis, was projected to generate hydropower for all of Europe and to dry up the sea, creating new land for settlement. Greeted with enthusiasm, it failed to materialize (Lehmann 2016). This drawing, from around 1930, depicts a proposed sea embankment between Gibraltar and Tangier, Morocco. (© Unknown, via Wikimedia Commons, CC-BY-SA-4.0).

Der Gibraltardamm im Bau.

The multidisciplinary literature on the unbuilt and unfinished focuses our attention on the forms of temporal reckoning and interplay that take place as planners, analysts, politicians, speculators, displaced peoples, and potential users are drawn into relation through infrastructure projects. As we explained earlier, these include, but are not limited to, the temporal orientation we call project time, which we might gloss as "the ideological positions that presuppose the materialization of blueprint plans in physical form" (MacLean 2017: 366). The stylized, stagewise timeline—plan, budget, procure, build, complete—is far from the only relevant temporal frame for understanding infrastructure and society, but it does do important work. It orients organizations, structuring activities, employment, investment, and resource distribution. Thus, adopting this orientation makes some consequences visible. A stalled project siphons resources from other priorities. Planning and implementation timelines also have a social poetics, engendering affective states from hope to anxiety and practices from speculation to protest.

Due to the temporal standardization and compression associated with industrial capitalism and modernity (Harvey 1989; Schivelbusch 2014; Thompson 1967) it is easy to assume that the contemporary experience of time is homogeneous, abstract, and linear. However, as anthropologists (Bear 2016; Kockelman and Bernstein 2012) argue, the time of capitalist modernity is not singular but remarkably diverse and heterogeneous. Approaching unbuilt and unfinished infrastructures as time-knots (Chakrabarty 2000) or timescapes (Bear 2016)—that is, sites where temporal practices articulate—provides a more expansive understanding of what these projects are, how they shape social life, and how they come to matter. There are, as we will discuss, nonlinear relationships between the plan and its implementation (Campbell 2012b; Smith 2017), as well as the imagined orders and realities produced (Abram and Weszkalnys 2011). Time-knots can become an empirical focus for archival research, a way of structuring fieldwork, and a point of departure for analysis.

Heuristics for Understanding Unbuilt and Unfinished Infrastructures

In this section, we develop a typology for interpreting the temporalities of unbuilt and unfinished infrastructures. The inherent limits to any classificatory framework notwithstanding, the heuristics that follow—shadow histories, present absences, suspended presents, nostalgic futures, and zombies—provide alternative vantage points for research and analysis. Drawing on different bodies of theory, each makes different temporal configurations visible and suggests different research questions. They also flag common arguments, or propositions, in the literatures concerned with infrastructure and time, while drawing attention to matters of positionality and methodology. How and where we encounter unfinished infrastructures—ethnographic fieldwork, archives, or elsewhere—shapes how we engage and understand those projects.

Shadow Histories

Shadow histories approach unbuilt and unfinished infrastructures as paths not taken. For the anthropologist Peter Redfield (2000: 16), shadow histories are "real alternatives to the primary ways things have been done or understood" (see also Powell 2018). Those plans and projects that failed to materialize invite us to grapple with contingency and question the narratives of inevitability that can calcify around infrastructures. Like the historian Kathryn Oberdeck's analysis of the unbuilt spaces of Kohler, Wisconsin, with its "paper streets, imaginary blocks, [and] fantasy buildings," this heuristic often "compares what was once possible to powerful versions of the inevitable" (2006: 252–253). In other words, shadow histories turn on a counterintuitive historiographical claim: to understand the relationships between past and present, we need to study what *did not* happen. They may examine the multiple visions of the future at play in the past to capture the range of ideas and practices that informed the construction of our world—what we might call the "embryonic contemporary" (Harle 2019: 20). The shadow history is therefore often a recovery project that makes use of historical materials—planning documents, media reports, architectural drawings, and other artifacts—to reconstruct the immediacy of the world in which a project emerged and, thus, its conditions of possibility.

Shadow histories of unbuilt and unfinished infrastructures complicate the "great historical confidence in progress," rendering it an anthropological problem (Ssorin-Chaikov 2016: 690). In his history of the Trans-Saharan Railway, an unbuilt nineteenth-century

Illustration 1.3. The Pan-Atomic Canal was proposed by the US government in the 1960s through Project Plowshare, a postwar US Atomic Energy Commission initiative to find peacetime uses for nuclear explosives (Kirsch 2005). The canal project was a response to the perceived looming obsolescence of the Panama Canal (a lock canal opened in 1914) and anti-colonial geopolitics on the isthmus (Keiner 2016, forthcoming). Here, US Senator Warren G. Magnuson, Lieutenant General W.K. Wilson Jr., and Lieutenant Colonel Robert W. McBride, discuss an artist's rendering of the project in 1964 (reprinted from the University of Washington Libraries, Special Collections with permission, Order Number SOC6742).

megaproject that was to link French colonies in North and West Africa across a vast expanse of desert, Mike Heffernan (2011) argues that analyses of unsuccessful grandiose projects are useful because they illuminate persistent ideologies, particularly related to modernism, science, and technology. The Pan-Atomic Canal (Illustration 1.3) is a case in point. The unbuilt sea-level channel was to be excavated using 200 buried nuclear charges. Seen as a shadow history, the Pan-Atomic Canal reveals what Christine Keiner (2016: 4) calls "a powerful technocratic worldview" in which faith in expertise eclipsed concern for environmental risk, at least initially. The project's eventual demise reveals how changing scientific and public perceptions eroded that worldview as the confident episteme of mid-century US techno-science was forced to reckon with problems of uncertainty and the rise of environmentalism as a social movement (Keiner forthcoming). Similarly, Shawn Miller (2014: 191) argues that the construction of the Pan-American Highway, long stalled at the Darién Gap (near a proposed site for the Pan-Aatomic Canal), runs "contrary to the dominant narrative of progress and development." Like Keiner's unbuilt nuclear canal, this seminal "nonevent" (Miller 2014) reveals the unsung successes of opposition to twentieth-century megaprojects.

As a project of recovery, the shadow history extends beyond the discipline of history, finding common ground with a vein of architectural thought. In *Unbuilt America*, Alison Sky and Michelle Stone (1976) coined "unbuiltism," identifying only one previous work—written a half-century before by the German architect Josef Ponten (1929)—that dealt exclusively with the phenomenon. At the time of its publication, the volume was an idiosyncratic salvage project, assembling two centuries of sketches and plans for buildings that were never realized, ranging from "hypothetical proposals" and nonwinning entries in architecture competitions to projects shelved for lack of funding. In retrospect, *Unbuilt America* seems prescient as architects have since embraced its central conceit, staging popular exhibitions and publishing books on "unbuilt" and "never built" versions of cities that highlight prior imaginaries of urban space (Goldin and Lubell 2013, 2016). The history of another significant work of the architectural imagination, the Atlantropa project (Illustration 1.2), serves as an alternative entry point into the political and scientific space of Weimar Germany and interwar Europe (Lehmann 2016). In the 1920s and 1930s, the German architect Herman Sörgel's proposed damming the Mediterranean Sea to generate an inexhaustible source of hydropower and create an "Afro-European super-continent." The evaporation of ocean water would, in turn, make new coastal land available for settlement. As a shadow history, Phillip Lehmann's analysis of Atlantropa reveals an "eclectic mix of attitudes towards technology" and "rich variety of utopian thought" in this period (2016: 73). In so doing, it adds historical nuance to contemporary concerns around climate and energy provisioning.

In opening up what might have been, shadow histories exist in dialectical relationship to what is. Shadows invoke obscured reflections and alter egos, inviting counterfactual histories that posit alternative presents. This is not only an intellectual exercise. As Richard White argues, "It is only by conceiving of alternative worlds that people in the past themselves imagined that we can begin to think historically, to escape the inevitability of the present, and get other perspectives on issues that concern us still" (2011: 517). Put simply, shadow histories cast the present in a new light. This is why Mike Davis opens a book about Los Angeles amid the ruins of Llano del Rio, an unfinished utopian community outside the city: "The best place to view the Los Angeles of the next millennium is from the ruins of its alternative future" (1990: 5).

Present Absences

The prefix "un-" implies absence, but unbuilt and unfinished infrastructures can be surprisingly consequential. Whereas shadow histories recover the past's forgotten possibilities, the present absences heuristic draws attention to what unbuilt and unfinished projects leave behind, including: institutional forms, knowledges, altered landscapes, social movements, and new subjectivities. In so doing, this work recasts a scholarly conversation around the failure of infrastructure projects. Moving beyond theories of "project noncompletion" (Williams 2017) that seek to ex-plain absence, including influential work on project failure (Latour 1996; Scott 1998), this scholarship foregrounds absence's political, material, and affective significance (Meier et al. 2013).

Unbuilt and unfinished projects can reshape social and political life. Dana Powell (2018) approaches Desert Rock, a proposed but unbuilt coal-fired power plant slated for Navajo territory, as a present absence. She argues that the plant, which was contested and ultimately blocked, reworked power in the Navajo Nation by acting on "imaginations, desires, hopes, and worst fears in a manner that gave it the moral weight to shape the politics of energy" (5). Similarly, the sociologist Wendy Espeland's (1998) study of a failed dam project in Arizona shows how bureaucracies construct constituencies and how struggles over unbuilt projects can change values and subjectivities. On the other side of the world, oil companies arrived in Murmansk, Russia, projecting prosperous natural resource futures and promoting corporate social responsibility (CSR) (Rowe 2017). When projects went unrealized, residents were left with a sense of disillusionment. Rather than instilling faith in corporate models of social welfare, CSR activities led, ironically, to a renewed appreciation of Soviet-era industrial practices (Rowe 2017: 10).

Infrastructure-planning processes can generate knowledges, networks, and forms of expertise that outlast the projects themselves, with potential second-order consequences. US scientists conducted research in Darién, Panama, to evaluate the impacts of the proposed Pan-Atomic Canal and Pan-American Highway. Neither project was completed, but the associated survey work generated lasting knowledge about the region's complex ecosystems, nevertheless (Covich 2015). In the same vein, failed Olympic bids can have surprisingly "durable outcomes" by generating networks and expertise that are later folded into urban planning and future projects (Lauermann 2016). Experts are not the only ones who come to see landscapes differently through the planning processes of unrealized projects. Jonathan Peyton argues that unbuilt dams in northern British Columbia reshaped local perspectives on conservation and native land rights (2011); they also persist in the extractive imaginaries of the mining industry (2017).

Finally, unfinished infrastructures can be in use, but not always as expected. For example, outsiders may narrate unpaved sections of a Brazilian highway as a "failed" development project, but for the colonists who use it, the road "has already realized its connective promise" (Campbell 2012b: 11). It may not be the imagined road, but it is a road. Some unbuilt and unfinished infrastructures are used in ways that are even further from initial plans. In the 1990s, decades after a long-running plan to excavate a Cross Florida Barge Canal—to connect the Atlantic Ocean and the Gulf of Mexico by means of a channel through the middle of the state—was canceled, land along the proposed route became a protected green belt named for an anti-canal environmental activist (Noll and Tegeder 2009). Today, that 110-mile-long strip is navigated by bikes and canoes, not barges. Similarly, scientific survey work on the ecological risks posed by the Pan-American Highway led to the creation of Panama's Darién National Park (Covich 2015: 55). In such cases, absent infrastructures are inscribed on the landscape.

Suspended Presents

Local opposition, cost overruns, political shifts, and lack of investment can elongate or discontinue project planning, assessment, and construction. The suspended presents heuristic is concerned with the varied social experiences and affective states associated with infrastructural delay, from hope and anxiety to waiting and disillusionment. This heuristic focuses attention on the emergence of "suspension" as a social fact (Rest 2018) that reworks experiences of past, present, and future. Researchers may employ ethnographic and qualitative methods to capture what it means to occupy "a temporary zone between the start of projects and their completion" (Gupta 2018: 70). Suspension, as understood here, is not a state of being but rather a social process associated with distinct temporal frames, rhythms, and conditions of possibility.

Infrastructures can become "promissory notes" that prompt people to imagine a future world and their place in it (Anand et al. 2018; Hetherington 2014; MacLean 2017). The anticipatory sentiments and practices surrounding roads have attracted particular attention in this regard (Campbell 2012a; Haines 2017; Reeves 2016), but this phenomenon unfold around many projects, from airports (Delgado 2018; Illustration 1.1) to potable water systems (Rest 2018; Illustration 1.4). Crucially, infrastructure projects enroll people in communities of aspiration and anxiety (Hetherington 2014). They may act in anticipation of unbuilt and unfinished projects, seeking to take advantage of the promised transformations and avoid or mitigate deleterious effects. But what happens when the temporal horizon of infrastructure's promise becomes protracted and completion is itself called into question? When the unfinished comes to seem like a permanent condition rather than a prelude to something else? When waiting becomes the norm?

Anticipation is a key feature of modern life (Adams et al. 2009), an affective state that orients practices toward uncertain, if probable, futures. For residents of Nairobi, Kenya, Constance Smith argues, the future is experienced as both close at hand and impossibly far off. Billboards and other images of spectacular urban megaprojects abound, but the projects have been slow to materialize. Thus, residents anticipate the future with a mix of hope and anxiety. It is described as "indefinitely out of reach," forestalled by an "endless" present (Smith 2017: 38). Nevertheless, this disjuncture leaves space "for residents to enact their own interpretations of promised futures, to reconfigure them and make them anew" (35). Suspension can signal what Austin Zeiderman (2016a: 170–171; 2016b) describes as a subjunctive state: an uncertain and indeterminate orientation involving contradictions between short- and long-term futures (see also Kneas 2016). In this same vein, Karen Hébert (2016: 123) outlines the unforeseen effects that emerged from participatory risk assessment associated with potential copper mining in Alaska. Due to the project's uncertainty, locals forecast a future of protracted mining debates rather than mining activities, opening the door for a reappraisal of a future that is increasingly in question.

Suspension can mean delay or hangover. Both characterize a temporal orientation defined, on the one hand, by uncertain horizons of project initiation, renewal, or closure and, on the other, the experience of deferral. The title of Elana Rowe's (2017) work on

Illustration 1.4. Construction of the Melamchi Water Supply Project, designed to deliver water and hydropower to Kathmandu's growing population, began in 2000. It has been delayed by opposition from affected communities and state officials pursuing different projects. Consequently, residents have become frustrated, the state has lost legitimacy, and small-to-medium-scale water solutions have been stymied because they would be wasteful if and when the project is complete (Rest 2018) (© Bijaya2043, via Wikimedia Commons, CC BY-SA 4.0).

Russia's unbuilt oil environment—"Promises, Promises"—captures the shift from hope to cynicism that may ensue. In São Tomé and Príncipe, where the anticipation of becoming an oil nation outpaced the chronology of exploration, Gisa Weszkalnys (2014) describes how temporal dispositions of "waiting" emerged alongside anticipation as ideologies of transparency morphed into suspicion. For others, deferral is a source of great anxiety. Julian Kirchherr and collaborators (2018) refer to the unbuilt Kaeng Suea Ten Dam in Thailand as a "Damocles project." After nearly four decades of waiting to be displaced by the project, community members live in a state marked by individual anxiety and limited economic development associated with the unbuilt dam.

A focus on suspended presents may also mean considering how actors draw on a sense of historicity that is de-linked from that promoted by infrastructure planners and builders. As Jeremy Campbell explains, three decades of living "suspended between" a planned road and the social worlds engendered by its unpaved materiality disposed Brazilian colonists "to pursue different livelihoods, paces of life, and visions of development in the region" (2012b: 3, see also 2015). While residents and state officials alike advocated for road completion, they also "longed for the realization of different development visions" (2012b: 15). Rosa Ficek's analysis of roads in Panama's Darién region, the location of the only unfinished stretch of the Pan-American Highway, echoes this insight. The layered elements of highway surface, sections of which were paved after two decades of incompletion, point "to other histories . . . that operate alongside (and entangled with) the timeline of progress but that refuse to be erased by the smooth silences of a modern road" (2014: 16). Long-term colonists insist on calling the Pan-American Highway "Main Street," situating their own histories alongside the homogeneous progress narrative of capitalism and development (112–113). As these examples reveal, thinking through the suspended presents heuristic is more than an effective means of holding assumptions of inevitability at bay; it also foregrounds social experiences that produce alternative renderings of project completion.

Nostalgic Futures

This heuristic attends to the promise and aspiration that once accompanied an infrastructure project. This is not a longing for the past, per se, but for the possibilities it once held. Whereas shadow histories may seek to recover the embryonic contemporary through archival research and position it against historiographical norms, nostalgic futures take shape around collective memory that is accessible through qualitative research and material culture. Ruins are one way to access the lingering remains of the past in the present. The remains of Detroit's auto industry and Henry Ford's utopian company town in the Brazilian Amazon, Fordlândia, are both seen as ruins. They are, however, remembered differently. Detroit's abandoned buildings evoke a history of what was; Fordlândia conjures what might have been (Grandin 2009). The industrial logic that motivated Ford's Amazonian project—an effort to conquer nature and tame capital—still persists along Brazil's ever-expanding industrial soy frontier, nearly a century since the experiment was abandoned in 1934. In the film *Beyond Fordlândia* (2017), writer-director Marcos Colón approaches Fordlândia as a harbinger of environmental hubris and risk; he is concerned with the lessons we can learn from its failure. However, the "cruelest legacy" of the short-lived, ill-fated endeavor is nostalgia, according to the poet Carlos Correia's interviews with residents who remember it. For them, "the American dream came, but didn't stay, and they've been waiting their whole lives for it to return" (Colón 2017). They are wistful for its unrealized promise.

In the 1960s, the Volta Resettlement Project symbolized a modern, post-independence era of Ghanaian development. The plan imagined rapid social and economic development

Illustration 1.5. Unfinished project, unknown location, North Korea
(© Unknown, via Wikimedia Commons, CC BY 2.0)

through mechanized agriculture and industrialization to be powered by a hydroelectric dam. Fifty-four resettlement townships were planned to receive displaced people. Due to shifts in domestic politics and international development priorities, however, construction ended with the townships occupied by only a fraction of the projected population. Like Fordlândia, the temporal dimensions of the Volta project are distinct from conventional approaches to ruins:

> Unlike the negative spaces of buildings that once existed and are now destroyed, these ruins exist as the negative time and space made present by an ideal: of what might have existed, even might still, but which does and has not. These are not absences presenced as the material remains of that which has gone, but as the remembered anticipation of a future. (Yarrow 2017: 568)

Whereas shadow histories are concerned with historical recovery, nostalgic futures are remembered. Although the boundaries are porous, the difference between recovery and remembrance, as we see it, stems from how the latter is mediated by the public sphere. Even as Yarrow narrates Volta as a failed project, he notes that residents continue to draw on promised plans in efforts to enlist infrastructure investment, holding onto the notion of Volta as a future possibility. In other words, the ruins of an imagined future resonate in contemporary social life in ways that can be studied ethnographically. This recalls what Gastón Gordillo (2011) captures in an essay on the local memories "woven around" steamships stranded in the forest after a failed nineteenth-century effort to turn Argentina's Bermejo River into a commercial navigation route, which some hoped would bring prosperity to the Gran Chaco region. Among the absences these ruins invoke in the present is nostalgia for the progress that the ships once promised.

Zombies

Zombies are alive and dead—of the world but stripped of social obligation. This heuristic draws attention to how unbuilt and unfinished infrastructures linger between the dissipation and reemergence of the social, political, and economic networks that give them life. The figure of the zombie invites analysis of infrastructure projects over multiple iterations and across temporal frames. For example, the idea of an interoceanic canal across what is now Nicaragua emerged under Spanish rule in the sixteenth century. Napoleon III resurrected the prospect in the early nineteenth century, which was pursued, yet again, during the twentieth century by British and US interests. Since the 1990s, there have been renewed proposals to construct an interoceanic route, including, most significantly, the establishment of a Hong Kong firm, HKND, in 2012 to construct a deepwater canal. Construction was to begin in 2014, but it never did. In an account of this unbuilt canal, Jennifer Goett (2016) writes that such megaprojects "have become zombies, as one after the other is proposed, approved by the state, eventually killed due to lack of feasibility or popular resistance, only to return from the grave to terrorize local populations with the specter of dispossession once again." Though unbuilt, the specter of the canal (Jewell 2017) haunts relations of rule in Nicaragua associated with shifting national and international power.

Analyses of this type track the ebbs and flows of project potential, and the shifting social and political configurations of activation. William Rankin uses the phrase "zombie project" to capture how cartographic projects associated with International Map of the World (IMW) endured for more than a century despite distinct, even competing, interests over time: "Each generation sought to align the IMW with its own assumptions about the goals of cartography and its own measures of success, and in each phase map production was sponsored by different institutions for different reasons" (2017: 358). As this suggests, the zombie heuristic invites work on projects over multiple iterations with a focus on changing contexts and potentials.

Zombies share characteristics with so-called shelf projects (d'Avignon 2018), which also persist in a prospective state between closure and renewal. Put on the shelf, they can be reactivated in different economic and political circumstances (Rowe 2017). In the case of failed Olympic bids, the shelf can be metaphorical or quite literal as old planning documents are dusted off for subsequent rounds of bidding. Robyn d'Avignon (2018) also frames gold prospecting efforts in Senegal as shelf projects, demonstrating how seemingly novel initiatives actually emerged from relaunching projects shelved in the 1960s. However, unlike the zombie heuristic described earlier, which emphasizes changing social networks over a project's multiple iterations, shelf projects emphasize how actors control project closure and revitalization.

Conclusion: New Propositions

Our intention in developing this typology is not to establish rigid boundaries between the heuristics. These are not "cubbyholes of classification" (Mintz 1974: 298). Their utility comes from juxtaposing and working through temporal propositions that suggest alternative analyses. Thinking about a given infrastructure as a zombie or shelf project piques the historical imagination (Comaroff and Comaroff 1992), fostering new lines of inquiry. Reflecting on specters of ruins and absent presences can add an ethnographic dimension to nominally historical questions. Theorizing the distinct ways that an unfinished project is recovered or remembered points to different sites for historical research and consideration of the multiple registers through which the past is encoded in the present. Both shadow histories and nostalgic futures bring alternative presents to the fore, but they do so from different temporal and methodological vantage points; working with both asks for whom that alternative is meaningful and in which ways. Thinking with suspended presents can be a means of ethnographic reckoning—a way to identify and track slippages or overflows related to the temporalities of anticipation.

Social scientific interest in infrastructure has focused on the socio-material artifacts and, in many cases, the spatial connections that create the conditions of possibility for modern life. As scholars foreground the roads, rails, pipelines, and cables that formerly occupied the background of social analysis—conducting what Geoffrey Bowker (1994) calls infrastructural inversion—we should also continue to develop new ways to make sense of complex processes of temporal transformation. Through exploring projects that were proposed but shelved or pursued but abandoned, research on the unbuilt and unfinished can be a focal point for understanding the "embryonic contemporaries" of previous eras and the suspended futures of the present.

▪ ACKNOWLEDGMENTS

We thank Jessica Barnes, Christine Keiner, Sayd Randle, Sara Safransky, Austin Zeiderman, and the anonymous reviewers for useful comments and suggestions on earlier drafts of this article.

▪ **ASHLEY CARSE** is Assistant Professor of Human and Organizational Development at Vanderbilt University. He is the author of *Beyond the Big Ditch: Politics, Ecology, and Infrastructure at the Panama Canal* (2014). Trained as an anthropologist, his work also engages geography, environmental history, and science and technology studies. Thematically, he focuses on global transportation, the social dimensions of infrastructure, and environmental politics. He has worked in Panama for more than a decade and is currently developing a multi-sited ethnography of the shipping industry that traces connections between the Panama Canal expansion and environmental change in the Southeastern United States. Email: ashley.carse@vanderbilt.edu

▪ **DAVID KNEAS** is Assistant Professor of Geography at the University of South Carolina, with a joint appointment in the School of Earth, Ocean, and Environment. His long-term research centers on the intersections between agrarian landscapes and mineral exploration in the Ecuadorian Andes. He is currently developing new research that focuses on the global mining industry and the practices of speculation associated with junior exploration companies. Recent publications include "Emergence and Aftermath: The (Un)becoming of Resources and Identities in Northwestern Ecuador" (*American Anthropologist*, 2018). Email: kneas@mailbox.sc.edu

▪ REFERENCES

Abram, Simone, and Gisa Weszkalnys. 2011. "Introduction: Anthropologies of Planning—Temporality, Imagination, and Ethnography." *Focaal* 61: 3–18.

Adams, Vincanne, Michelle Murphy, and Adele E. Clarke. 2009. "Anticipation: Technoscience, Life, Affect, Temporality." *Subjectivity* 28 (1): 246–265.

Adas, Michael. 1989. *Machines as the Measure of Men: Science, Technology, and Ideologies of Western Dominance.* Ithaca, NY: Cornell University Press.

ASCE (American Society of Civil Engineers). 2017. Report Card for America's Infrastructure.

Anand, Nikhil. 2017. *Hydraulic City*. Durham, NC: Duke University Press.

Anand, Nikhil, Akhil Gupta, and Hannah Appel, eds. 2018. *The Promise of Infrastructure*. Durham, NC: Duke University Press.

Barry, Andrew. 2017. "Infrastructure and the Earth." In Harvey et al. 2017a: 187–197.

Baumgardt, Laurin. 2017. "Unfinished Futures: Ethnographic Reflections on Infrastructure and Aspirations in an Informal Settlement in South Africa." *Moment Journal* 4 (1): 73–91.

Bear, Laura. 2007. *Lines of the Nation: Indian Railway Workers, Bureaucracy, and the Intimate Historical Self*. New York: Columbia University Press.

Bear, Laura. 2016. "Time as Technique." *Annual Review of Anthropology* 45: 487–502.

Biehl, João. 2013. "Ethnography in the Way of Theory." *Cultural Anthropology* 28 (4): 573–597.

Biehl, João, and Peter Locke, eds. 2017. *Unfinished: The Anthropology of Becoming*. Durham, NC: Duke University Press.

Blok, Anders, Moe Nakazora, and Brit Ross Wintherreik. 2016. "Infrastructuring Environments." *Science as Culture* 25 (1): 1–22.

Bowker, Geoffrey C. 1994. *Science on the Run: Information Management and Industrial Geophysics at Schlumberger, 1920–1940*. Cambridge, MA: MIT Press.

Campbell, Jeremy M. 2012a. "Brazil's Deferred Highway: Mobility, Development, and Anticipating the State in Amazonia." *Boletín de Antropología Universidad de Antioquia* 27 (44): 102–126.

Campbell, Jeremy M. 2012b. "Between the Material and the Figural Road: The Incompleteness of Colonial Geographies in Amazonia." *Mobilities* 7 (4): 481–500.

Campbell, Jeremy M. 2015. Conjuring Property: Speculation and Environmental Futures in the Brazilian Amazon. Seattle: University of Washington Press.

Carse, Ashley. 2012. "Nature as Infrastructure: Making and Managing the Panama Canal Watershed." *Social Studies of Science* 42 (4): 539–563.

Carse, Ashley. 2014. *Beyond the Big Ditch: Politics, Ecology, and Infrastructure at the Panama Canal*. Cambridge, MA: MIT Press.

Carse, Ashley. 2017. "Keyword: Infrastructure." In Harvey et al. 2017a: 27–39.

Carse, Ashley. 2019. "Dirty Landscapes: How Weediness Indexes State Disinvestment and Global Disconnection." In Hetherington 2019: 97–114.

Chakrabarty, Dipesh. 2000. *Provincializing Europe: Postcolonial Thought and Historical Difference*. Princeton, NJ: Princeton University Press.

Colón, Marcos. 2017. "Five Reasons Why Henry Ford's Failure in Brazil Still Matters Today." *Edge Effects*, 14 December. http://edgeeffects.net/fordlandia.

Comaroff, John, and Jean Comaroff. 1992. *Ethnography and the Historical Imagination*. Boulder, CO: Westview Press.

Covich, Alan P. 2015. "Projects That Never Happened: Ecological Insights from Darién, Panama." *Bulletin of the Ecological Society of America* 96 (1): 54–63.

Cowen, Deborah. 2014. *The Deadly Life of Logistics*. Minneapolis: University of Minnesota Press.

d'Avignon, Robyn. 2018. "Shelf Projects: The Political Life of Exploration Geology in Senegal." *Engaging Science, Technology, and Society* 4: 111–130.

Davis, Mike. 1990. *City of Quartz: Excavating the Future in Los Angeles*. London: Verso.

Deleuze, Gilles. 1995. "Control and Becoming." In *Negotiations: 1972–1990*, trans. Martin Joughin. New York: Columbia University Press.

Deleuze, Gilles, and Félix Guattari. 1987. *A Thousand Plateaus: Capitalism and Schizophrenia*. Minneapolis: University of Minnesota Press.

Delgado, Andrea. 2018. "Sumaq Kawsay, Allin Kawsay: Conceptions of Well-Being among Quechua Female Vendors in the Face of Change in Chinchero, Peru." MA thesis, Vanderbilt University.

Donovan, Kevin P. 2015. "Infrastructuring Aid: Materializing Humanitarianism in Northern Kenya." *Environment and Planning D: Society and Space* 33 (4): 732–748.

Dove, Michael. 2000. "The Life-Cycle of Indigenous Knowledge, and the Case of Natural Rubber Production." In *Indigenous Environmental Knowledge and Its Transformations: Critical Anthropological Perspectives*, ed. Roy Allen, Peter Parkes, and Alan Bicker, 213–251. Amsterdam: Harwood Academic Publishers.

Edwards, Paul N. 2003. "Infrastructure and Modernity: Force, Time, and Social Organization in the History of Sociotechnical Systems." In *Modernity and Technology*, ed. Thomas J. Misa, Philip Brey and Andrew Feenberg, 185–226. Cambridge, MA: MIT Press.

Espeland, Wendy Nelson. 1998. *The Struggle for Water: Politics, Rationality and Identity in the American Southwest.* Chicago: University of Chicago Press.

Ficek, Rosa E. 2014. "The Pan-American Highway: An Ethnography of Latin American Integration." PhD diss., University of California, Santa Cruz.

Ficek, Rosa E. 2016. "Imperial Routes, National Networks and Regional Projects in the Pan-American Highway, 1884–1977." *Journal of Transport History* 37 (2): 129–154.

Flyvbjerg, Bent. 2014. "What You Should Know about Megaprojects and Why: An Overview." *Project Management Journal* 45 (2): 6–19.

Fortun, Kim. 2001. *Advocacy after Bhopal: Environmentalism, Disaster, New Global Orders.* Chicago: University of Chicago Press.

Furlong, Kathryn. 2014. "STS beyond the 'Modern Infrastructure Ideal': Extending Theory by Engaging with Infrastructure Challenges in the South." *Technology in Society* 38: 139–147.

Gellert, Paul K., and Barbara D. Lynch. 2003. "Mega-Projects as Displacements." *International Social Science Journal* 55 (175): 15–25.

Goett, Jennifer. 2016. "In Nicaragua, the Latest Zombie Project." *NACLA*, 20 May. https://nacla.org/news/2016/05/20/nicaragua-latest-zombie-megaproject.

Goldin, Greg, and Sam Lubell. 2013. *Never Built Los Angeles.* New York: Metropolitan Books.

Goldin, Greg, and Sam Lubell. 2016. *Never Built New York.* New York: Metropolitan Books.

Gordillo, Gastón. 2011. "Ships Stranded in the Forest." *Current Anthropology* 52 (2): 141–167.

Gordillo, Gastón. 2014. *Rubble: The Afterlife of Destruction.* Durham, NC: Duke University Press.

Graham, Stephen, and Simon Marvin. 2001. *Splintering Urbanism: Networked Infrastructure, Technological Mobilities and the Urban Condition.* London: Routledge.

Grandin, Greg. 2009. *Fordlandia: The Rise and Fall of Henry Ford's Forgotten Jungle City.* New York: Metropolitan Books.

Guldi, Jo. 2012. *Roads to Power: Britain Invents the Infrastructural State.* Cambridge, MA: Harvard University Press.

Gupta, Akhil. 2018. "The Future in Ruins: Thoughts on the Temporality of Infrastructure." In Anand et al. 2018: 62–79.

Haines, Sophie. 2017. "Imagining the Highway: Anticipating Infrastructural and Environmental Change in Belize." *Ethnos* 83 (2): 392–413.

Harbison, Robert. 2001. *The Built, the Unbuilt, and the Unbuildable: In Pursuit of Architectural Meaning.* Cambridge, MA: MIT Press.

Harle, Matthew. 2019. *Afterlives of Abandoned Work: Creative Debris in the Archive.* New York: Bloomsbury Academic.

Harvey, David. 1989. *The Condition of Postmodernity: An Enquiry into the Origins of Cultural Change.* Cambridge: Blackwell.

Harvey, Penny, and Hannah Knox. 2015. *Roads: An Anthropology of Infrastructure and Expertise.* Ithaca, NY: Cornell University Press.

Harvey, Penny, Casper Bruun Jensen, and Atsuro Morita, eds. 2017a. *Infrastructures and Social Complexity: A Routledge Companion.* London: Routledge.

Harvey, Penny, Casper Bruun Jensen, and Atsuro Morita. 2017b. "Introduction: Infrastructural Complications." In Harvey et al. 2017a: 1–22.

Hébert, Karen. 2016. "Chronicle of a Disaster Foretold: Scientific Risk Assessment, Public Participation, and the Politics of Imperilment in Bristol Bay, Alaska." *Journal of the Royal Anthropological Institute* 22 (S1): 108–126.

Heffernan, Mike. 2011. "Shifting Sands: The Trans-Saharan Railway." In *Engineering Earth: The Impacts of Megaengineering Projects*, ed. Stanley D. Brunn, 617–626. Dordrecht: Springer.

Hetherington, Kregg. 2014. "Waiting for the Surveyor: Development Promises and the Temporality of Infrastructure." *Journal of Latin American and Caribbean Anthropology* 19 (2): 195–211.

Hetherington, Kregg. 2017. "Surveying the Future Perfect: Infrastructure, Development, and the Promise of Infrastructure." In Harvey et al. 2017a: 40–50.

Hetherington, Kregg, ed. 2019. *Infrastructure, Environment, and Life in the Anthropocene.* Durham, NC: Duke University Press.

Howe, Cymene, Jessica Lockrem, Hannah Appel, Edward Hackett, Dominic Boyer, Randal Hall, Matthew Schneider-Mayerson, et al. 2015. "Paradoxical Infrastructures: Ruins, Retrofit, and Risk." *Science, Technology & Human Values* 41 (3): 547–565.

Hughes, Thomas P. 1983. *Networks of Power: Electrification in Western Society, 1880–1930.* Baltimore, MD: Johns Hopkins University Press.

Hughes, Thomas P. 1987. "The Evolution of Large Technological Systems." In *The Social Construction of Technological Systems: New Directions in the Sociology and History of Technology,* ed. Thomas P. Hughes, Wiebe E. Bijker and Trevor Pinch, 51–82. Cambridge, MA: MIT Press.

Jensen, Casper Bruun, Andrea Ballestero, Marisol de la Cadena, Michael Fisch, and Miho Ishii. 2017. "New Ontologies? Reflections on Some Recent 'Turns' in STS, Anthropology and Philosophy." *Social Anthropology* 25 (4): 525–545.

Jewell, Kendra. 2017. "Another Big Ditch: The Prospect of a Nicaragua Canal." MA thesis, University of British Columbia.

Johnson, Andrew Alan. 2013. "Progress and Its Ruins: Ghosts, Migrants, and the Uncanny in Thailand." *Cultural Anthropology* 28 (2): 299–319.

Karasti, Helena, Karen S. Baker, and Florence Millerand. 2010. "Infrastructure Time: Long-Term Matters in Collaborative Development." *Computer Supported Cooperative Work* 19 (3–4): 377–415.

Keiner, Christine. 2016. "The Panatomic Canal and the US Environmental Management State." *Environmental History* 21 (2): 75–85.

Keiner, Christine. forthcoming. *Deep Cut: The Failed Plan to Build a Sea-Level Canal in Central America from Humboldt to the Oil Crisis.* Athens: University of Georgia Press.

Kermode, Frank. 1967. *The Sense of an Ending: Studies in the Theory of Fiction.* Oxford: Oxford University Press.

Kirchherr, Julian, Teerapong Pomun, and Matthew J. Walton. 2018. "Mapping the Social Impacts of 'Damocles Projects': The Case of Thailand's (as yet Unbuilt) Kaeng Suea Ten Dam." *Journal of International Development* 30: 474–492.

Kirsch, Scott. 2005. *Proving Grounds: Project Plowshare and the Unrealized Dream of Nuclear Earthmoving.* New Brunswick, NJ: Rutgers University Press.

Kirsch, Stuart. 2014. *Mining Capitalism: The Relationship between Corporations and Their Critics.* Berkeley: University of California Press.

Kneas, David. 2016. "Subsoil Abundance and Surface Absence: A Junior Mining Company and its Performance of Prognosis in Northwestern Ecuador." *Journal of the Royal Anthropological Institute* 22 (S1): 67–86.

Kneas, David. 2018. "Emergence and Aftermath: The (Un)Becoming of Resources and Identities in Northwestern Ecuador." *American Anthropologist* 120 (4): 752–764.

Kockelman, Paul, and Anya Bernstein. 2012. "Semiotic Technologies, Temporal Reckoning, and the Portability of Meaning, Or: Modern Modes of Temporality—Just How Abstract Are They?" *Anthropological Theory* 12 (3): 320–348.

Koselleck, Reinhart. 2004. *Futures Past: On the Semantics of Historical Time.* New York: Columbia University Press.

Landry, David G. 2018. "The Belt and Road Bubble Is Starting to Burst." *Foreign Policy,* 27 June. https://foreignpolicy.com/2018/06/27/the-belt-and-road-bubble-is-starting-to-burst.

Larkin, Brian. 2013. "The Politics and Poetics of Infrastructure." *Annual Review of Anthropology* 42: 327–343.

Latour, Bruno. 1996. *Aramis, or the Love of Technology.* Cambridge, MA: Harvard University Press.

Lauermann, John. 2016. "Temporary Projects, Durable Outcomes: Urban Development through Failed Olympic Bids?" *Urban Studies* 53 (9): 1885–1901.

Lehmann, Philipp Nicolas. 2016. "Infinite Power to Change the World: Hydroelectricity and Engineered Climate Change in the Atlantropa Project." *American Historical Review* 121 (1): 70–100.

Levinson, Marc. 2006. *The Box: How the Shipping Container Made the World Smaller and the World Economy Bigger.* Princeton, NJ: Princeton University Press.

MacLean, Ken. 2017. "Unbuilt Anxieties: Infrastructure Projects, Transnational Conflict in the South China/East Sea, and Vietnamese Statehood." *TRaNS: Trans-Regional and -National Studies of Southeast Asia* 4 (S2): 365–85.

Mayntz, Renate, and Thomas P. Hughes. 1988. *The Development of Large Technical Systems.* Boulder, CO: Westview Press.

Mbembe, Achille, and Janet Roitman. 1995. "Figures of the Subject in Times of Crisis." *Public Culture* 7 (2): 323–352.

Meier, Lars, Lars Frers, and Erika Sigvardsdotter. 2013. "The Importance of Absence in the Present: Practices of Remembrance and the Contestation of Absences." *Cultural Geographies* 20 (4): 423–430.

Miller, Shawn W. 2014. "Minding the Gap: Pan-Americanism's Highway, American Environmentalism, and Remembering the Failure to Close the Darién Gap." *Environmental History* 19 (2): 189–216.

Millington, Nate. 2018. "Producing Water Scarcity in São Paulo, Brazil: The 2014–2015 Water Crisis and the Binding Politics of Infrastructure." *Political Geography* 65: 26–34.

Mintz, Sidney. 1974. "The Rural Proletariat and the Problem of Rural Proletarian Consciousness." *Journal of Peasant Studies* 1 (3): 291–325.

Noll, Steven, and David Tegeder. 2009. *Ditch of Dreams: The Cross Florida Barge Canal and the Struggle for Florida's Future*. Gainesville: University of Florida Press.

Oberdeck, Kathryn T. 2006. "Archives of the Unbuilt Environment: Documents and Discourses of Imagined Space in Twentieth-Century Kohler, Wisconsin." In *Archive Stories: Facts, Fictions and the Writing of History*, ed. Antoinette Burton, 251–274. Durham, NC: Duke University Press.

Peyton, Jonathan. 2011. "Corporate Ecology: BC Hydro's Stikine-Iskut Project and the Unbuilt Environment." *Journal of Historical Geography* 37 (3): 358–369.

Peyton, Jonathan. 2017. *Unbuilt Environments: Tracing Postwar Development in Northwest British Columbia*. Vancouver: University of British Columbia Press.

Pipek, Volkmar, and Volker Wulf. 2009. "Infrastructuring: Towards an Integrated Perspective on Design and Use of Information Technology." *Journal of the Association of Information Systems* 10 (5): 306–332.

Ponten, Josef. 1925. *Architektur die Nicht Gebaut Wurde* [Architecture that was not built]. Berlin: NP.

Porter, Gina. 2002. "Living in a Walking World: Rural Mobility and Social Equity Issues in Sub-Saharan Africa." *World Development* 30 (2): 285–300.

Powell, Dana. 2018. *Landscapes of Power: Politics of Energy in the Navajo Nation*. Durham, NC: Duke University Press.

Rankin, William. 2017. "Zombie Projects, Negative Networks, and Multigenerational Science: The Temporality of the International Map of the World." *Social Studies of Science* 47 (3): 353–375.

Redfield, Peter. 2000. *Space in the Tropics: From Convicts to Rockets in French Guiana*. Berkeley: University of California Press.

Reeves, Madeleine. 2016. "Infrastructural Hope: Anticipating 'Independent Roads' and Territorial Integrity in Southern Kyrgyzstan." *Ethnos* 82 (4): 711–737.

Rest, Matthäus. 2018. "Dreaming of Pipes: Kathmandu's Long-Delayed Melamchi Water Supply Project." *Environment and Planning C: Politics and Space*. Published online 30 August. https://doi.org/10.1177%2F2399654418794015.

Rowe, Elana Wilson. 2017. "Promises, Promises: The Unbuilt Petroleum Environment in Murmansk." *Arctic Review on Law and Politics* 8: 3–16.

Schivelbusch, Wolfgang. 2014. *The Railway Journey: The Industrialization of Time and Space in the Nineteenth Century*. Berkeley: University of California Press.

Scott, James C. 1998. *Seeing Like a State: How Certain Schemes to Improve the Human Condition Have Failed*. New Haven, CT: Yale University Press.

Simone, AbdouMaliq. 2004. "People as Infrastructure: Intersecting Fragments in Johannesburg." *Public Culture* 16 (3): 407–429.

Sky, Alison, and Michelle Stone. 1976. *Unbuilt America: Forgotten Architecture in the United States from Thomas Jefferson to the Space Age*. New York: McGraw-Hill.

Smith, Constance. 2017. "'Our Changes'? Visions of the Future in Nairobi." *Urban Planning* 2 (1): 31–44.

Ssorin-Chaikov, Nikolai. 2016. "Soviet Debris: Failure and the Poetics of Unfinished Construction in Northern Siberia." *Social Research* 83 (3): 689–721.

Star, Susan Leigh. 1999. "The Ethnography of Infrastructure." *American Behavioral Scientist* 43 (3): 377–391.

Star, Susan Leigh, and Karen Ruhleder. 1996. "Steps toward an Ecology of Infrastructure: Design and Access for Large Information Spaces." *Information Systems Research* 7 (1): 111–134.

Stoler, Ann Laura, ed. 2013. *Imperial Debris: On Ruins and Ruination*. Durham, NC: Duke University Press.

Summerton, Jane. 1994. *Changing Large Technical Systems*. Boulder, CO: Westview Press.

Thompson, E. P. 1967. "Time, Work-Discipline, and Industrial Capitalism." *Past & Present* 38: 56–97.

Von Schnitzler, Antina. 2016. *Democracy's Infrastructure: Techno-politics and Protest after Apartheid*. Princeton, NJ: Princeton University Press.

Wallen, James Ramsey. 2015. "What Is an Unfinished Work?" *New Literary History* 46 (1): 125–142.

Weisman, Alan. 2007. *The World Without Us*. New York: Picador.

Weszkalnys, Gisa. 2014. "Anticipating Oil: The Temporal Politics of Disaster yet to Come." *Sociological Review* 62 (S1): 211–235.

White, Richard. 2011. *Railroaded: The Transcontinentals and the Making of Modern America*. New York: W. W. Norton & Co.

Williams, Martin J. 2017. "The Political Economy of Unfinished Development Projects: Corruption, Clientelism, or Collective Choice?" *American Political Science Review* 111 (4): 705–723.

Yarrow, Thomas. 2017. "Remains of the Future: Rethinking the Space and Time of Ruination through the Volta Resettlement Project, Ghana." *Cultural Anthropology* 32 (4): 566–591.

Zeiderman, Austin. 2016a. *Endangered City: The Politics of Security and Risk in Bogota*. Durham, NC: Duke University Press.

Zeiderman, Austin. 2016b. "Prognosis Past: The Temporal Politics of Disaster in Colombia." *Journal of the Royal Anthropological Institute* 22 (S1): 163–180.

CHAPTER 2

———————■———————

Biomimicry as a Meta-Resource and Megaproject
A Literature Review

Veronica Davidov

This article focuses on biomimicry, which is broadly understood as an emergent field that uses biological processes found in nature as inspirational sources for deriving or optimizing technologies for military engineering, robotics, architecture, and industrial design. In this review, I take the broad scope view on biomimicry and look at production of knowledge, as well as academic discourses and debates that span disciplines around a wide range of projects that, in one way or another, imitate nature in a solution-oriented way. In the process, nature is positioned as an exceptional mega- and meta-resource, seemingly untethered to its sociopolitical entanglements, and infinite in its abundance.

First, I review the history of biomimicry and provide an overview of its fundamental tenets and working definitions. Biomimicry is interesting in its existence as a praxis that straddles several bodies of literature, and I structure this review following the logic of its "multi-locality." The first part of the review comes out of the way in which biomimicry itself functions as a discipline—a practitioner-oriented, eclectic discipline, but one that has its own principles, hermeneutics, conferences, publications, and, recently, even online graduate and certificate courses. The beginning of that section is dedicated to, in a sense, "biomimicry in its own words." Contemporary biomimicry as a field of knowledge production about itself—and about nature—is (arguably)[1] grounded in a foundational text by Janine Benyus (1997) and appendant publications through her project the Biomimicry Institute and the consultancy she cofounded, Biomimicry 3.8 (formerly the Biomimicry Guild), where the figure 3.8 refers to the billions of years that evolution has been taking place. The opening of this article therefore reviews what can be gleaned about the subject through a recapitulation of that literature with a particular focus on how the paradigm of biomimicry reenvisions the human-nature relationship. What can be gleaned through other bodies of literature I then go on to discuss is disciplinary perspectives on biomimicry as a praxis and its function as a hermeneutic paradigm from efficacy to ethics in various academic and practitioner contexts. These literatures can be split into two sets: disciplines that instrumentalize and apply biomimicry as a model or a method, and those that take a critical approach grounded in humanities, social sciences, and STS to biomimicry and treat it as a cultural and epistemological phenomenon. This review tackles these sets of literatures with an emphasis on the exploration and treatment of the phenomenon in humanities and social sciences. Finally, I discuss two environmental management phenomena that are not conventionally grouped under the umbrella of biomimicry but, I argue, fall under its aegis in ethos and methods and thus warrant mention in a broad-based literature overview of biomimicry. These phenomena are geoengineering (and particularly its subset, solar radiation management, known as SRM) and rewilding. I conclude by calling for a deeper exploration of the ways in which the nexus of knowledge production around nature as an infinite meta-resource of intellectual inspiration, as is the case with biomimicry, paradigmatically shifts our understanding of what a natural resource is and what it means for nature to be a resource.

Background

I want to start with a caveat that biomimicry is not a coherent and clearly delineated set of ideas and practices: it is an umbrella term that has come to represent a loose aggregation of practices and approaches that pursue analogic but not necessarily homologic goals depending on, for example, whether they are deployed in a "sustainability" context or a military research and development context. Furthermore, they may diverge ontologically in terms of how they are informed by concepts like "nature," "culture," "technology," and "innovation." The term biomimicry is derived from the term biomimetics, generally attributed to Otto Schmitt (1969: 80), a biophysicist who coined it in 1969,[2] though he himself noted it was hardly a new concept, as he pointed out that "all humanly created mathematical models may properly be considered biomimetic:[3] in imitation of life, as they are created by biological creatures who have only biological figures of thought at their disposal" (quoted in Johnson and Goldstein 2015).

The contemporary field of biomimicry evolved at least in some ways out of the project of ecological design (Anker 2010; Gross 2010), which helps explain why much of the applied uptake of the concept and much of the literature produced around it lies within the fields of design and architecture. But it was also preceded by a proto-cousin of sorts—bionics—a term coined in the 1960s by the US Air Force engineer J. E. Steele. Although it is commonly associated with the creation of artificial body parts (in particular, limbs), bionics initially had a broader scope and, according to D C. Wahl (2006), is rooted in the process of "learning from nature as an inspiration for independent technical design" based on 10 principles[4] outlined by the German zoologist and biologist Werner Nachtingal. While bionics and biomimicry have a lot in common, bionics, historically, has been practiced as a more technocratic and engineering-oriented endeavor. As Wahl notes, in bionics, technological innovation has at times "almost actively tried to discourage ecological concerns and the issue of sustainability," whereas from his perspective, biomimicry distinguishes itself with its essential commitment to the first principles of ecological design, namely, design committed to minimizing environmentally destructive impacts by integrating itself with living processes (Van der Ryn and Cowan 1996). Wahl continues: "This list of biological design precepts [underpinning the vision of biomimicry] clearly reflects the holistic and participatory worldview that informs integrated sustainable design . . . [which] reintegrates culture and nature [and] has to emulate nature's way of dealing with unpredictability, fundamental interconnectedness and dynamic transformation" (2006: 293).

Biomimicry in its current incarnation is a field that has gained legibility and momentum since the 1990s and has been both invested in and promoted by the US Department of Defense while also branding itself as an ally to environmental concerns and as a way to integrate green sensibilities and economic growth. It has yielded inventions such as robot bees, bullet trains designed to emulate the beaks of kingfisher birds, hydrophobic and self-cleaning fabrics inspired by morpho butterfly wings and lotus leaves, camouflage techniques based on cephalopods, and wind turbines modeled after humpback whales.[5] These technologies, among many others, fall into one of three core biomimicry classifications within the Benyus paradigm—imitation of form, process, or ecosystem, which are all grounded in the foundational logic of biomimicry's three "pillars": nature as model (to be imitated to solve design problems), nature as measure (biomimicry using ecological standards to judge the "rightness" of innovations), and nature as mentor (biomimicry regarding nature as a "genius").

Biomimicry claims a "green" and "sustainable" identity and discourse for itself, but I argue it does so while positioning nature as a mega-resource (a cornucopia of solutions for a wide variety of problems) and a meta-resource, where it functions as a kind of library or apothecary that can be drawn upon by different areas of expertise. In resourcifying nature in and of itself, I contend that the relationship which biomimicry mediates between humans and nature is fundamentally extractive, though not in the way that easily fits into common tropes of resource extraction, which involve material transfers of monetized parts of nature out of their original context. It is closer to being extractive in the way, as I have argued elsewhere, that bioprospecting is extractive in part because it represents extraction of information and knowledge, not just extraction of genetic information from flora and fauna (Davidov 2013).

As a concept and an object of inquiry, biomimicry brushes up against recent research in environmental anthropology, which, seeking to move beyond the classic studies of resource extraction, has engaged with new forms of commodification of nature, including work on neoliberal conservation and enclosures (Büscher et al. 2012; Fletcher 2010; Igoe and Brockington 2007; Münster and Münster 2012; West 2005, 2006), the spectacle of nature (Igoe 2010), and the natural capital and financialization of conservation (Sullivan 2013). However, while most of these studies take as their subject processes that position nature as governed by an economy of scarcity, biomimicry is a discourse and praxis within which nature, reified as life itself, is construed as an infinitely renewable and generative resource and is thus governable by an economy of abundance instead. As promotional material for the Biomimicry Institute at AskNature.org states in language evocative of open-source projects, "imagine 3.8 billion years of design brilliance available for free, at the moment of creation to any sustainability innovator in the world." Academic literature on biomimicry, which is the main subject of this article, plays a role in positioning it as an industry and a project that is reframing natural resources as a site of abundance rather than scarcity, shifting our cultural understanding of a "natural resource" away from something that is material, territorial, and finite.

Biomimicry in Its Own Words

Before delving into aggregating and analyzing commentary on biomimicry, I want to cite how biomimicry is conceptualized by sources understood to be its "authors"; that primarily includes biologist Janine Benyus and her organizations, the Biomimicry Institute and Biomimicry 3.8. In her foundational book on biomimicry, Benyus (1997: 6) writes, in a section subtitled "In Vivo Genius":

> We realize that all our inventions have already appeared in nature in more elegant form and at a lot less cost to the planet. Our most clever architectural struts and beams are already featured in lily pads and bamboo shoots. Our central heating and air-conditioning are bested by the termite tower's steady 86 degrees F. Our most stealthy radar is hard of hearing compared to the bat's multifrequency transmission. And our new "smart materials" can't hold a candle to the dolphin's skin or the butterfly's proboscis.

The 3.8 website recapitulates the ethos and philosophy that Benyus reiterates throughout the book and the rest of her writings, both persuasively and technically: "Biomimicry ushers in an era based not on what we can extract from nature, but on what we can learn from her."[6] So, given its depth and breadth, how does one categorize biomimicry? Is it a design discipline, a branch of science, a problem-solving method, a sustainability ethos, a movement, a stance toward nature, or a new way of viewing and valuing biodiversity? Yes, yes, and yes . . . Biomimicry is the conscious emulation of life's genius. "Conscious" refers to intent: it is not enough to design something without nature's help and then in retrospect say, "This reminds me of something in the natural world." That is called convergent evolution, but it is not biomimicry. Biomimicry implies conscious forethought, an active seeking of nature's advice before something is designed. The nature of the consultation is also important. Seeking nature's blueprints and recipes is only part of the process; the intent should be to create products, processes, and policies that fit seamlessly within the larger natural system and that embody Life's Principles.[7]

Such texts and primers are augmented by Biomimicry Institute's books, primers, and an "open-source" database called Ask Nature that invites aspiring biomimeticians to "find biological strategies and inspired ideas relative to your innovation challenges, so you can emulate time-tested forms, processes, and systems" aided by a "biomimicry taxonomy" chart, which is a classification system that "categorizes the different ways that organisms and natural systems meet functional challenges into groups of related functions." And as the website for the first graduate and certificate program in biomimicry offered by Arizona State University (developed in collaboration with Biomimicry 3.8) states in its overview: "The Biomimicry Center offers educational programs for students and professionals across disciplines to learn to create sustainable solutions by answering the question: *What would nature do?*"[8]

Biomimicry as Praxis and Method

The fields that have yielded the lion's share of existing substantial literature on biomimicry—meaning, the uses of biomimicry—have largely been architecture and design (and I am including urban planning, which also makes considerable use of the biomimicry paradigm within the broad understanding of those two fields), and science and biomedicine. Much of the purpose of works within this field is characterized by discussion of how to accomplish the transfer of biological parameters into technological ones. For instance, an edited volume by Akhlesh Lakhtakia and Raúl Martín-Palma (2013: xiii) aggregates work by scholars from disciplines that include materials science, engineering, and optics, and develops four approaches to this task: the first one is a "classical biological one, where one particular functional system is comparatively studied in various organisms" enabling the researchers to recognize the same functional solutions that evolve over time. The second approach is grounded in the idea of a "model organism" where

"different methods can be applied to one particular organism/system," revealing information about structure-function relationships in a system. The third approach relies on
virtual theoretical and empirical modeling, enabling exploration of ideas in a wide set
of hypothetical experimental conditions. And the fourth approach involves mimicking
an organism in an artificial but partially real model "keeping some essential features of
the biological original and then performing experiments with this artificial model." This
text exemplifies a level of academic discussion that, although comparativist in nature, is
ultimately concerned with refining methodologies for the biology-to-technology transfer
but does not challenge its core assumptions and or disrupt the teleological order of how
such transfer is supposed to work (ending with laboratory prototypes). It is a rich body
of literature, though; and one that goes beyond Western academia and demonstrates the
uptake of biomimicry across various sociocultural contexts. For instance, Aliyu Barau
(2012) "coupled the relevant verses of the Quran on the habitats of the three insects [ant,
bee, and spider] to develop a nine-component sustainable urban design template."

At the same time, specifically within such instrumentally oriented contexts, one issue
that recurs in the literature is the simultaneous cooptation and marginalization of the idea
of indigenous knowledge. Particularly in its treatment of nature as "mentor," biomimicry
literature engages in discursive work to relate this form of engagement with nature to
traditional indigenous knowledge processes and frequently invokes explicit parallels with
indigenous subsistence-dwelling cultures (onto which Western fantasies of harmonious
human-nature relations are commonly projected). For instance, the Biomimicry Institute
website features the following commentary:

> Most indigenous cultures share a participatory awareness of nature as the ground of
> our being . . . learning from traditional indigenous wisdom—or Traditional Ecological
> Knowledge (TEK)—is an important aspect of biomimicry practice . . . As we move to-
> wards a synthesis of ancient wisdom and modern scientific and technological capabilities
> . . . among the many lessons we can learn from indigenous cultures around the world are
> the understanding that the world is alive and meaningful and our relationship with the
> rest of life is one of participation, communion, and co-creation; the practice of accessing
> the collective intelligence of community through modes of communication that involve
> deep listening and sharing from the heart in a council circle; the insight that the rest of
> the natural world is in continuous communication with us if we only learn to listen.[9]

This kind of rhetoric is typical of green primitivism—the problematic[10] yet persistent
postcolonial era construction of the exotic other as an "ecologically noble savage" (Redford 1991) who must "know something that we don't or that we have lost" (Gaćeša 2008).
And it casually permeates many uncritically written "applied biomimicry" pieces, which,
invoking indigenous knowledge, tend to reproduce this Western fantasy of indigenous
epistemologies and/or construct indigenous peoples as historical artifacts located firmly
in the past, somewhere vaguely before Leonardo da Vinci (who makes a regular appear-
ance in biomimicry literature because of his fascination with flying technologies and his
codex on the flight of birds). For example, Allen Marshall and Silvia Lozeva (2009: 2),
in their article "Questioning the Theory and Practice of Biomimicry," answer their own
question "Is biomimicry all that new?" by claiming:

> Numerous historical examples can easily be cited of bio-inspired design: 1. Indigenous
> management of landscapes that mimicked natural processes; 2. Leonardo Da Vinci's
> bird-like flying machine designs; 3. some of the 19th century architectural ideas of
> Gottfried Semper who worked with the anatomical studies of renowned French naturalist
> George Cuvier; 4. the turn-of-the-century biomorphic style of Art Nouveau; 5. George
> de Mistrals invention of Velcro based upon the attachment properties of cockle burs.

Other authors, still falling within this "applied" category, may explore not just methods but meta-methods, as it were, considering different first principles that can inform a biomimicry endeavor, and their work could be said to at least complexify if not completely intervene in the teleology of biomimicry. For instance, Salma El Ahmar (2012) notes, "approaches to biomimicry as a design process typically fall into two categories: problem-based approach (top-down approach) and solution-based approach (bottom-up approach)." She contrasts the two approaches: in the first one, designers identify problems and biologists match them to organisms that have solved similar issues. In a solution-based approach, "biology may influence humans in a way that might be outside a predetermined design problem, resulting in previously unthought of technologies, systems, or even approaches to design solution . . . [for that] biological research must be conducted and identified as relevant to a design context."

Incidentally, design as a project that makes use of biomimicry is not limited to the field of design but also extends to urban planning (Taylor Buck 2015), as well as organizational design and business, as seen in pieces like the one by Samir Patel and Khanjan Mehta (2011), who treat biomimicry's "life principles" as a framework for designing "successful social enterprises" and the practitioner-oriented book written by the investment expert Katherine Collins (2016), *Nature of Investing: Resilient Investment Strategies through Biomimicry*, in which she writes, "Applying the principles of biomimicry (life's principles) gives us an approach that realigns and reintegrates our investment activity with the world around us."[11] Specifically within architecture, the literature on biomimicry spans both case studies (López et al. 2017; Pedersen Zari 2015) and "best practices" and theoretical inquiries, for example, contrasting biomimicry with humanism in its implications for architectural innovation as in the case of Joe Kaplinsky, who takes an anti-biomimicry approach, arguing that biological analogies devalue the achievement of designers and calling for a humanistic approach instead. While Kaplinsky's pro-humanism argument reads as antiquated (for him, humanism seems to be the legacy of the Enlightenment, which the principles of biomimicry in his opinion contradict (2006: 68)), he does provide an interesting line of critique from the standpoint of evolutionary biology:

> Architecture can never be alive. Nor does nature optimise. At least it rarely optimizes what it is that we are interested in. Evolution can only proceed by small steps. It can never start from scratch. Instead, it must optimise incrementally, which can produce some distinctly suboptimal results. For example, no designer would make the nerve connection between the brain and larynx of a giraffe by looping it all the way down the neck and back up to the throat. But evolution was constrained by the anatomy of the giraffe ancestor, in which the nerve looped around a blood vessel at the base of the neck. (69)

Biomimicry in architecture is a relatively new concept, and while seen as potentially valuable to design, it is also recognized as philosophically underdeveloped, indistinct, and ad hoc in the application of its theories, as noted by Freya Mathews (2011: 3), who warns that until its "critical ambiguities" are brought to light and resolved, "biomimicry remains vulnerable to co-optation by as powerful an anthropocentric mentality as that which launched the original industrial revolution and ravaged, in our time, the living constituency of the biosphere."

There is a lot of discussion about potential application (Brownell and Swackhamer 2015; Gruber 2011; Gruber and Jeronimidis 2012; Kuhlmann 2011) and some discussion about comparative ways to deploy biomimicry. For example, Nina Volstad and Casper Boks discuss "reductive" and "holistic" approaches to biomimicry (the distinction maps onto the different levels of biomimicry proposed by Benyus, so the reductive view correlates to the imitation of form while the holistic view correlates to the system-imitation level of biomimicry). As they elaborate, "the reductive approach to biomimicry focuses on simulation of a small number of features of a particular organism or biological process, moreover this approach doesn't necessarily aim to achieve sustainability as a result. In contrast, the holistic approach involves emulation of entire natural systems, encouraging hermeneutical and phenomenological solutions within the field of biomimicry" (2008: 3). So, such discussions create space and vocabulary for distinguishing biomimicry as a technocratic solution from biomimicry as a multilevel praxis animated by a particular understanding of human relationality and experience vis-à-vis the natural world. This kind of literature can be thought of as providing a meso-level critical perspective—treating biomimicry as a cluster of practices and worldviews and judging some to be preferable to others. But that body of literature neither critically examines the first principles of biomimicry nor explores biomimicry's ontololgical trajectory as a particular form of cultural capital. It also fails to locate biomimicry within the power structures made legible by political economy and political ecology. In that, it falls short of a higher-order critical discourse on biomimicry.

In other words, while there is a substantive level of theoretical debates around biomimicry within architecture and design, much of it focuses on interpretation or optimization—in some way engaging with the question of what is the "right" way to do biomimicry. But there is little work in these disciplinary contexts that engages with how biomimicry is situated within the broader social, political, and economic context as both an epistemic paradigm and an economy of value.

Affective Relationships

It must be noted that one salient aspect of biomimicry literature is what could be termed affect—stemming from the valorization and, in a somewhat ironic sense, anthropomorphization of nature, and the projection of hopes and aspirations onto it as a domain. Eva Hayward (2010), in her ethnography of the Long Marine Laboratory, where studies of cup corals take place, in making her argument that species are "impressions" that carry structural, behavioral, and textural traces—of those other species with whom they are entangled—brings in the idea of bioenvy as a precursor to biomimicry: "I am reminded of *Sensory Exotica* by Howard C. Hughes (1999). Working through the biomechanics of animal senses, Hughes maintains that technologies such as sonar and electroreception bespeak a human envy of nonhuman sensoria" and links it to work by Steven Connor (2005: 580), who "posits that as bioenvy transforms into biomimicry, compounding eyes of flies are turned into figures of lenses—as a part of the shift that finds mechanisms taking over animal roles as sentinels such as—literally—canaries in the mines, for example."

Biomimicry also figures in the body of literature that spans from psychology to environmental architecture that pertains to biophilia, though scholars also note the chief distinction between the two. As Stephen Kellert writes:

> Both the concepts of biophilia and biomimicry focus on the human relationship to nature, based on the belief that by better understanding the processes of evolutionary adaptation, we will be able to utilize this knowledge to advance human interests, particularly in the design of the built environment and in fostering a more sustainable world. These two concepts differ, however, in their respective emphases on human evolutionary adaptation versus that of other species and natural processes (2014: 1)

even as they "both . . . reflect a respect and affinity for the ingenuity and intelligence of solutions hammered into a species genes following countless adaptations to the requirements of survival" (5).

But this emotional connection to and valorization and admiration of nature figures prominently in the deployment of the concept of biomimicry in contexts that, if one had to construct a dyad, could be seen as "uncritical" applications of it rather than critical interrogations of it as a hermeneutic and heuristic system. The "affective dimension" of biomimicry is particularly prominent in education literature, especially (but not exclusively) in sustainability education literature, which demonstrates the uses of biomimicry in educational projects. An example of one such project is the "Study away experience in Costa Rica focused around the Life Principles of Biomimicry for the purpose of stimulating connection with and affection for nature," which names as its goals "to stimulate a sense of wonder in and affection for the natural world, to utilize Life Principles in everyday decision-making and to represent good global citizenship by developing an appropriate relationship with nature" as discussed by Cosette Armstrong (2016). The author notes in her article, reflecting on this pedagogical experiment:

> from a teaching perspective, focusing on solutions stemming from affection and adoration of nature set a different tone for students, much different from the often depressing facts about the state of the planet, which are no less true but have a propensity to overwhelm and disempower learners . . . Emphasizing the affective domain during the learning process was . . . effective to engage students in sustainability in a positive way.

An article by Constance Soja in the *Journal of Geoscience Education* about the pedagogical setup and outcomes of a field-based biomimicry exercise within the framework of a course themed on the Sixth Extinction concludes:

> [The biomimicry exercise] . . . helps students acquire the necessary tools to proceed with the final research project on bioinspired design innovations, many of which have real potential for solving human problems in a sustainable way. In essence, appreciating the causes and consequences of global biodiversity loss in the past can help students learn and then teach others about the value of species and ecosystem services at the onset of the Sixth Extinction. (2014: 698)

Here, affective themes of appreciation and the cultivation of what Arun Agrawal (2005) termed "environmentality" are linked to the uses of biomimicry in the classroom. And another example, also more oriented at pedagogical practice than producing new knowledge per se, is a piece by Dorna Schroeter (2010) in *Green Teacher*, a publication for and by educators, which also attests to the trend of viewing biomimicry as an affectively powerful mobilizing device in educational settings:

> Looking for a way to capture your students' attention and encourage creativity and critical thinking skills? Try this: ask them to explain the connection between a moth's eye and a cell phone screen, or between the Blue Morpho butterfly and fabric. If you do not know the answers yourself, then welcome to the amazing and inspiring world of biomimicry. Both are examples of how humans are looking at designs and processes in nature for solutions to many of the problems we are facing. At a time when an overload of news about environmental crises often creates fear and hopelessness, the science of biomimicry is a beacon of light.

Science

In the context of STEM fields, the line between biomimicry and biomimetics is hazier than it is in the design and design-adjacent fields. And in these fields, the intentional imitation of nature, by either name, found a vocal champion (and thus biomimicry literature found a prolific author) in Yoseph Bar-Cohen, a notable physicist at the Jet Propulsion

Laboratory. He published the volume *Biomimetics: Nature-Based Innovation* and wrote in the introduction:

> Through evolution, nature came up with effective solutions to its challenges, and they were improved over millions of years. Nature is effectively a giant laboratory where trial-and-error experiments are made, and through evolution the results are implemented, self-maintained, and continually evolving to address the changing challenges . . . Researchers are seeking rules, concepts, and principles of biology to inspire new possibilities including materials, mechanisms, algorithms, and fabrication processes. Some of the benefits from these studies are improved structures, actuators, sensors, interfaces, control, software, drugs, defense, intelligence, and many others. (2016: vi–vii)

The author then develops these themes, persuading the reader through concrete and easy-to-visualize examples like "Furniture and Many Animals Have Four Legs: Is It a Coincidence?"; "The Need to Feed Our Babies: Inspiring the Design of Bottles"; and "Thorns, Spines, and Prickles: Possibly Inspired Barbwire," among others. The volume itself features work on the application of biomimetics to medical implants (Müller 2016), medical devices design (Argunsah and Davis 2016), plant cell wall architecture (Rey et al. 2016), optics (Lee 2016), and flying technology (Kulfan and Colozza 2016), among others.

Biomimicry as method and praxis figures routinely in articles across a variety of fields pertaining to medicine, biotechnology, nanotechnology, etcetera. For instance, Ge Zhang (2012) provides an overview of what biomimicry can contribute to biomedical research in areas such as regenerative medicine or in tissue engineering where skin grafts have been designed to mimic the cell composition and layered structure of native skin. In nanobiotechnology, for example, biomimicry is used for making an enzymatic reaction converting glucose to lactate more efficient (Mukai et al. 2016) or imitating amelogenesis (the process of developing tooth enamel) (Uskoković 2010). Yanfei Liu and K. M. Passino (2002) study the biology and physics underlying the foraging behavior of *E. coli* bacteria and discuss the uses of biomimicry of social foraging as a component of the study. Biomimicry has also been used in public health initiatives, for instance in developing a primary care model (Whitehouse 2013).

Scientists like Joseph Ayers and his collaborators are using biomimetic approaches to intervene in the standard approach in robotics that is grounded in rule-based finite state machines. Instead, they are creating robots with electronic nervous systems "composed of analog and computed neurons and synapses for biomimetic robots based on neurobiological model systems, the lobster and the lamprey" (Ayers and Rulkov 2008). Robert Full (2002), an integrative biologist focused on comparative biomechanics, uses gecko physiology to make advances in an area of engineering known as inertial assisted robotics and has long stressed the importance of discernment for biomimetic experimentations. As he notes, as many living things are "over-engineered," it is important to only imitate what is necessary. The Wyss Institute at Harvard University, which precedes the Benyus biomimicry initiative, works on a range of projects from biomimetic adaptive materials that respond to environmental cues like living organisms to bioinspired therapeutics and diagnostics.

A meta-analysis of biomimicry research successes (largely within the STEM context) by Elena Lurie-Luke provides an "ecosystem-based" analysis of various aspects of biomimicry from how many species have been imitated to what the most popular applications have been. The author says material development seems to be the largest area of biomimicry research, accounting for approximately 50 percent of all reviewed references, and this research has yielded innovations across a range of fields including optical materials, medicine, agriculture, textiles, and coating materials. The second-largest area of biomimicry application, according to her findings, is animal locomotion models: "Insights into the general principles that underlie movement, the mechanisms and structures of muscular and skeletal systems provide insights that can be applied to increase the efficiency of moving vehicles, especially in robotics, or help to inspire entirely new modes of transport" (2014: 1499).

Deconstructing Biomimicry

The body of literature that specifically engages biomimicry from a critical humanities and social science perspective is more nascent but is already characterized by certain discernible trends. For example, much of it focuses on the militarization of the biological life aspect of biomimicry (Johnson 2010; Zerner 2012), which is unsurprising, given the somewhat occluded but highly relevant history of biomimicry as a research megaproject within DARPA. In response, Charles Zerner develops the concept of "stealth nature" to analyze DARPA projects involving biomimetics[12] as a part of the militarized deployment of nature that include vivisystems (e.g., using bees or moths for environmental tracking) and hybrid biosystems designed to create animal-robot cyborgs for surveillance purposes. Biomimetics in this trifecta are the "mechanical devices that mimic the abilities and structures of living beings, particularly insects (Masco 2004: 537, quoted in Zerner 2010: 297). Zerner contextualizes biomimicry within a long history of intellectual enchantment with biological structures and processes, and, in discussing the work of the aforementioned champion of biomimicry, he states:

> Bar-Cohen's reverence . . . reflects a recent branch in the long genealogy of scientific inspiration from natural structure and operations . . . It is linked to Fabre's meditative gaze at the structures and behaviors of spiders, wasps, and mantises. It is related to Leonardo da Vinci's observations on and drawings of the fight of birds; awe at a world ingeniously constructed . . . DARPA, in this sense of stealth nature, is involved in a mimetic mode, or, more precisely, a biomimetic mode, imitating not only the structure or appearance of a certain organism, but the evolutionary strategy of stealth nature—nature as weapon against perceived threats being rescaled down and harder and harder to detect" (315, 295)

Biomimetics, according to Zerner, is a part of new frontiers that "unsettle how we wage war and how we fashion nature and the social." These new frontiers bring with them new ethical challenges; for instance, in the case of human casualties facilitated by biomimetic entities, who is responsible? Can one speak of responsibility? In case of casualties, "would this be a violation of the Geneva Convention or a product liability case?" (321).

Colin Salter analogously focuses on the intersection of biomimicry and the US military project in his exploration of the return of animals to the battlefield and the intersection of the animal-industrial complex—"a set of economic, cultural and social relations and networks spanning agribusiness, governments and scientific bodies"—and the military-industrial complex: "Animals have been integrated into human warfare in a dearth of ways, including as transport, weapons platforms, weapons in themselves, and surveillance. In many ways, the introduction and proliferation of drones, the central focus of . . . the robotics revolution are bioinspired robots: what amounts to biomimesis or biomimicry" (2015: 13).

Elizabeth Johnson, in a theoretically rigorous and thoughtful overview of biomimicry, also engages its military history but then goes beyond it to situate this field in global neoliberal biopolitics, highlighting the apolitical camouflage or veneer through which the promise of biomimicry obscures its complexities: "It is a discourse that invigorates thoroughly deposed interpretations of nonhuman natures and pre-human pasts as 'harmonious' and 'balanced.' As biomimetic production is made to promise a 'return' to such a state, it is charged with generating the environmental and social security required to get there." As she continues to point out, another component of her critique highlights that the Benyus vision in biomimicry departs from post-human theorists like Donna Haraway and Giorgio Agamben, who see life as inherently and explicitly political, to instead inadvertently

> revive the essentialism of nature, reinscribing the notion that nonhumans—and, by extension, their reinvention—are righteous and apolitical. Biomimetic production so conceived does not merely open new avenues for production; it imagines instead that it opens up access to the 'right ones,' eliminating the potential for ecological, geopolitical, and economic contestations. The 'political will' that such a view engenders is one of acquiescence and blind acceptance of 'nature's wisdom' however it may be taken up and applied. (2010: 191)

Elsewhere, Elizabeth Johnson and Jesse Goldstein (2015: 8) focus on biomimicry as a force of—though they do not call it that specifically—a kind of new modernism, that remakes the relationship between nature and production, in the process both enabling and, in a sense, falling prey to the "recuperative powers of capital's logic and its tendency to evacuate the political from notions of progress," as well as producing "inadvertent erasure of nonindustrial ways of knowing."

In a related direction, Mathews (2011: 2) notes, "critical ambiguities lurk in this concept. Until these are brought to light and resolved, biomimicry remains vulnerable to co-optation by as powerful an anthropocentric mentality as that which launched the original industrial revolution and ravaged, in our time, the living constituency of the biosphere." She points to an ethical contradiction that inhabits the uninterrogated concept of biomimicry as it is deployed and claimed by various factions today:

> For some theorists, biomimicry is a vehicle by which we can save the parliament of species; for others it is a vehicle by which we can replace that parliament with a "new nature" of our own design. Both parties agree that we need to re-situate ourselves morally inside nature, but for the former party this translates into moral respect for the biological beings and systems that currently constitute the biosphere whereas for the latter it translates into respect for abstract principles of self-genesis and regeneration. Both positions seem equally biomimetic: they both agree on the generative principles that shape nature and hence underpin bio-design. Both announce themselves, justifiably, as models of sustainability. The choice between them comes down to ethics. (8)

Vincent Blok and Bart Gremmen take a philosophical interrogation of biomimicry into the realm of semiotic categories and their implications. They point out, "it is striking that the ambition of biomimicry is to mimic nature, but that nature is in fact already understood in technological terms" (i.e., as "natural technology"). The ambiguity they highlight is the following: "We encounter a first ambiguity here regarding the concept of nature. On the one hand, the concept of nature is rooted in a technological concept of nature: natural technology or nature as artist, tektoon, techne, technology. On the other hand, the traditional dichotomy between nature and technology is ignored in biomimetical approaches" (2016: 205). They distinguish between a "strong concept of biomimetics"—one that is didactically focused on duplication—and contrast it with "the weaker concept of biomimetics," which is grounded in inspiration, concluding that the strong concept is more problematic partially because it commits the naturalistic fallacy but also because it is grounded in problematic assumptions, whereas the weaker concept sees mimicry not as the duplication of natural solutions but primarily as a creative solution inspired by nature such that, "therefore, the complexity and temperamentality of natural phenomena are acknowledged, as well as the necessity of translation in order to transfer natural problem solving to technological problem solving" (209).

Further from the realm of philosophy, there is work by Henry Dicks (2016) that proposes an analytical framework for biomimicry, where he first "translates" each of Benyus's three principles of biomimicry into philosophical principles. So, "nature as model" becomes the "poetic principle" (referring to the Greek concept of *poiesis*, meaning "creating" or "bringing forth"). "Nature as measure" becomes the "ethical principle" affirming it as the standard against which the "rightness" of innovations should be judged. "Nature as mentor" becomes the "epistemological principle" reflecting the fact that in biomimicry, nature is the ultimate source of knowledge. Dicks then adds the fourth "ontological" field of inquiry, which is a particularly welcome one, as it explicitly integrates the discussion of "the nature of nature" into the discourse of biomimicry, highlighting the occluded first principles or fundamental assumptions in this field, which, in reifying nature, obscures its existence as a fundamentally historically and culturally contingent construct. Elsewhere, Dicks (2014) further problematizes the reified and un-interrogated monolith, or megaproject, of "nature" that at times seems to be the animating ethos of biomimicry. So, Dicks recapitulates Benyus's nine basic "laws, strategies, and principles" of nature that are designed to undergird the practice of biomimicry:

> Nature runs on sunlight.
> Nature uses only the energy it needs.
> Nature fits form to function.
> Nature recycles everything.
> Nature rewards cooperation.
> Nature banks on diversity.
> Nature demands local expertise.
> Nature curbs excesses from within.
> Nature taps the power of limits. (Benyus 1997: 7)

But, as Dicks points out, while "without some sort of characterization of Nature biomimicry would be radically incomplete and ill-defined," attention must be paid to the differences between "'laws,' 'strategies,' and 'principles.'" He continues:

> Whereas a law is either something that is always followed or something whose transgression will be penalized, a strategy is rather a course of action that it may prove advantageous to adopt. To take a simple example, it is clearly not the case that Nature always "runs on sunlight" or that organisms will necessarily be penalized if they do not do so. Certain deep sea organisms, for example, depend on hydrothermal vents to produce organic material via chemosynthesis. So, even when indirect use of solar energy (wind, hydro, biomass) is factored in, the claim that "Nature runs on sunlight" is clearly not a *law*, though this is not to say that it is not the *principal strategy* for energy procurement adopted by life on earth. (2014: 238)

Elsewhere, Dicks (2017) further develops this strand of thought when he writes:

> It is . . . evident that underlying the totality of biomimicry is what Heidegger (1995) calls our "pre-ontological" understanding of Being, that is to say, our ability to understand the "as" prior to the formulation of any explicit ontology, for this underlies our understanding of Nature and natural phenomena "as" this or that, as well as our understanding of the principles of Nature *as* model, Nature *as* measure, and Nature *as* mentor.

Overall, his work is significant in pointing to the haze surrounding the ontological assumptions and their articulations when it comes to biomimicry.

One of the schisms in the broad concept of biomimicry is attentively analyzed by Michael Fisch (2017), who maps the ideological and praxis differences between the Benyus approach and the version of biomimicry emerging out of MIT through the work of the media ecologist Neri Oxman—two directions animated by the ethos of imitation and inspiration, respectively, according to the author. Fisch argues the Benyus way, fo-cused as it is on nature as a source for innovative design that can be emulated in tech-nologies, is problematic in valorizing the organic form and reifying the separation of nature and technology. Oxman's work, according to Fisch, is neomaterialist in ethos and treats biomimicry as a technology of nature, and its relational orientation results in a new and, in a way inductive (though he does not use the term) system of ethics, "emergent within a system of relations rather than something that is realized under a binding logic [of Benyus's approach]" (2017: 22). Fisch's critique dovetails with Karen Barad's piece that also critiques Benyus's "hard distinction" between nature and human—and further expands the critique to point out the division between "nature" and "culture" in Benyus's vision, and the presumption that "the material designs can be separated from the agential practices that produce them" (2008: 318).

Two (Out of Many) Potential Directions in Exploring Biomimicry

The last set of literatures I want to mention (though each of them could easily be the subject of its own literature review) consists of two macroscale environmental practices that aren't "officially" legible as biomimicry but arguably fall within the scope of bio-mimicry, and there is some (very limited) recognition of that, at least in case of the first, in academic literature. While there are many practices reliant on imitating processes of nature as a part of environmental future-making and the emergent and accelerating bio-economy—all that it encompasses across various scales of planetary management—and a full review of them could easily be its own article, I want to highlight the two practices, as I contend that they represent the logics and processes of biomimicry but with scales and temporalities that bring into question how to use nature as a standard, given that in a scenario where they are followed to the logical conclusion of their respective visions, they would interpolate the entire global ecosystem.

The first practice I am referring to is geoengineering—in particular, the strand of geoengineering known as SRM (solar radiation management) via a technique called stratospheric aerosol injection—a controversial (Poumadère et al. 2011; Szerszynski et al. 2013) process that, in injecting reflecting aerosol particles into the stratosphere, replicates the effect of volcanic eruptions blasting reflecting sulphate particles there. The particles (either "real" or mimicked do, or in theory would) reflect some amount of sunlight, thus temporarily cooling the planet. As Leslie Thiele notes in his overview, "SRM might be embraced by Gaians as a form of biomimicry, as it effectively reproduces the albedo modi-fication generated by volcanic eruptions that inject vast amounts of (sulfate) aerosols into the stratosphere. As such, it might be likened to the construction of artificial reefs that stimulate the regeneration of aquatic life in human-degraded seas" (2018: 16). But others specifically juxtapose SRM with biomimicry, like Byron Williston, who writes in his piece on geoengineering that

> albedo modification appears to be a relatively cheap and technically feasible set of options . . . But surely there are alternatives to this sort of large-scale manipulation of planetary systems. Biomimicry, for example, seeks to learn lessons from nature at the micro-scale and apply them to our own problems. For example, we might better learn how to keep our buildings cool by studying the way termite colonies keep internal temperatures relatively low for the structure's inhabitants. (2016: 206)

It is possible that, in line with Williston's argument, there is an under-recognition of pro-posed geoengineering protocols as biomimicry because they challenge the assumptions of the scale that biomimicry is imagined to occupy. However, it would be intriguing and worthwhile to bring the literature on geoengineering into dialogue with literature on biomimicry and to discuss the convergences and divergences of their ontologies and teleologies.

The other practice I want to mention, which is actually not recognized as biomimicry at the moment but is one I would argue falls under its aegis, is the philosophy and practice of trophic rewilding (Svenning and Faurby 2017; Svenning et al. 2015). Trophic rewilding is a controversial updated version of the no less controversial "Pleistocene rewilding" (Donlan 2005; Donlan et al. 2006) or "resurrection ecology"—a concept that is made literal in the media-garnering project of the resurrection or "de-extinction" of the wooly mammoth in the Pleistocene Park of Yakutia[13] and explored in a more tempered form through "'back-breeding': the selective breeding of domestic animals in an attempt to achieve an animal breed with a phenotype that resembles an extinct wild ancestor" (Keulartz and Bovenkerk 2016). Trophic here "refers to a 'trophic cascade'—when the removal of a top predator or herbivore has indirect and cascading effects on lower tropic level" (Rubenstein and Rubenstein 2016: 113). Rewilding facilitates the restoration of keystone species (as a rule, large-bodied carnivores and herbivores) that help restore and self-regulate ecosystems via impact on land. Rewilding—which, like biomimicry itself, is "a plastic term with several different meanings" (Lorimer et al. 2015: 55)—does not strictly follow the systematic protocol of biomimicry in "biologizing the question" and following the trail to solutions. Rather, the question in a sense folds in on itself because learning from nature's processes and using technological interventions to imitate them here is sup-posed to result in a final product that is not something other-than-nature mimicking nature but is, rather, nature mimicking an earlier version of itself. It can be argued, though, that trophic rewilding is animated by the ethos of and comprised of elements of biomimicry, and uses the logic of biomimicry, making it a kind of meta-biomimicry phenomenon. It would be a valuable contribution to conceptualizing bio-mimicry as a paradigm to use trophic rewilding as a kind of generative theoretical engine to help think through its underlying principles and implications.

Conclusion

This article synthesized and reviewed the various strands of literatures on biomimicry—a task that involved bringing together representative (though not exhaustive) examples of literature from different disciplines that have categorically different epistemic relation-ships with the concept of biomimicry: an object of philosophical inquiry, an arena for ethical exploration, a praxis for design that ranges in its applications from military to environmental, and more. The result is necessarily somewhat eclectic, owing to this radi-cally different existence that biomimicry as an epistemic object has across different fields. To me, as an environmental anthropologist and political ecologist, what I termed "critical literature" on biomimicry is of particular interest—and going forward, I want to identify a lacuna in the production of knowledge on biomimicry that can best be remedied by critical social sciences working on environmental topics. The most fruitful directions I see for future exploration of the topic involve further developing the important work on how biomimicry fits within the political economy of biotechnology in general (Goldstein and Johnson 2015) and engaging with biomimicry as a praxis that radically reframes, or has the potential to reframe, our understanding of resources and the human-nature relations as constituted by the process of the resourcification of nature. While Johnson and Gold-stein do link the critique of biomimicry with the critique of capitalism, beyond their work, there is a dearth of links between the critique of biomimicry and critique of, specifically, green capitalism (Büscher et al. 2012; Igoe 2010; Sullivan 2013) and the financialization of nature (Bakker 2010; Brockington and Duffy 2010; West 2006). Goldstein and Johnson (2015: 71) open the door to and lay a foundation for a discussion about this set of issues when they write, "With the shift from nature characterized by material resources to immaterial inspiration, biomimetic enclosures produce life's extant objects—in the form of organisms, cells, DNA, etc.—through a new lens of Intellectual property, paralleling similar movements within the disciplines of neurology, micro-biology, bio-technology, and genetics." But overall, the body of literature I reviewed does not explore in depth what it means that biomimicry instrumentalizes nature into a meta-resource and mega-resource that is uniquely dematerializing and deterritorializing, or the ways in which biomimicry's promise of "free inspiration for all" aims to erase the positionality of nature within specific cultural and political contexts of power relations. It would also be valuable to explore the ways in which the paradigm of biomimicry uses discourses and stereotypes of indigenous knowledge and indigenous human-nature relations. Multiple ethnographies of biomimetic projects and initiatives would, of course, be incredibly valuable in pushing the critical literature on biomimicry in that direction, as ethnographic methods could rise to the challenge of locating invisible and covert forms of dispossession that may arise from the commodification of conceptual, rather than materialized, nature.

▪ **VERONICA DAVIDOV** is Associate Professor of Anthropology at Monmouth University. She holds a PhD from New York University and is an environmental and visual anthropologist. She is the author of *Ecotourism and Cultural Production: An Anthropology of Indigenous Spaces in Ecuador* (2013) and *Long Night at the Vepsian Museum: The Forest Folk of Russia and the Struggle for Cultural Survival* (2017). Email: vdavidov@monmouth.edu

▪ **NOTES**

1. This "origin story" is contested by various factions within biomimicry, but for the purposes of this article, I am starting with the site of the most ubiquitous "name recognition," which is the Benyus project.
2. Although searching through Google Scholar citations revealed the synonymous "biomemesis" was used as early as 1968 by E. O. Attinger "Biomedical Engineering: From Biomimesis to Biosynthesis" (1968).
3. Despite homological origins, biomimicry and biomimetics are, at present, neither identical nor interchangeable as spaces of innovation or denotative terms; biomimetics is a broader umbrella term that can signify any kind of imitation of nature in general, in particular in STEM contexts, while biomimicry, especially with its increasing self-branding as a "green" industry, particularly in the fields of science and engineering, and biomimicry by this point presupposes a commitment to a certain ecologically and sustainably oriented sensibility and praxis.
4. (1) Integrated instead of additive construction; (2) Optimization of the whole, rather than maximization of individual elements; (3) Multifunctionality instead of monofunctionality
5. This list regularly appears in mainstream media features on biomimicry, in dozens of articles, e,g., Bird (2008); Brown (2018).
6. "What Is Biomimicry?" Biomimicry 3.8, accessed 30 March 2019, https://biomimicry.net/what-is-biomimicry.
7. Life's Principles, according to the Biomimicry Institute guidelines, are design lessons from nature—a set of survival strategies and overarching patterns found amongst the species surviving and thriving on Earth. They include "evolve to survive," "adapt to changing conditions,"

"be locally attuned and responsive," "use life-friendly chemistry," "be resource-efficient," and "integrate development with growth." "Biomimicry DesignLens: A Visual Guide," Biomimicry 3.8, released 12 November 2015, https://biomimicry.net/the-buzz/resources/designlens-lifes-principles.
8. "Biomimicry Thinking: A Skill Set for the 21st Century," Biomimicry Center at Arizona State University, accessed 30 May 2019, http://biomimicry.asu.edu/education.
9. "Learning from Nature and Designing as Nature: Regenerative Cultures Create Conditions Conducive to Life," Biomimicry Institute, 6 September 2016, https://biomimicry.org/learning-nature-designing-nature-regenerative-cultures-create-conditions-conducive-life.
10. For critiques of this concept across the disciplines, see Argyrou (2005); Driessen (2005); Ellen (1986); Sillitoe (1993).
11. No page reference is available, as the author released the book as an e-book.
12. Although, as I note at the beginning, there is an etymological and contextual difference between biomimicry and biomimetics, the terms are used interchangeably by other scholars working on the topic, including those who write about it in a military context (Salter, Johnson), and I follow their lead here.
13. See http://www.pleistocenepark.ru/en.

■ REFERENCES

Agrawal, Arun. 2005. *Environmentality: Technologies of Government and the Making of Subjects*. Durham, NC: Duke University Press.
Anker, Peder. 2010. *From Bauhaus to Ecohouse: A History of Ecological Design*. Baton Rouge: Louisiana State University Press.
Argunsah, Hande, and Brian L. Davis. "Application of Biomimetics in the Design of Medical Devices." In Bar-Cohen 2016: 445-461.
Argyrou, Vassos. 2005. *The Logic of Environmentalism: Anthropology, Ecology and Postcoloniality*. Oxford: Berghahn Books.
Armstrong, Cosette Marie. 2016. "'Don't Step on the Ants!' Biomimetic Pedagogy for Sustainability in a Costa Rica Study Away Experience." *Journal of Sustainability Education* 11. http://www.susted.com/wordpress/content/dont-step-on-the-ants-biomimetic-pedagogy-for-sustainability-in-a-costa-rica-study-away-experience_2016_05.
Ayers, Joseph, and Nikolai Rulkov. 2008. "Controlling Biomimetic Underwater Robots with Electronic Nervous Systems." In *Bio-mechanisms of Swimming and Flying*, ed. Naomi Kato and Shinji Kamimura, 295-306. Tokyo: Springer.
Bakker, Karen. 2010. "The limits of 'neoliberal natures': Debating green neoliberalism." *Progress in human geography* 34 (6): 715-735.
Bar-Cohen, Yoseph. 2016. *Biomimetics: Nature-Based Innovation*. Boca Raton: CRC Press.
Barad, Karen. 2008. "Queer causation and the ethics of mattering." Pp. 311-338 in *Queering the non/human*, edited by Myra Herd and Noreen Gaffney, New York: Routledge
Barau, Aliyu Salisu. 2012. "Habitats of Ant, Bee and Spider in the Qur'an: Exploring Clues for Sustainable Urban Design." Paper presented at "Sustainability Through Biomimicry: Discovering a World of Solutions Inspired by Nature," University of Dammam, College of Design, 28-30 October.
Benyus, Janine. 1997. *Biomimicry: Innovation Inspired by Nature*. New York: Harper Perennial.
Bird, Winfried. 2008. "Biomimicry: Natural by Design." *Japan Times*, 24 August. https://www.japantimes.co.jp/life/2008/08/24/general/natural-by-design/#.XPBxCnt7ln4.
Blok, Vincent, and Bart Gremmen. 2016. "Ecological Innovation: Biomimicry as a New Way of Thinking and Acting Ecologically." *Journal of Agricultural and Environmental Ethics* 29 (2): 203-217.
Brockington, Dan and Rosaleen Duffy. 2010. Capitalism and conservation: the production and reproduction of biodiversity conservation. *Antipode, 42* (3): 469-484.
Brown, Sass. 2018. "Inspired by Nature: Design That Imitates Life." *The National*, 8 December. https://www.thenational.ae/lifestyle/fashion/inspired-by-nature-design-that-imitates-life-1.800318.

Brownell, Blaine E., and Marc T. Swackhamer. 2015. *Hypernatural: Architecture's New Relationship with Nature*. Princeton, NJ: Princeton Architectural Press.

Büscher, Bram, Sian Sullivan, Katja Neves, James Igoe, and Dan Brockington. 2012. "Towards a Synthesized Critique of Neoliberal Biodiversity Conservation." *Capitalism Nature Socialism* 23 (2): 4–30.

Collins, Katherine. 2016. *Nature of Investing: Resilient Investment Strategies through Biomimicry*. New York: Routledge.

Connor, Steven. 2005. "The Menagerie of the Senses." Paper presented at the 6th Synapsis Conferences "I cinque sensi (per tacer del sesto)," Bertinoro, Italy, 1 September.

Davidov, Veronica. 2013. "Amazonia as Pharmacopia." *Critique of Anthropology* 33 (3): 243–262.

Dicks, Henry. 2014. "Aldo Leopold and the Ecological Imaginary: The Balance, the Pyramid, and the Round River." *Environmental Philosophy* 11 (2): 175–209.

Dicks, Henry. 2016. "The Philosophy of Biomimicry." *Philosophy & Technology* 29 (3): 223–243.

Dicks, Henry. 2017. "The Poetics of Biomimicry: The Contribution of Poetic Concepts to Philosophical Inquiry into the Biomimetic Principle of Nature as Model." *Environmental Philosophy* 14 (2): 191–219.

Donlan, Josh. 2005. "Re-wilding North America." *Nature* 436 (7053): 913–914.

Donlan, C. Josh, Joel Berger, Carl E. Bock, Jane H. Bock, David A. Burney, James A. Estes, Dave Foreman, et al. 2006. "Pleistocene Rewilding: An Optimistic Agenda for Twenty-First Century Conservation." *American Naturalist* 168 (5): 160–183.

Driessen, Paul. 2005. *Eco-Imperialism: Green Power, Black Death*. Bellevue: Merrill Press.

El Ahmar, Salma Ashraf Saad. 2011. "Biomimicry as a Tool for Sustainable Architectural Design: Towards Morphogenetic Architecture." MA thesis, Alexandria University.

Ellen, Roy F. 1986. "What the Black Elk Left Unsaid: On the Illusory Images of Primitivism." *Anthropology Today* 2 (6): 8–12.

Fisch, Michael. 2017. "The Nature of Biomimicry: Toward a Novel Technological Culture." *Science, Technology, & Human Values* 42 (5): 795–821.

Fletcher, Robert. 2010. "Neoliberal Environmentality: Towards a Poststructuralist Political Ecology of the Conservation Debate." *Conservation and Society* 8 (3): 171–181.

Full, Robert. 2002. "Robots Inspired by Cockroach Ingenuity." TED Talk. Video, 20:11. https://www.ted.com/talks/robert_full_on_engineering_and_evolution/details.

Gaćeša, Dijana. 2008. "Eco-savages Are Conquering the World: The Creation of Ecological Sensibility Through the Construction of the 'Other.'" *Teme* 32 (3): 541–556.

Goldstein, Jesse, and Elizabeth Johnson. 2015. "Biomimicry: New Natures, New Enclosures." *Theory, Culture & Society* 32 (1): 61–81.

Gross, Matthias. 2010. *Ignorance and Surprise: Science, Society, and Ecological Design*. Cambridge, MA: MIT Press.

Gruber, Petra. "Biomimetics in Architecture." In Gruber et al. 2011: 127–148.

Gruber, Petra, and George Jeronimidis. 2012. "Has Biomimetics Arrived In Architecture?" *Bioinspiration & Biomimetics* 7 (1): 010201.

Gruber, Petra, Dietmar Bruckner, Christian Hellmich, Heinz-Bodo Schmiedmayer, Herbert Stachelberger, and Ille C. Gebeshuber, eds. 2011. *Biomimetics: Materials, Structures and Processes—Examples, Ideas and Case Studies*. Berlin: Springer.

Hayward, Eva. 2010. "Fingeryeyes: Impressions of Cup Corals." *Cultural Anthropology* 25 (4): 577–599.

Igoe, Jim. 2010. "The Spectacle of Nature in the Global Economy of Appearances: Anthropological Engagements with the Spectacular Mediations of Transnational Conservation." *Critique of Anthropology* 30 (4): 375–397.

Igoe, Jim, and Dan Brockington. 2007. "Neoliberal Conservation: A Brief Introduction." *Conservation and Society* 5 (4): 432–449.

Johnson, Elizabeth. 2010. "Reinventing Biological Life, Reinventing 'the Human.'" *Ephemera* 10 (2): 177–193.

Johnson, Elizabeth R., and Jesse Goldstein. 2015. "Biomimetic Futures: Life, Death, and the Enclosure of a More-Than-Human Intellect." *Annals of the Association of American Geographers* 105 (2): 387–396.

Kaplinsky, Joe. 2006. "Biomimicry versus Humanism." *Architectural Design* 76 (1): 66–71.

Kellert, Stephen. 2016. "Biophilia and Biomimicry: Evolutionary Adaptation of Human Versus Nonhuman Nature." *Intelligent Buildings International* 8 (2): 51–56.

Keulartz, Jozef, and Bernice Bovenkerk. 2016. "Changing Relationships with Non-Human Animals in the Anthropocene: An introduction." In *Animal Ethics in the Age of Humans: Blurring Boundaries in Human-Animal Relationships*, ed. Bernice Bovenkerk and Jozef Keulartz, 1–22. Dordrecht: Springer.

Kuhlmann, Dörte, "Biomorphism in Architecture: Speculations on Growth and Form." In Gruber et al. 2011: 149–178.

Kulfan, Brenda M., and Anthony J. Colozza. 2016. "Biomimetics and Flying Technology." In Bar-Cohen 2016: 527–674.

Lakhtakia, Akhlesh, and Raúl José Martín-Palma. 2013. *Engineered Biomimicry*. Amsterdam: Elsevier.

Lee, David W. 2016. "Biomimicry of the Ultimate Optical Device: The Plant." In Bar-Cohen 2016: 307–361.

Liu, Yanfei, and K. M. Passino. 2002. "Biomimicry of Social Foraging Bacteria for Distributed Optimization: Models, Principles, and Emergent Behaviors." *Journal of Optimization Theory and Applications* 115 (3): 603–628.

López, Marlén, Ramón Rubio, Santiago Martín, and Ben Croxford. 2017. "How Plants Inspire Façades: From Plants to Architecture—Biomimetic Principles for the Development of Adaptive Architectural Envelopes." *Renewable and Sustainable Energy Reviews* 67: 692–703.

Lorimer, Jamie, Chris Sandom, Paul Jepson, Chris Doughty, Maan Barua, and Keith J. Kirby. 2015. "Rewilding: Science, practice, and politics." *Annual Review of Environment and Resources* 40: 39–62.

Lurie-Luke, Elena. 2014. "Product and Technology Innovation: What Can Biomimicry Inspire?" *Biotechnology Advances* 32 (8): 1494–1505.

Marshall, Alan, and Silvia Lozeva. 2009. "Questioning the Theory and Practice of Biomimicry." *International Journal of Design & Nature and Ecodynamics* 4 (1): 1–10.

Mathews, Freya. 2011. "Towards a Deeper Philosophy of Biomimicry." *Organization & Environment* 24 (4): 364–387.

Mukai, Chinatsu, Lizeng Gao, Jacquelyn L. Nelson, James P. Lata, Roy Alan Cohen, Lauren Wu, Meleana M. Hinchman, et al. 2017. "Biomimicry Promotes the Efficiency of a 10-Step Sequential Enzymatic Reaction on Nanoparticles, Converting Glucose to Lactate." *Angewandte Chemie International Edition* 56 (1): 235–238.

Müller, Bert. 2016. "Biomimetics for Medical Implants." In Bar-Cohen 2016: 431–445.

Münster, Daniel, and Ursula Münster. 2012. "Consuming the Forest in an Environment of Crisis: Nature Tourism, Forest Conservation and Neoliberal Agriculture in South India." *Development and Change* 43 (1): 205–227.

Patel, Samir, and Khanjan Mehta. 2011. "Life's Principles as a Framework for Designing Successful Social Enterprises." *Journal of Social Entrepreneurship* 2 (2): 218–230.

Pedersen Zari, Maibritt. 2015. "Ecosystem Processes for Biomimetic Architectural and Urban Design." *Architectural Science Review* 58 (2): 106–119.

Poumadère, Marc, Raquel Bertoldo, and Jaleh Samadi. 2011. "Public Perceptions and Governance of Controversial Technologies to Tackle Climate Change: Nuclear Power, Carbon Capture and Storage, Wind, and Geoengineering." *Wiley Interdisciplinary Reviews: Climate Change* 2 (5): 712–727.

Redford Kent H. 1991. "The ecologically noble savage." *Cultural Survival Quarterly* 15 (1): 46–48.

Rey, Alejandro D., Damiano Pasini, and Yogesh Kumar Murugesan 2016. "Multiscale Modeling of Plant Cell Wall Architecture and Tissue Mechanics for Biomimetic Applications." In Bar-Cohen 2016: 131–169.

Rubenstein, Dustin R., and Daniel I. Rubenstein. 2016. "From Pleistocene to Trophic Rewilding: A Wolf in Sheep's Clothing." *Proceedings of the National Academy of Sciences* 113 (1): E1.

Salter, Colin. 2015. "Animals and War: Anthropocentrism and Technoscience." *NanoEthics* 9 (1): 11–21.

Schroeter, Dorna L. 2010. "Introducing Biomimicry." *Green Teacher* 88. https://greenteacher.com/introducing-biomimicry.

Sillitoe, Paul. 1993. "Local Awareness of the Soil Environment in the Papua New Guinea Highlands." In *Environmentalism: The View from anthropology*, ed. Milton Kaye, 160-173. London: Routledge.

Soja, Constance M. 2014. "A Field-Based Biomimicry Exercise Helps Students Discover Connections among Biodiversity, Form and Function, and Species Conservation during Earth's Sixth Extinction." *Journal of Geoscience Education* 62 (4): 679–690.

Sullivan, Sian. 2013. "Banking Nature? The Spectacular Financialisation of Environmental Conservation." *Antipode* 45 (1): 198–217.

Svenning, Jens-Christian, and Søren Faurby. 2017. "Prehistoric and Historic Baselines for Trophic Rewilding in the Neotropics." *Perspectives in Ecology and Conservation* 15 (4): 282–291.

Svenning, Jens-Christian, Pil B. M. Pedersen, C. Josh Donlan, Rasmus Ejrnæs, Søren Faurby, Mauro Galetti, Dennis M. Hansen, et al. 2015. "Science for a Wilder Anthropocene: Synthesis and Future Directions for Trophic Rewilding Research." *Proceedings of the National Academy of Sciences* 113 (4): 898–906.

Szerszynski, Bronislaw, Matthew Kearnes, Phil Macnaghten, Richard Owen, and Jack Stilgoe. 2013. "Why Solar Radiation Management Geoengineering and Democracy Won't Mix." *Environment and Planning A* 45 (12): 2809–2816.

Taylor Buck, Nick. 2017. "The Art of Imitating Life: The Potential Contribution of Biomimicry in Shaping the Future of Our Cities." *Environment and Planning B: Urban Analytics and City Science* 44 (1): 120–140.

Thiele, Leslie Paul. 2018. "Geoengineering and Sustainability." *Environmental Politics* 28 (3): 460–470. https://doi.org/10.1080/09644016.2018.1449602.

Uskoković, Vuk. 2010. "Prospects and Pits on the Path of Biomimetics: The Case of Tooth Enamel." *Journal of Biomimetics: Biomaterials and Tissue Engineering* 8: 45–78.

Van der Ryn, Sim, and Stuart Cowan. (1996) 2013. *Ecological Design*. Washington, DC: Island Press.

Volstad, Nina Louise, and Casper Boks. 2008. "Biomimicry: A Useful Tool for the Industrial Designer?" *DS 50: Proceedings of NordDesign 2008 Conference*, Tallinn, Estonia, 21–23 August.

Wahl, D. C. 2006. "Bionics vs. Biomimicry: From Control of Nature to Sustainable Participation in Nature." *Design and Nature III: Comparing Design in Nature with Science and Engineering* 87: 289–298.

West, Paige. 2005. "Translation, Value, and Space: Theorizing an Ethnographic and Engaged Environmental Anthropology." *American Anthropologist* 107 (4): 632–642.

West, Paige. 2006. *Conservation Is Our Government Now: The Politics of Ecology in Papua New Guinea*. Durham, NC: Duke University Press.

Whitehouse, Peter J. 2013. "InterWell: An Integrated School-Based Primary Care Model." *London Journal of Primary Care* 5 (2): 106–110.

Williston, Byron. 2017. "The Question Concerning Geo-Engineering." Techne: Research in Philosophy and Technology. Online First. DOI: 10.5840/techne201772166

Zerner, Charles. 2010. "Stealth Nature: Biomimesis and the Weaponization of Life." In *In The Name of Humanity: The Government of Threat and Care*, ed. Ilana Feldman and Miriam Tinktin, 290–324. Durham, NC: Duke University Press.

Zhang, Ge. 2012. "Biomimicry in Biomedical Research." *Organogensis* 8 (2): 101–102.

CHAPTER 3

The Urban Politics of Mega-Events
Grand Promises Meet Local Resistance

John Lauermann

Sports mega-events have long been promoted as drivers of urban development, based on their potential to generate physical, economic, and social legacies for host cities (see reviews in Andranovich and Burbank 2011; Essex and Chalkley 1998; Gold and Gold 2008; Kassens-Noor et al. 2015; Smith 2012). Yet the mega-event industry is increasingly struggling to find cities willing to host. Between 2013 and 2018, 13 cities canceled their bids to host the Olympics, either in response to negative referenda or after political pressure on city leaders.[1] In response, the International Olympic Committee (IOC) made unprecedented concessions to recruit host cities, offering subsidies to the municipalities of Paris and Los Angeles to convince them to host the 2024 and 2028 Games, respectively. Similarly, less prominent event franchises like the Commonwealth Games, Universiade, and regional Olympic franchises (Asian Games, Pan American Games, etc.) must now contend with a dearth of interest, often receiving no more than one or two bids from potential host cities. The lack of willing host cities reflects a shift in the urban politics of mega-events, as critics and boosters debate whether cities should pursue such projects—debates that the critics are frequently winning.

This article reviews recent scholarship on the urban politics of mega-events, comparing the promises made by promoters with the critiques made by opponents. The promises hinge on the idea that mega-events can act as a catalyst for urban development: a temporary project that can unleash long-term benefits by facilitating infrastructure investment, prompting policy innovation, or bolstering civic engagement. More specifically, these promises focus on mega-event "legacy"—the idea that mega-event investments can be repurposed after an event—and mega-event "leveraging"—the idea that the mega-event planning process can be strategically co-opted to facilitate non-sport agendas. In contrast, mega-event critics express skepticism toward these promises, especially toward the concept of legacy. Recent scholarship analyzes mounting evidence that mega-event legacies are uncertain and tend to be oriented toward elite interests, and documents growing public skepticism toward promises made by boosters. This skepticism increasingly extends beyond activist communities, as city leaders and the general public question the wisdom of government investment in mega-events. There is a growing political hesitance toward risks like cost overruns and project delays, and the public sector subsidies on which event planners rely to manage those risks. Recent scholarship demonstrates that local governments are increasingly unwilling to subsidize mega-events and are demanding cost- and risk-sharing agreements from event owners.

Recent history suggests a power shift in favor of mega-event opponents. City leaders who may have traditionally supported mega-events now face skeptical voters and vocal protest campaigns, resulting in canceled projects and an apparent decline in interest among potential host cities. In a general sense, this reflects a climate of political skepticism toward the promises made by promoters of grand projects, as part of a broader political climate of populism and distrust of urban elites (Gaffney 2015; Lauermann and Vogelpohl 2019). In a more specific sense, this is driven by increasingly robust and organized political opposition to mega-events. Recent scholarship documents the development of new kinds of protest movements against mega-events, in particular by anti-Olympics protests and allied urban social movements (Boykoff 2014a; Dart and Wagg 2016).

This article contributes by examining the declining appeal of mega-events for cities, linking it to broader debates over the urban politics of megaprojects. While there is a growing global interest in megaprojects (Datta and Shaban 2017; Lauermann 2018), not all types of megaprojects fare so well. The mega-event industry has entered a period of crisis due to skepticism among urban citizens and a weak support from city leaders. This has upended the dynamics of the industry, as franchises that were historically able to demand grandiose promises from cities are now struggling to make their mega-events more appealing to city governments. The article analyzes the interaction of a general climate of political skepticism toward grand projects and the emergence of often-successful political opposition. It evaluates parallels between the urban politics of mega-events and those of other types of megaprojects. Mega-event protests have significantly disrupted the urban political status quo, and their techniques could have broad impacts if borrowed by other urban social movements.

In the following review, I first examine the promises made by mega-event promoters to host cities. Namely, I review scholarship on mega-event legacy and leveraging, with emphasis on their role in urban politics. Next, the I review political critiques of these promises—especially critiques of mega-event legacy. I also introduce emerging research on protests against mega-events and analyze how those protests impact mega-event governance. The article concludes by evaluating the implications of these shifts for the urban politics of other kinds of megaprojects.

Grand Promises: Mega-Event Legacy and Leveraging

Mega-events have long been promoted as a means to achieve urban development: an opportunity to facilitate urban regeneration (Smith 2012), construct major infrastructure (Kassens-Noor 2013), improve transit networks (Pereira 2018), invest in environmental sustainability (Gold and Gold 2013), bolster tourism industries (Fourie and Santana-

Gallego 2011), preserve architectural and cultural heritage (Jones and Ponzini 2018), improve residents' quality of life (Kaplanidou et al. 2013), or promote urban place brands (Zhang and Zhao 2009), to name only a few examples (see also Viehoff and Poynter 2016). These benefits are achieved through "financial gigantism" (Preuss 2004) as cities spend in order to outbid each other for hosting rights and respond to the ever-increasing expectations of event owners like the IOC. While some of that investment is funded through private sources (e.g., broadcast revenue, ticket sales, sponsorships, and donations), most comes from public sector subsidies, in particular from municipal governments (Baade and Matheson 2016; Boykoff 2014b; Zimbalist 2015). This creates political pressure for mega-event promoters to justify public expenditures by articulating how mega-events benefit a host city.

The benefits of mega-events are promoted by members of urban "growth machines," loose coalitions of civic boosters like business leaders and politicians who mobilize to support many types of urban development projects (Hall 2006; Lauermann and Vogelpohl 2017; Surborg et al. 2008; Zhang and Wu 2008). They are also promoted by interconnected global industries that advise cities on bid, event, and legacy planning (Cashman and Harris 2012; Salazar et al. 2017) and through "policy tourism" in which city leaders travel to other host cities for conferences and technical exchanges (Cook and Ward 2011; González 2011; McCann 2013). Host cities intentionally design planning "models" that can be circulated among future host cities through policy transfer and consulting: the "Los Angeles model" of fiscal responsibility (Andranovich and Burbank 2011), the "Barcelona model" of urban regeneration (Degen and García 2012), the "London model" of urban sustainability (Raco 2013), and so on. These types of civic boosterism benefit from knowledge transfer networks and a small industry of consultants providing research that validates development promises. For example, there is an interlocking knowledge transfer system surrounding Olympics planning, including IOC workshops (for bidding and hosting cities) and databases (e.g., the Olympic Games Knowledge Management System), and several consulting firms founded by former IOC and host city staff to advise cities on event planning and management (Cook and Ward 2011; Oliver and Lauermann 2017; Silvestre 2013).

Mega-events' unique project timelines are promoted as a key benefit. By definition, a mega-event happens at a particular time, so mega-event planning must work around a hard deadline. While other megaprojects might remain useful even if they fall behind schedule, preparations for mega-events are all in vain unless they are completed before the opening ceremony. The political imperative created by this hard deadline creates a "catalyst" for urban development (Essex and Chalkley 1998), providing a window of opportunity to change policies, purchase and rezone land, or secure financing. That window of opportunity creates momentum in urban politics as city leaders attempt to push through projects before enthusiasm dissipates. Once set in motion, mega-event planning reorients urban governance toward deadlines, creating a "delivery imperative," that is, "the growing imperative in many contexts to 'get things done' and deliver 'on time' and 'to budget'" (Raco 2014: 181). In this sense, the catalyst effect is one of political fast-tracking: urban planning processes that would typically require years of deliberation, extensive public participation, and numerous studies can instead be accelerated in light of looming deadlines and global media exposure. The research literature on mega-event benefits identifies two types of catalyst effects: producing an event legacy or providing an opportunity for event leveraging.

Legacy

Legacy is the idea that a megaproject designed for one purpose can later be repurposed for other applications. In the case of sports mega-events, this means investments designed to support a few weeks of elite sport can be repurposed for more ordinary urban uses: stadiums can be rented out to local teams, pools and arenas can be converted into community centers, athlete housing can be renovated as residential real estate, staff can receive training that will improve their employability after the games, and the like. Mega-event planners have a long history of promoting the general benefits of hosting, a narrative which gradually evolved to discuss the term legacy by the 1980s (Leopkey and Parent 2012). The geographer Andrew Smith (2012: chap. 3) classifies the history of the "legacy agenda" into several periods. Mega-event planning before World War II involved relatively small-scale events in which few permanent facilities were constructed. This changed in the postwar period as mega-events grew bigger and more expensive and as political pressure mounted to justify larger spending. By the 1960s, mega-event planners were promoting the role of events for facilitating urban renewal and modernization. By the 1980s, event investment was promoted as a means to address deindustrialization in the Global North. Mega-events became increasingly commercialized and privatized as cities turned to public-private partnerships and other types of neoliberal urban management in the 1990s, which necessitated increasingly elaborate political arguments for why public money should support private sector stakeholders. A fully articulated legacy concept finally emerged by the early 2000s, when mega-event hosts began to conceptualize legacy not as a fortuitous unintended outcome but as something that should be explicitly planned for from the outset.

There are numerous definitions of mega-event legacy in the research literature. Holger Preuss (2007) distinguishes between "hard" and "soft" legacies, with the former seen in tangible infrastructure left for a city after an event, while the latter involve intangible benefits like workforce development or improved civic engagement. Summarizing various definitions used in the literature, Scarlett Cornelissen and colleagues (2011: 311) identify seven broad legacy categories, offering both positive and negative examples: economic legacies like the growth of local industries, infrastructure legacies like transit investment, social legacies like civic pride, political legacies like displacement, environmental legacies like pollution and sustainability investments, sports legacies like venues for community teams, and brand legacies used for place marketing. In a more recent review of the mega-event legacy literature, Alana Thomson and colleagues (2018: 9) classify hundreds of peer-reviewed articles on legacy into a similar set of categories, including impacts on the built environment (sport and non-sport construction); economic impacts; impacts on public life, public health, and culture; sport development through education, financing, elite performance, or symbolism; and environmental improvements. They show, however, that most of the research literature discusses soft legacies like investment in cultural institutions, community sport development, or economic impacts. Eva Kassens-Noor and colleagues (2015: 667–668) likewise identify similar content in legacy agendas but note significant distinctions within the mechanisms that lead to legacies. They distinguish, for example, between "mega-event accelerated legacy," in which an event accelerates urban projects, and "mega-event motivated legacy," in which an event creates political momentum in support of projects. They also note that mega-events can delay or even cancel other urban megaprojects, as the mega-event delivery imperative overwhelms other urban planning priorities.

Thus, mega-event legacy is an extraordinarily broad concept. The eclectic nature of the concept is often viewed as a weakness of legacy planning. There is a tendency for mega-event planners to "bring it under the legacy umbrella" (Gold and Gold 2013: 3527) by linking any number of marginally related initiatives to a legacy agenda. It is common for city leaders to engage in "high frequency bidding" (Lauermann 2016: 1895), pursuing numerous sport and non-sport mega-events while proposing largely the same legacies in each plan, slowly building the legacy regardless of whether the events actually occur.

As a result, legacy is no longer considered solely a secondary or unintended conse-quence. Rather, it is conceptualized as something that can and indeed should be planned. However, this tendency to plan specifically for legacy contributes to cost overruns because cities face pressure to make investments that are not necessary for hosting an event. As Smith (2012: 60–61) puts it, this "new legacy agenda" prioritizes the planning of legacies over planning for the main event, thereby escalating costs:

> Legacy is now focused on producing tangible legacies, not merely restricting negative impacts. Therefore, legacy is a justification for increasing expenditure, thus perhaps—counter-productively—increasing the likelihood of wasteful spending . . . The idea that the new legacy focus has put more pressure on cities for permanent physical changes contradicts the wider academic literature on event regeneration where there is more recognition of intangible legacies.

He goes on to distinguish between "event-led" and "event-themed" legacy planning. The former type prioritizes event planning, while the latter prioritizes urban investments that—while beneficial for a city—may be only tangentially related to the mega-event itself. This latter type of planning is increasingly common as cities put the legacy cart in front of the mega-event horse. Indeed, this reprioritization is described in industry and academic circles as "leveraging," a concept explained in a growing research literature.

Leveraging

Leveraging is the idea that the process of megaproject planning has strategic potential beyond the obvious goal of delivering the project. Related agendas can be linked to the core megaproject, such that those agendas can be moved forward by its momentum. The sports policy analyst Laurence Chalip (2014: 6) distinguishes between the legacy framework, which emphasizes post-event impacts, and the leveraging framework, which strategically pursues particular kinds of impacts from the very beginning:

> The legacy framework holds that events should be planned and administered in a manner that will engender positive outcomes which will last beyond the time of the event . . . Rather than focusing on the necessary alliances for strategic leverage of events—which can be achieved with or without the engagement of event organizers—the focus remains on the event, its elements, and its organizers.

In contrast, taking a strategic approach to mega-event planning involves both economic leveraging—"endeavours to optimize total trade and revenue from the event"—and social leveraging—which "utilizes the limnoid feeling events can engender in order to enable targeted social outcomes" (5). Examples include branding sport to promote a country's image (Grix 2012) or using event planning as a way to develop networks that extend into related professional communities (O'Brien and Gardiner 2006).

Analysis of leveraging examines why governments choose to host mega-events. It digs beneath the "manufactured consent that surrounds SME [sports mega-event] discourse . . . upbeat and uncritical, and those who question the sanity of SME spending are more often than not labelled as 'naysayers'" (Grix 2014: x–xi). Instead, research on leverag-ing takes an investigative approach to why stakeholders choose a risky investment like mega-events, exploring the motivations of real estate investors, aspiring politicians, and corporate sponsors. This type of analysis has a long history in the mega-events literature, for example, literature that examined the use of mega-events as a form of "strategic plan-ning" for urban regeneration (Bramwell 1997), city leaders' use of "mega-event strategy" to pursue local economic growth (Andranovich et al. 2001), or attempts at linking events to place branding and community development (Chalip 2006).

Given its focus on the underlying motivations of mega-event boosters, recent research has retained a critical perspective on leveraging. While leveraging is promoted as a way to extend mega-event benefits to diverse stakeholder communities, it is also filtered through power structures that skew benefits toward elites (Ziakas 2015). For example, analysts of Russian mega-events like the 2014 Sochi Olympics and 2018 FIFA World Cup point to "event seizure" by local elites, suggesting that leveraging discourse was used to justify elite co-optation of plans and legislation supporting the event (Müller 2017). Indeed, there is debate over whether leveraging is a new mega-event planning model at all or if it is simply a rhetorical justification for controversial megaprojects that disproportionately benefit their boosters (Smith 2014). Regardless, the leveraging narrative has appeal for cities because it offers a rationale for pursuing benefits immediately, in contrast to the legacy narrative, which is based on the assumption of future benefits.

In sum, mega-events are promoted as a catalyst for urban development, a temporary project that can generate long-term benefits for a city. Two broad narratives are used to promote mega-events in urban politics. First, legacy narratives identify tangible and intangible outcomes that follow a mega-event. While legacies were historically viewed as fortuitous but largely unintended outcomes, today's mega-event planners explicitly plan for legacy from the very beginning of the project. Second, leveraging narratives further expand the idea that legacies can and should be planned. These narratives argue city stakeholders should strategically use the mega-event planning process as an institutional platform for pursuing related investments and programs. While these narratives are important tools in the politics of promoting mega-events, they also encounter criticism, and the critics are increasingly successful at contesting mega-event boosterism.

Urban Resistance: Skepticism and Protest

Mega-events increasingly encounter political opposition. A recent wave of protests against them has achieved high rates of political success by forcing cities to cancel their bids to host and by pressuring city leaders to more carefully scrutinize event management practices (Lauermann and Vogelpohl 2019). The mega-event industry has attempted to implement reforms in response to this pressure, seen, for instance, in the IOC's "new norm" policies which aim to decrease Olympics hosting costs (ESC 2018) or in FIFA's decision to increase transparency by publishing World Cup bids and contracts (FIFA 2017).

The underlying driver of these changes is a shift in the *urban* politics of mega-events: a realignment of the terms of political debate, as cities debate not just how to host but whether to host at all. Recent protests focus on distinctively urban issues related the role of mega-events within urban planning, and mega-events' impact on urban topics like gentrification, traffic, public space, or municipal finances. While there is a long history of political protest during mega-events (Cottrell and Nelson 2011), widespread protest against mega-event planning is a relatively new phenomenon (Boykoff 2014a). Protests historically focused on the actors involved (e.g., corporate sponsors) or the impacts of hosting (e.g., social displacement), but today's political debates increasingly focus on the more fundamental question of why a city should participate in mega-events at all. This shift is driven by urban protest movements and by skeptical city leaders, including many of the same types of urban elites who might have historically supported mega-events. Since these are relatively new trends, the research literature on mega-event protest is still developing. However, recent research emphasizes two shifts that are changing the urban politics of mega-events: skepticism toward mega-event promises, and protest against mega-event bids.

Skepticism

First, there is a growing skepticism among urban stakeholders toward the narratives used by mega-event boosters, in particular toward narratives that promise legacies. There is ample evidence that mega-events can generate positive legacies for a city, and, with careful planning, negative legacies can be avoided. Yet it is unclear whether a city actually needs to go through the inconvenience of hosting a mega-event in order to achieve legacy effects. Using a mega-event to secure a nonevent benefit is a rather indirect form of public policy: to get the legacy benefit, a city must first develop a bid, win a bid, plan the event, host the event, and then successfully wind down event operations. If the public wants a particular investment, why not simply make it directly? Legacy is a political justification for mega-events, so it is no surprise their promoters build political campaigns around the promise of legacies. Indeed, a key political argument in favor of mega-events is that they provide a catalyst for the city to pursue projects that would otherwise be politically impossible to achieve. Yet even this catalyst argument struggles to articulate the necessity of mega-events. If a city were able to muster the political will to catalyze urban development in order to host a mega-event, why wouldn't it be able to do the same thing without the event?

There is well-established academic literature critiquing mega-event legacy narratives. Economists document methodological problems in the studies that purport to find positive economic legacies, studies that are often conducted by consultants who are paid by mega-event boosters. Critics argue such boosterish studies are typically conducted ex ante with minimal post hoc follow up (Baumann and Matheson 2013), routinely overestimate multiplier effects (Matheson 2009), and fail to model well-known dynamics like crowding out and substitution effects (Baade and Matheson 2016). Urbanists likewise question the wisdom of municipal spending on events, mapping a landscape of abandoned or underused facilities and showing a range of negative legacies like gentrification (Casaglia 2018; Gaffney 2016; Paton et al. 2012), aggressive policing (Giulianotti and Klauser 2011; McMichael 2012; Samatas 2007), and the privatization of public spaces (Davidson 2013; Eick 2010). Still other critics note the uneven distribution of legacies, highlighting the limited reach among social minorities (McGillivray et al. 2018; Minnaert 2012) and elite capture of the event planning process (Kassens-Noor and Lauermann 2017; Müller 2017).

There is a growing public awareness of these critiques, as new alliances emerge between academics, activists, and city leaders. Activists publicize research literature through online repositories like GamesMonitor.org.uk, NOlympia.de, and city-specific research websites built to address individual Olympic bids; protesters in Boston also published a book through a university press (Dempsey and Zimbalist 2017). Likewise, books that summarize the research literature for general audiences—like Andrew Zimbalist's (2015) *Circus Maximus* and Jules Boykoff's (2016) *Power Games*—are widely read and cited in activist circles. Collectively, these sources cast doubt on the claims made by mega-event promoters. This feeds skepticism not only among activists and opposition movements but also among local boosters including business leaders, elected officials, and local media (Lauermann and Vogelpohl 2017; Kassens-Noor and Lauermann 2018).

Skepticism generates conflict between host governments and event franchises over the distribution of financial responsibilities. Like many megaprojects, mega-events conform to what the management scholar Bent Flyvbjerg (2014: 6) has called the "iron law of mega-projects": they will be "over budget, over time, over and over again." In another study, Flyvbjerg and colleagues (2016) found that every single Olympics since 1960 has run over budget, at an average of 156 percent overrun. Host governments—and by extension, taxpayers—typically cover the risk of these overruns. Even without cost overruns, host governments are typically responsible for most mega-event costs. While operating costs are usually funded through private sources (e.g., ticket sales, corporate sponsorships, sale of broadcast rights), capital costs (for infrastructure and venues) are often financed and guaranteed by a host government.

Historically, host governments have stepped in to fill funding gaps, engaging in what the political scientist Jules Boykoff (2014b: 3) terms "celebration capitalism." He shows that city leaders offer generous public subsidies for construction costs and sign hosting contracts that commit taxpayers to cover overruns. In this way, he argues:

> celebration capitalism manipulates state actors as partners, pushing us toward economics rooted in so-called public-private partnerships. All too often, though, these public-private partnerships are lopsided: the public pays and the private profits. In a smiley-faced bait and switch, the public takes the risks and private groups scoop up the rewards.

He goes on to invert the argument made by mega-event promoters, casting events not as a catalyst for development but as a threat to democracy. Promoters argue the temporary nature of mega-event planning is an asset: a relatively short project with a clear deadline creates political momentum for cities to realize their goals, thereby catalyzing development. Boykoff, on the other hand, argues the all-out push to deliver the project on time creates a "state of exception" in urban politics, which "opens space for opportunism whereby the powerful can press through policies on their wish lists that they wouldn't dream of putting forward during normal political times" (11).

City leaders who may have traditionally supported mega-events are increasingly confronted with "uncomfortable knowledge" (Stewart and Rayner 2016) about cost overruns, unbudgeted risk, and disproportionate distribution of profits. Historically, local elites may have been able to overlook questionable contracts, or at least to counter uncomfortable knowledge with arguments about future benefits. The economist Andrew Zimbalist (2015: 55) argues legacy narratives in particular provided cover for political leaders, since opposition to present-day subsidies could be countered with promises of future legacies. He argues this creates a crisis of political accountability:

> Those who promised economic and other advantages from hosting become basically unaccountable. If there are no apparent gains, the politicians can always proclaim that the benefits on their way. Thus, in the short run the games' boosters can appeal to the promise of long-run legacy benefits, while in the long run the boosters can appeal to the expectation of still longer-run benefits down the road. By this time the politicians who originally appropriated public funds to finance the games may be long gone.

Such a model only works politically, however, as long as the public remains unaware of systemic discrepancies in mega-event planning. As the geographer Martin Müller (2015) argues, mega-events become politically untenable when the public becomes aware of what he terms "the mega-event syndrome"—a set of symptoms that first seem to be unrelated but actually share an underlying cause. Political support wanes once city leaders and the public draw connections between strong evidence of risks like cost overruns, weak evidence of legacy benefits, and knowledge about hosting contracts that disproportionately burden taxpayers.

Protest

These currents of discontent have culminated in a second shift in the urban politics of mega-events: the emergence of urban protest campaigns. Mega-events attract global media coverage and thus have a long history of attracting political protests. John Horne and Garry Whannel (2016: chap. 9) trace the origin of modern mega-event protests to Olympics politics of the Cold War, and identify three types of protest that have characterized mega-event politics since then. One type used mega-events as a stage for political theater, seen in various boycotts during the latter half of the twentieth century. These include, for example, American and Soviet boycotts of Olympics hosted by the opposing side (e.g., the Moscow 1980 and Los Angeles 1984 Olympics), and anti-apartheid boycotts in the 1960s and 1970s that protested the segregated South African teams' participation in the Olympics. A second type contested the facade that governments sought to project to the world through mega-events, drawing attention to issues like human rights abuses or political repression. For example, this kind of protest included athletes' display of the Black Power salute during the 1968 Mexico City Olympics to protest racism in the United States, and Tibetan rights activists who protested China's human rights record during the Beijing 2008 Olympics. A third type protested the role of mega-events as a tool for neoliberal development, and parallels broader protest of social inequalities. These were more broadly conceived protests, aimed at issues like the commercialization of sport at the Atlanta 1996 Olympics or corruption scandals at various Olympics including Salt Lake City 2002.

For these types of protests, mega-events provided a "platform for protest" (Timms 2012) or a temporary "opportunity structure" (Cottrell and Nelson 2011) for activists to campaign against topics that are related to an event, for instance, the practices of corporate sponsors or the human rights records of participant countries. Some of the protests focused on the negative impacts of the mega-event on a host city—especially related to issues like gentrification and neighborhood displacement—but the mega-event itself was not typically the primary focus. The goal was often to use a mega-event as a platform (e.g., to heighten awareness of a topic or pressure political leaders) but not necessarily to cancel the event itself.

In contrast, recent years have witnessed the growth of protests that directly contest mega-event bidding, planning, and hosting. These campaigns are distinct because they are explicitly *urban* protests (Oliver and Lauermann 2017: chap. 7). Built by local co-alitions and concerned with urban themes like gentrification, housing affordability, or transit planning, they are focused on one particular urban policy question: should our city host the games? This kind of protest employs relatively novel methods like online activism (Millington and Darnell 2014), and while it draws from ideologically diverse coalitions, the focus is squarely on the mega-event itself (Giulianotti et al. 2015). These urban protest campaigns are not completely new: there are precedents in Denver's referendum against hosting the 1976 Olympics (Boykoff 2014a: 22–24) and in Toronto's "Bread not Circuses" protests against Olympic bids in the 1990s (Tufts 2004). Yet early urban campaigns rarely grew beyond small pockets of "piecemeal resistance" (Burbank et al. 2000), in part because the protests began only after hosting contracts were signed by the host governments.

Recent protests mobilize early in the mega-event planning process, when cities are still developing bids and—crucially—before host governments have signed contracts that lock in commitments to deliver infrastructure and fund construction. These protests have been most common in cities bidding to host the Olympics. While protests against other mega-events are less common, there is some evidence that anti-Olympics activists turn out to protest non-Olympics events when relevant (Casaglia 2018; Weber-Newth et al. 2017). Nonetheless, these campaigns generally do not travel well: by definition they are local campaigns rooted in a particular city's political debates, so strategies that work in one city may not transfer to others (Timms 2017).

They are not urban social movements per se, but operate rather as temporary political campaigns that contest a specific urban policy—the decision over whether a city should host an event. Contrasting them with conventional social movements, Boykoff (2014a: 26) characterizes Olympics protests as a "moment of movements," temporary coalitions that emerge from existing urban social movements:

The Games pop up in one city, generating dissent, and then quickly plunge beneath the discursive surface, rearing their head in another city two years later. Protesters meanwhile fall back into their pre-Games patterns of protest, returning to their main targets and objectives . . . During the Olympics moment, extant activist groups come together using the Olympics as their fight-back focal point.

Lauermann and Vogelpohl (2019) classify these urban protest movements as a form of "fast activism," which has three characteristics: first, it is necessarily temporary because protesters must mobilize quickly to match the speed of mega-event planning. Coalitions often disband just as quickly after a bid is defeated. Second, fast activists adopt a relationally local rhetorical strategy, framing problems through the lens of local urban concerns (e.g., gentrification, environmental impacts) but with careful reference to debates and terminology used in the international mega-event industry. Third, fast activist coalitions tend to be ideologically diverse, rooted in leftist movements and parties but extending to include sometimes-uncanny assemblies of local business leaders, skeptical politicians, and fiscal conservatives.

In sum, mega-event opponents are increasingly successful at mobilizing against mega-events, forcing cities to cancel bids and prompting city leaders to carefully scrutinize mega-event spending. That shift in the urban politics of mega-events has two dimensions. First, there is a growing skepticism toward the promises made by mega-event proponents, especially toward narratives about legacy. There is a well-established academic literature critiquing concepts like legacy, and new alliances between scholars, activists, and city leaders help share knowledge with the general public and cast doubt on boosterish claims. As a result, city leaders increasingly question the financial relationship between governments and event owners. As they face mounting evidence of planning risks like cost overruns, these local leaders are negotiating more favorable contracts. Second, these general trends have been catalyzed by the growth of protest campaigns against mega-events, in particular anti-Olympics protests. While there is a long history of political activism surrounding mega-events, these recent campaigns are distinct because they focus their strategy on specifically urban policy questions.

Conclusion

Mega-events are often promoted as drivers of urban development, and historically cities engaged in fierce competition to win hosting rights. Yet mega-events appear to be losing their appeal, as fewer cities are willing to bid on events and as city leaders demand more favorable hosting contracts from event franchises. This article reviews recent research on the urban politics of mega-events, comparing arguments for and against them commonly used in urban politics, and reviewing new types of political opposition. Mega-events are promoted to urban stakeholders as a development catalyst: a temporary project that will unleash long term benefits as they generate various legacies—tangible and intangible benefits that emerge after the games—and as the planning process is leveraged to advanced non-sport agendas. These grand promises are increasingly met with skepticism and protest, as urban stakeholders question the promises made by event boosters and as protest campaigns call for cities to eschew mega-events entirely. In recent years, numerous cities have canceled their bids for the Olympics, and less prominent event franchises struggle to find any willing host cities at all. Recent scholarship has documented the evolving urban politics of mega-events, analyzing the impact of skepticism and protest while debating the implications for mega-event governance.

Questions remain about the broader implications of the political backlash against mega-events. While mega-event protesters have attempted to build international networks with other activist communities (Dempsey and Zimbalist 2017), there is also evidence that their model of protest does not travel easily (Boykoff 2014a; Lauermann and Vogelpohl 2019; Timms 2017). The success of the opposition is rooted in its local character: networks within extant urban social movements, relationships with local politicians and journalists, and ties to neighborhood communities. Most importantly, the critics have been able to portray mega-events as an urban political issue: for them, the debate is not about international sport but about the future of their city. This has proved effective on a localized scale, but by definition, locally embedded politics is difficult to replicate in other places. Future research might monitor whether protest campaigns can scale up into international activist networks or durable social movements. It might also evaluate the broader impact of urban protests on the mega-event industry, in particular on the relationship between host governments and event owners.

The political headwinds against mega-events have implications for the urban politics of other types of megaprojects. Mega-events are a unique type of megaproject, in particular because of their hard deadlines, intense global media exposure, and heavy involvement of international institutions. Yet they are also part of a broader pattern of urban development through major-scale projects (Lauermann 2018). Megaprojects are an increasingly common vehicle for urban development, especially in cities of the Global South and Global East (Datta and Shaban 2017; Moser et al. 2015). Yet urban megaprojects retain many of the same problems that critics have long highlighted. While the aspiration may be one of "grand urbanism" (Enright 2016) delivering "world class" infrastructure (Watson 2014), the reality is more likely a "dysfunctional urbanism" (McNeill 2005) defined by megaproject planning that routinely overpromises and under-delivers. Likewise, today's urban megaprojects suffer the same problems that dogged an earlier generation of modernist architects and planners, namely that the rush to construct megaprojects can rob cities of community-oriented, human-scaled places and deliver instead what the urbanist Jane Jacobs (1961) once famously critiqued as "unurban urbanization."

Mega-event protests exemplify a disruptive form of activism that could have broad impacts if borrowed by urban social movements concerned with other kinds of megaprojects. Future research might examine the potential for such crossover. Mega-event opposition makes demands that would be disruptive to any megaproject: for transparent budgeting of cost overruns and project delays, for public participation in the planning of large scale construction, and for local leaders to be more assertive in their dealings with international institutions. Likewise, the international impact of primarily local protests suggests that even small, uncoordinated campaigns can disrupt global industries. Given their cost and complexity, megaprojects are vulnerable to locally targeted political opposition. Mega-event protesters have discovered that contesting international organizations like the IOC may yield only superficial results, but pressuring local elected officials can have enormous impact. Other urban megaprojects are susceptible to similar forms of local targeting (at least in the context of urban democracies). While megaproject opponents may have little impact on the practices of multinational corporations or international institutions, applying political pressure to local officials can significantly slow, change, or derail a project.

▪ **ACKNOWLEDGMENTS**

Thanks to the editors for organizing this issue of *Environment and Society* and to the anonymous reviewers for their comments. Any errors or omissions are solely my own.

▪ **JOHN LAUERMANN** is Assistant Professor of Geography at Medgar Evers College of the City University of New York. He is an urban geographer interested in the planning and impacts of urban megaprojects. His recent writing has appeared in *Progress in Human Geography*, *Journal of the American Planning Association*, *Antipode*, and *Urban Studies*. Email: jlauermann@mec.cuny.edu

▪ **NOTE**

1. These cancellations were caused by negative referendums (Calgary, Canada; Davos, Switzerland; Hamburg, Germany; Innsbruck, Austria; Munich, Germany; Sion, Switzerland), after protesters lobbied for a referendum (Boston, US; Budapest, Czech Republic; Graz, Austria), or after city leaders experienced more general forms of political opposition (Krakow, Poland; Oslo, Norway; Rome, Italy; Stockholm, Sweden).

▪ **REFERENCES**

Andranovich, Greg, and Matthew Burbank. 2011. "Contextualizing Olympic legacies." *Urban Geography* 32 (6): 823–844.

Andranovich, Greg, Matthew Burbank, and Charles Heying. 2001. "Olympic Cities: Lessons Learned from Mega-Event Politics." *Journal of Urban Affairs* 23 (2): 113–131.

Baade, Robert A., and Victor A. Matheson. 2016. "Going for the Gold: The Economics of the Olympics." *Journal of Economic Perspectives* 30 (2): 201–218.

Baumann, Robert, and Victor A. Matheson. 2013. "Estimating Economic Impact Using ex post Econometric Analysis: Cautionary Tales." In *The Econometrics of Sport*, ed. Plácido Rodríguez, Stefan Késenne, and Jaume García, 169–188. Northampton, MA: Edward Elgar Publishers.

Boykoff, Jules. 2014a. *Activism and the Olympics: Dissent at the Games in Vancouver and London.* New Brunswick, NJ: Rutgers University Press.

Boykoff, Jules. 2014b. *Celebration Capitalism and the Olympic Games.* London: Routledge.

Boykoff, Jules. 2016. *Power Games: A Political History of the Olympics.* London: Verso.

Bramwell, Bill. 1997. "Strategic Planning before and after a Mega-Event." *Tourism Management* 18 (3): 167–176.

Burbank, Matthew J., Charles H. Heying, and Greg Andranovich. 2000. "Antigrowth Politics or Piecemeal Resistance? Citizen Opposition to Olympic-Related Economic Growth." *Urban Affairs Review* 35 (3): 334–357.

Casaglia, Anna. 2018. "Territories of Struggle: Social Centres in Northern Italy Opposing Mega-Events." *Antipode* 50 (2): 478–497.

Cashman, Richard I., and Rob Harris. 2012. *The Australian Olympic Caravan from 2000 to 2012: A Unique Olympic Events Industry.* Sydney: Walla Walla Press.

Chalip, Laurence. 2006. "Towards Social Leverage of Sport Events." *Journal of Sport & Tourism* 11 (2): 109–127.

Chalip, Laurence. 2014. "From legacy to leverage." In *Leveraging Legacies from Sports Mega-Events: Concepts and Cases*, ed. Jonathan Grix, 2–12. New York: Palgrave Macmillan.

Cook, Ian R., and Kevin Ward. 2011. "Trans-Urban Networks of Learning, Mega-Events and Policy Tourism." *Urban Studies* 48 (12): 2519–2535.

Cornelissen, Scarlett, Urmilla Bob, and Kamilla Swart. 2011. "Towards Redefining the Concept of Legacy in Relation to Sport Mega-Events: Insights from the 2010 FIFA World Cup." *Development Southern Africa* 28 (3): 307–318.

Cottrell, M. Patrick, and Travis Nelson. 2011. "Not Just the Games? Power, Protest and Politics at the Olympics." *European Journal of International Relations* 17 (4): 729–753.

Dart, Jon, and Stephen Wagg, eds. 2016. *Sport, Protest and Globalisation.* New York: Palgrave Macmillan.

Datta, Ayona, and Abdul Shaban, eds. 2017. *Mega-Urbanization in the Global South: Fast Cities and New Urban Utopias of the Postcolonial State*. London: Routledge.

Davidson, Mark. 2013. "The Sustainable and Entrepreneurial Park? Contradictions and Persistent Antagonisms at Sydney's Olympic Park." *Urban Geography* 34 (5): 657–676.

Degen, Mónica, and Marisol García. 2012. "The Transformation of the 'Barcelona Model': An Analysis of Culture, Urban Regeneration and Governance." *International Journal of Urban and Regional Research* 36 (5): 1022–1038.

Dempsey, Christopher, and Andrew Zimbalist. 2017. *No Boston Olympics: How and Why Smart Cities Are Passing on the Torch*. Lebanon, NH: University of New England Press.

Eick, Volker. 2010. "A Neoliberal Sports Event? FIFA from the Estadio Nacional to the Fan Mile." *City: Analysis of Urban Trends, Culture, Theory, Policy, Action* 14 (3): 278–297.

Enright, Teresa. 2016. *The Making of Grand Paris: Metropolitan Urbanism in the Twenty-First Century*. Cambridge, MA: MIT Press.

Essex, Stephen, and Brian Chalkley. 1998. "Olympic Games: Catalyst of Urban Change." *Leisure Studies* 17 (3): 187–206.

ESC (Executive Steering Committee for Olympic Games Delivery). 2018. *Olympic Games: The New Norm*. Lausanne: International Olympic Committee.

FIFA (Fédération Internationale de Football Association). 2017. *Guide to the Bidding Process for the 2026 FIFA World Cup*. Zurich: FIFA.

Flyvbjerg, Bent. 2014. "What You Should Know About Megaprojects and Why: An Overview." *Project Management Journal* 45 (2): 6–19.

Flyvbjerg, Bent, Allison Stewart, and Alexander Budzier. 2016. "The Oxford Olympics Study 2016: Cost and Cost Overrun at the Games." Said Business School Research Paper 2016-20. Last revised 18 August.

Fourie, Johan, and María Santana-Gallego. 2011. "The Impact of Mega-Sport Events on Tourist Arrivals." *Tourism Management* 32 (6): 1364–1370.

Gaffney, Christopher. 2015. "Virando o jogo : The Challenges and Possibilities for Social Mobilization in Brazilian Football." *Journal of Sport & Social Issues* 39 (2): 155–174.

Gaffney, Christopher. 2016. "Gentrifications in Pre-Olympic Rio de Janeiro." *Urban Geography* 37 (8): 1132–1153.

Giulianotti, Richard, and Francisco Klauser. 2011. "Introduction: Security and Surveillance at Sport Mega Events." *Urban Studies* 48 (15): 3157–3168.

Giulianotti, Richard, Gary Armstrong, Gavin Hales, and Dick Hobbs. 2015. "Sport Mega-Events and Public Opposition: A Sociological Study of the London 2012 Olympics." *Journal of Sport & Social Issues* 39 (2): 99–119.

Gold, John, and Margaret Gold. 2008. "Olympic Cities: Regeneration, City Rebranding and Changing Urban Agendas." *Geography Compass* 2 (1): 300–318.

Gold, John, and Margaret Gold. 2013. "'Bring It under the Legacy Umbrella': Olympic Host Cities and the Changing Fortunes of the Sustainability Agenda." *Sustainability* 5 (8): 3526–3542.

González, Sara. 2011. "Bilbao and Barcelona 'in Motion': How Urban Regeneration 'Models' Travel and Mutate in the Global Flows of Policy Tourism." *Urban Studies* 48 (7): 1397–1418.

Grix, Jonathan. 2012. "'Image' leveraging and sports mega-events: Germany and the 2006 FIFA World Cup." *Journal of Sport & Tourism* 17 (4): 289–312.

Grix, Jonathan, ed. 2014. *Leveraging Legacies from Sports Mega-Events: Concepts and Cases*. New York: Palgrave Macmillan.

Hall, C. Michael. 2006. "Urban Entrepreneurship, Corporate Interests and Sports Mega-Events: The Thin Policies of Competitiveness within the Hard Outcomes of Neoliberalism." *Sociological Review* 54 (S2): 59–70.

Horne, John, and Garry Whannel. 2016. *Understanding the Olympics*. 2nd ed. New York: Routledge.

Jacobs, Jane. 1961. *The Death and Life of Great American Cities*. New York: Vintage Books.

Jones, Zachary M., and Davide Ponzini. 2018. "Mega-Events and the Preservation of Urban Heritage: Literature Gaps, Potential Overlaps, and a Call for Further Research." *Journal of Planning Literature* 33 (4): 433–450.

Kaplanidou, Kyriaki, Kostas Karadakis, Heather Gibson, Brijesh Thapa, Matthew Walker, Sue Geldenhuys, and Willie Coetzee. 2013. "Quality of Life, Event Impacts, and Mega-Event Support among South African Residents before and after the 2010 FIFA World Cup." *Journal of Travel Research* 52 (5): 631–645.

Kassens-Noor, Eva. 2013. "Transport Legacy of the Olympic Games, 1992–2012." *Journal of Urban Affairs* 35 (4): 393–416.

Kassens-Noor, Eva, and John Lauermann. 2017. "How to Bid Better for the Olympics: A Participatory Mega-Event Planning Strategy for Local Legacies." *Journal of the American Planning Association* 83 (4): 335–345.

Kassens-Noor, Eva, and John Lauermann. 2018. "Mechanisms of Policy Failure: Boston's 2024 Olympic Bid." *Urban Studies* 55 (15): 3369–3384.

Kassens-Noor, Eva, Mark Wilson, Sven Müller, Brij Maharaj, and Laura Huntoon. 2015. "Towards a Mega-Event Legacy Framework." *Leisure Studies* 34 (6): 665–671.

Lauermann, John. 2016. "Temporary Projects, Durable Outcomes: Urban Development through Failed Olympic bids?" *Urban Studies* 53 (9): 1885–1901.

Lauermann, John. 2018. "Geographies of Mega-Urbanization." *Geography Compass* 12 (8): e12396.

Lauermann, John, and Anne Vogelpohl. 2017. "Fragile Growth Coalitions or Powerful Contestations? Cancelled Olympic bids in Boston and Hamburg." *Environment and Planning A* 49 (8): 1887–1904.

Lauermann, John, and Anne Vogelpohl. 2019. "Fast Activism: Resisting Mobile Policies." *Antipode*, published online 26 April. https://doi.org/10.1111/anti.12538.

Leopkey, Becca, and Milena M. Parent. 2012. "Olympic Games Legacy: From General Benefits to Sustainable Long-Term Legacy." *International Journal of the History of Sport* 29 (6): 924–943.

Matheson, Victor A. 2009. "Economic Multipliers and Mega-Event Analysis." *International Journal of Sport Finance* 4 (1): 63–70.

McCann, Eugene. 2013. "Policy Boosterism, Policy Mobilities, and the Extrospective City." *Urban Geography* 34 (1): 5–29.

McGillivray, David, Gayle McPherson, and Laura Misener. 2018. "Major Sporting Events and Geographies of Disability." *Urban Geography* 39 (3): 329–344.

McMichael, Christopher. 2012. "Hosting the World: The 2010 World Cup and the New Military Urbanism." *City: Analysis of Urban Trends, Culture, Theory, Policy, Action* 16 (5): 519–534.

McNeill, Donald. 2005. "Dysfunctional Urbanism." *International Journal of Urban and Regional Research* 29 (1): 201–204.

Millington, Rob, and Simon C. Darnell. 2014. "Constructing and Contesting the Olympics Online: The Internet, Rio 2016 and the Politics of Brazilian Development." *International Review for the Sociology of Sport* 49 (2): 190–210.

Minnaert, Lynn. 2012. "An Olympic Legacy for All? The Non-infrastructural Outcomes of the Olympic Games for Socially Excluded Groups (Atlanta 1996–Beijing 2008)." *Tourism Management* 33 (2): 361–370.

Moser, Sarah, Marian Swain, and Mohammed H. Alkhabbaz. 2015. "King Abdullah Economic City: Engineering Saudi Arabia's post-oil future." *Cities* 45: 71–80.

Müller, Martin. 2015. "The Mega-Event Syndrome: Why So Much Goes Wrong in Mega-Event Planning and What to Do About It." *Journal of the American Planning Association* 81 (1): 6–17.

Müller, Martin. 2017. "How Mega-Events Capture Their Hosts: Event Seizure and the World Cup 2018 in Russia." *Urban Geography* 38 (8): 1113–1132.

O'Brien, Danny, and Sarah Gardiner. 2006. "Creating Sustainable Mega Event Impacts: Networking and Relationship Development through Pre-Event Training." *Sport Management Review* 9 (1): 25–47.

Oliver, Robert, and John Lauermann. 2017. *Failed Olympic bids and the Transformation of Urban Space*. London: Palgrave Macmillan.

Paton, Kirsteen, Gerry Mooney, and Kim McKee. 2012. "Class, Citizenship and Regeneration: Glasgow and the Commonwealth Games 2014." *Antipode* 44 (4): 1470–1489.

Pereira, Rafael H. M. 2018. "Transport Legacy of Mega-Events and the Redistribution of Accessibility to Urban Destinations." *Cities* 81: 45–60.

Preuss, Holger. 2004. *The Economics of Staging the Olympics: A Comparison of the Games, 1972–2008*. Cheltenham: Edward Elgar Publishers.

Preuss, Holger. 2007. "The Conceptualisation and Measurement of Mega Sport Event Legacies." *Journal of Sport & Tourism* 12 (3–4): 207–228.

Raco, Mike. 2013. "Governance as legacy: project management, the Olympic Games and the creation of a London model." *International Journal of Urban Sustainable Development* 5 (2): 172–173.

Raco, Mike. 2014. "Delivering flagship projects in an era of regulatory capitalism: state-led privatization and the London Olympics 2012." *International Journal of Urban and Regional Research* 38 (1): 176–197.

Salazar, Noel, Christiane Timmerman, Johan Wets, and Van den Broucke, eds. 2017. *Mega-event Mobilities: A Critical Analysis*. London: Routledge.

Samatas, Minas. 2007. "Security and Surveillance in the Athens 2004 Olympics: Some Lessons From a Troubled Story." *International Criminal Justice Review* 17 (3): 220–238.

Silvestre, Gabriel. 2013. "Mobile Olympic Planning: The Circulation of Policy Knowledge between Barcelona and Rio de Janeiro 1993–1996." Paper presented at "Geografias, Políticas Públicas e Dinâmicas Territoriais," Campinas, Spain, 7–10 October.

Smith, Andrew. 2012. *Events and Urban Regeneration: The Strategic Use of Events to Revitalise Cities*. London, New York: Routledge.

Smith, Andrew. 2014. "Leveraging Sport Mega-Events: New Model or Convenient Justification?" *Journal of Policy Research in Tourism, Leisure and Events* 6 (1): 15–30.

Stewart, Allison, and Steve Rayner. 2016. "Planning Mega-Event Legacies: Uncomfortable Knowledge for Host Cities." *Planning Perspectives* 31 (2): 157–179.

Surborg, Björn, Rob VanWynsberghe, and Elvin Wyly. 2008. "Mapping the Olympic Growth Machine." *City* 12 (3): 341–355.

Thomson, Alana, Graham Cuskelly, Kristine Toohey, Millicent Kennelly, Paul Burton, and Liz Fredline. 2018. "Sport Event Legacy: A Systematic Quantitative Review of Literature." *Sport Management Review* 22 (3): 295–321. https://doi.org/10.1016/j.smr.2018.06.011.

Timms, Jill. 2012. "The Olympics as a Platform for Protest: A Case Study of the London 2012 'Ethical' Games and the Play Fair Campaign for Workers' Rights." *Leisure Studies* 31 (3): 355–372.

Timms, Jill. 2017. "The Relay of Mega-Event Activism: Why Campaign Gains Do Not Travel Well." In *Mega-Event Mobilities: A Critical Analysis*, ed. Noel B. Salazar, Christine Timmerman, Johan Wets, and Sarah Van den Brooke. London: Routledge.

Tufts, Steven. 2004. "Building the 'Competitive City': Labour and Toronto's Bid to Host the Olympic Games." *Geoforum* 35 (1): 47–58.

Viehoff, Valerie, and Gavin Poynter, eds. 2016. *Mega-Event Cities: Urban Legacies of Global Sports Events*. London: Routledge.

Watson, Vanessa. 2014. "African Urban Fantasies: Dreams or Nightmares?" *Environment and Urbanization* 26 (1): 215–231.

Weber-Newth, Francesca, Sebastian Schlüter, and Ilse Helbrecht. 2017. "London 2012: 'Legacy' as Trojan Horse." *ACME: An International Journal for Critical Geographies* 16 (4): 713–739.

Zhang, Jingxiang, and Fulong Wu. 2008. "Mega-Event Marketing and Urban Growth Coalitions: A Case Study of Nanjing Olympic New Town." *Town Planning Review* 79 (2–3): 209–226.

Zhang, Li, and Simon Xiaobin Zhao. 2009. "City Branding and the Olympic Effect: A Case Study of Beijing." *Cities* 26 (5): 245–254.

Ziakas, Vassilios. 2015. "For the Benefit of All? Developing a Critical Perspective in Mega-Event Leverage." *Leisure Studies* 34 (6): 689–702.

Zimbalist, Andrew. 2015. *Circus Maximus: The Economic Gamble behind Hosting the Olympics and the World Cup*. Washington, DC: Brookings Institution Press.

CHAPTER 4

Mega-Plantations in Southeast Asia
Landscapes of Displacement

Miles Kenney-Lazar and Noboru Ishikawa

Southeast Asia has become one of the world's hot spots for industrial agriculture and tree plantation development. The region is the source of 76 percent of the world's natural rubber, 86 percent of the world's palm oil, and 59 percent of the world's coconuts. Agricultural crop production covers more than 122 million hectares (ha) of land (FAO 2016), established in a diverse range of environments including tropical rainforests, peatlands, and lowland agricultural zones. In Malaysia and Indonesia, more than 16 million ha of oil palm plantations have been established (Cramb and McCarthy 2016b; Hawkins et al. 2016), while 1 million ha of rubber plantations have been planted in areas of China, Laos, Thailand, Vietnam, Cambodia, and Myanmar where rubber was not traditionally grown (Li and Fox 2012). Cash crop plantations were first established across the region by colonial powers for purposes of expanding and solidifying territorial control, pacifying civil unrest in rural areas, and creating new sources of capital accumulation, via natural rubber, coffee, sugarcane, and coconut plantations (Byerlee 2014; De Koninck 2011; Ishikawa 2010; Moore 2000; Murray 1992; Stoler 1995; Wolf 1982). Yet, their rapid expansion in the past few decades represents a new era in plantation development across Southeast Asia in scale and scope.

Plantation development in Southeast Asia has led to dramatic transformations of the countryside. The region has become one of the epicenters of the contemporary "Plantationocene," a term coined by Donna Haraway and fellow anthropologists including Noboru Ishikawa (Haraway 2015; Haraway et al. 2016; Ishikawa and Soda 2019). The

Plantationocene builds on ideas of the Anthropocene and Capitalocene to demonstrate how one of the primary ways in which human societies are driving transformations of the earth is through extractive and enclosed plantations. Plantations, or "factories in the fields" (McWilliams 2000) that originated in the colonial period, have been an integral element to the expansion of capitalism and transformed rural areas and modern life, whether in the case of coffee (Paige 1997), sugar (Mintz 1985; Moore 2000), or rubber (Bunker 1985, Ishikawa 2010; Weinstein 1983).

In Southeast Asia, millions of hectares of land have been granted and developed into plantations (Bissonnette and De Koninck 2017; Byerlee 2014; Ingalls et al. 2019), dispossessing peasants of their land and generating widespread deforestation (Schoenberger et al. 2017). Social dynamics of the countryside have been radically transformed as some households have become landless (Hall et al. 2011), others have made money from their own investments in plantation crops (Feintrenie et al. 2010; Fox and Castella 2013), and migrant workers have arrived in the countryside from other regions and countries (Baird et al. 2019; Pye et al. 2012). Complex systems of agricultural processing, manufacturing, and trade have been established, built on new forms of rural and national infrastructure. The outcomes for rural peoples and economies are contradictory. On the one hand, those who have invested in their own plantations or have found gainful employment have seen their incomes rise and benefited from the new waves of plantations (Rist et al. 2010). On the other hand, those who have been displaced from their land have lost access to common forest and grazing lands, while those who have been heavily exploited by unfair contracting and employment schemes are much worse off (Fox and Castella 2013; Lee et al. 2014). Similarly, the biodiverse environments of Southeast Asia have been subject to untold destruction with global implications due to the massive amounts of carbon emitted (Ahrends et al. 2015; Carlson et al. 2013; Fox et al. 2014).

The development of plantations in the region is characterized by both large-scale land concessions or estates and the conversion of land by millions of smallholders. For rubber, a crop that is more conducive to small-scale cultivation, 83 percent of the area cultivated in Thailand, Indonesia, Malaysia, and India (which comprise 78 percent of world production) was in the hands of smallholders in 2005 (Byerlee 2014). Oil palm is a more difficult crop for smallholders to grow because of expensive agricultural inputs and rapid processing demands, yet, as of 2015, 42 percent of the 11 million hectares planted with oil palm in Indonesia was grown by smallholders (Bissonnette and De Koninck 2017). When it comes to estate plantations, astonishingly large-scale projects have been developed. For example, the Malaysian conglomerate Sime Darby Berhad owns more than 620,000 ha of land dedicated for oil palm development in Malaysia and Indonesia (Byerlee 2014). In 1996, the Suharto regime initiated the Mega Rice Project, which planned to transform one million hectares of peat swamp forest into rice paddy land, which eventually failed in part because of its considerable environmental impacts (Riely 2001). Echoing such projects, in 2010 the Indonesian government announced the Merauke Integrated Food and Energy Estate in Papua, to develop an expected 1.2 million ha of food crop and biofuel plantations through large-scale corporate investments (Ito et al. 2014). On the other hand, smaller- and medium-scale farmers and operators have developed plantations that individually cover relatively limited amounts of land but in the aggregate have transformed and completely altered landscapes (Bissonnette and De Koninck 2017; Byerlee 2014; Koizumi 2016).

A long-standing and prominent debate within agrarian studies, particularly regarding Southeast Asia, concerns whether smallholder versus large-holder estate plantations will dominate the cash crop sector and what are the relative merits and faults of each in terms of efficiency, livelihood development, and environmental impact (Bissonnette and De

Koninck 2017; Byerlee 2014). Known as the "agrarian question," originally formulated by Karl Kautsky ([1899] 19988) and advanced by contemporary scholars of agrarian change (Akram-Lodhi and Kay 2010; Goodman and Watts 1997; Mcmichael 1997), the debate is concerned with the degree to which capitalist social relations have and will continue to penetrate the agricultural sector and transform farming into a corporate-led form of production. Recent scholarship on global land grabbing (Borras and Franco 2012; De Schutter 2011; White et al. 2012; Zoomers 2010) has reignited concern for the loss of the smallholder form in favor of large-scale estate plantations.

In this article, we contend that the distinction between large and small plantations, while useful for disaggregating certain social-economic dynamics of cash crop production, can also obscure similarities across these forms of plantation development. This is particularly the case when smallholder plantations developed contiguously across a landscape reproduce the same social and environmental impacts of the large-scale estate. Furthermore, there is a much greater diversity of arrangements of plantation development across the region, such as managed smallholder schemes, joint ventures between communities and investors, contract farming, nucleus estate, and smallholder arrangements, all of which can involve widespread displacement of prior landscapes and replacement with monoculture plantations. Thus, in this article, we choose to instead focus on the development of "mega-plantations" to capture the landscape-scale transformation of social and environmental landscapes by plantations. Terms such as large-scale, estate, monoculture, and mono-crop fail to capture the broader dynamic of change that is underway across the region. "Large-scale" and "estate" reference single-owner plantations of a large size at the scale of the project or plot but miss the aggregate impacts of medium- and small-scale plantations. "Monoculture" and "mono-crop" denote that a single crop is planted in an area or on the same land each year, respectively, but do not address the size or political, social, and economic dynamics of the plantation.

"Mega-plantations," we contend, captures these dynamics and more that are critical to the transformation of rural landscapes—large-scale and small-scale, single crops that are combined with complex transnational commodity chains, and various forms of ownership that in combination to lead to a mega-transformation of the countryside. We use the term mega-plantations to capture the ideologies, politics, and economies of large-scale and complex forms of plantation development that are inscribed upon rural environments at the landscape level. We develop this concept with reference to the literature on megaprojects. This literature has largely focused on large construction projects that involve the creation of significant infrastructures, such as ports, railways, hydropower dams, mines, special economic zones, real estate developments, tourist attractions, and sporting stadiums, among others.

Although industrial plantations are sometimes listed as a type of megaproject (e.g., Gellert and Lynch 2003), there has yet to be an exploration of what it would mean to rigorously apply the idea of megaprojects to plantations. Some have sought to develop a specific definition of megaprojects as in the recently released *Oxford Handbook of Megaproject Management* (Flyvbjerg 2017: 2): "large-scale, complex ventures that typically cost $1 billion or more, take many years to develop and build, involve multiple public and private stakeholders, are transformational, and impact millions of people." Naomi Brookes and Giorgio Locatelli (2015) have said megaprojects have "long-lasting impact on the economy, the environment, and society." Others have focused on the symbolic significance of megaprojects or the complexity of their contents, such as combining residential, service, industrial, and transport dimensions (Orueta and Fainstain 2009). Here, however, we follow Paul Gellert and Barbara Lynch's more abstract characterization of "mega-projects as displacements," as they frame it clearly in their title. They argue:

> Mega-projects entail "creative destruction" in a material sense: they transform landscapes rapidly and radically, displacing mountaintops, rivers, flora, and fauna, as well as humans and their communities. We argue that displacement is intrinsic to mega-project development and that both are socio-natural phenomena . . . We define mega-projects as projects which transform landscapes rapidly, intentionally, and profoundly in very visible ways and require coordinated applications of capital and state power. (2003: 15)

Applying these characteristics of megaprojects to plantations, we define mega-plantations as the development of plantations that either through a single plantation project or in the aggregate of many smaller plantation projects, and all sorts of production arrangements in between, rapidly and radically transforms entire landscapes in ways that displace or transform local communities and rural environments that previously existed there. We intend not to romanticize the social-environmental landscapes that existed before mega-plantation development but merely to highlight the abrupt transformations that take place. Mega-plantations require the application of large amounts of capital and political power to achieve such transformations. Mega-plantations are created at a scale beyond that of the prior landscape, especially because of their often-complex connections with the regional, national, and global economy, tending to take on a transnational character (Pye 2013b). They become what Tania Li (2018) calls "plantation zones," a distinct kind of space, such as districts with significant areas of land devoted to plantations, in which land, livelihoods, law, and government are monopolized by, colonized by, and folded into the plantation system—a phenomenon that is both historical and contemporary. Furthermore, they are driven by ideological motivations that prioritize large-scale transformation over small-scale, incremental changes, viewing the large as characteristic of modernism and progress, what James Scott (1998) refers to as the logic of high modernism. Finally, megaprojects create a hitherto unseen degree of complexity and connectivity, through new flows of capital, labor, and commodities across national borders (Cramb and McCarthy 2016a).

The previous paragraphs logically explain why we preface plantations with the qualifier "mega." However, in reflecting on our choice of terminology, we also identify a deeper, more affective reason. "Mega" evokes a certain type of reaction we have experienced when encountering plantation development in Southeast Asia, which other terms such as estate or large-scale fail to capture. Miles Kenney-Lazar vividly remembers his first encounter with a transformed plantation landscape in southern Laos. Arriving at the edge of an area cleared in preparation for the development of a rubber plantation by a Vietnamese multinational corporation, he was struck by the seemingly unending expanse of empty land, cleared of all agricultural fields, forests (apart from a few remaining stands of trees), and people (see Illustration 4.1). The newly cut plantation road led into the distance, where it and the plantation landscape disappeared from view, seemingly running up against the mountains that were just visible in the smoggy haze. He remembers thinking, "So this is what 10,000 hectares looks like," reflecting on the size of the land granted to the company. It turned out that this particular plot was only 1,000 ha, not all of which is visible in the image. Similarly, the term mega-plantation captures Ishikawa's experiences of moving through endless oil palm plantation expanses in Sarawak, Malaysia, as can be seen in Illustration 4.2. What these experiential dimensions capture is the vast scale of the mega-plantation, which is ordered and developed beyond the scale of the human. Not only does the plantation go beyond the scale of the foreign researcher; more importantly, it also operates beyond the scale of the people that live in or near plantation spaces—farmers, migrants, workers, and even plantation managers. It is a landscape transformation that strikes both awe and unease for the viewer, especially in providing a sense of the dramatic changes that are underway, and what they mean for rural communities and environments.

The remainder of this article is dedicated to investigating how mega-plantations have been pursued in Southeast Asia, what are their contemporary social and environmental

Illustration 4.1. Land cleared in preparation for a Vietnamese rubber plantation, southern Laos (© Miles Kenney-Lazar, 2009).

dynamics, and what types of political reactions they have generated. First, we examine the historical drivers of mega-plantation development, particularly their ideological motivations and political-economic drivers during colonial, nationalist, and neoliberal historical periods. Following that, we focus on the contemporary aspects of mega-plantation development and maintenance, particularly the scope and scale of mega-plantations across the region, transnational linkages, and social-environmental transformations. Then, we write about the ways in which rural people, civil society groups, government institutions, and plantation companies have reacted to the trends of mega-plantation development, with a particular focus on efforts to emphasize small-scale over large-scale plantations, legal and regulatory reforms, and various forms of social movements and resistance. We conclude by reflecting on potential future trends for mega-plantations. The article is largely based on a review of the available literature and simultaneously aims to provide

Illustration 4.2. Young oil palm plantation in Sarawak, Malaysia (© Noboru Ishikawa, 2007)

a comprehensive review of plantation expansion in Southeast Asia. However, it is also built on our own research experiences in Laos and southern Myanmar (Kenney-Lazar) and Sarawak, Malaysia (Ishikawa), and thus we recognize that our particular research backgrounds may influence the issues, trends, and regions we focus on.

Historical Drivers of Plantation Expansion in Southeast Asia

In this section, we outline the driving historical forces behind the expansion of mega-plantations throughout Southeast Asia. Research on plantations in the region has shown that these forces are multiple and interactive. While the expansion of global capitalism is often framed as the dominant driver of resource extraction, including plantation development, the ways in which capitalism has integrated with forces of colonialism, nationalist modernism, the interests of national and local elites, discourses of taming unruly natures and populations in the countryside, and forestry management are critically important.

Colonial Origins of Mega-Plantations (Late Nineteenth–Mid-Twentieth Century)

The plantation, "producing tropical cash crops based on hired labor" (Hayami 2010: 3305), first emerged during the colonial period, including in Southeast Asia, to serve the resource and capital accumulation interests of European powers. Before colonial intervention, subsistence and cash crops, traded regionally and internationally, were produced by smallholders. Colonial plantations were dominated by estates at the time, and economic turbulence led to unprecedented conglomerations of ownership. Although much smaller in scale compared to contemporary mega-plantations, they were mega-plantations in their own right, as they significantly transformed rural landscapes across the region, created new labor relations of agricultural production, and established a model for plantation expansion in the later postcolonial and neoliberal periods. While the mega-plantations of the time were for the most part not comprised of smallholders, they did initiate the expansion of smallholder food crops, particularly rice, that were used to support estate plantations and an expanding urban workforce.

Such transformations of social-environmental relations in the tropics had their origins in a crisis of capital accumulation in Western Europe (Wolf 1982: 311). These are seemingly distant forces, but the genesis of the plantation mode of production, the increase of smallholdings, regional specialization, and the spread of a worldwide network of commodities were all related to the long depression of the European economy from 1873 to 1896. After an economic boom between 1848 and 1873, Europe experienced a significant economic depression characterized by high wages, the high cost of raw materials, and declining rates of profit. The outcome was that several European capitalist nation-states embarked upon an intense search for new investments, markets, raw materials, and cheap labor across the world, including Southeast Asia (312). From the 1880s onward, agricultural expansion in Southeast Asia quickened (De Koninck 2011: 5). The advent of new crops and new products altered the relations between regions; some specialized in producing foodstuffs or industrial materials; others processed the raw materials, consumed the food grains or meat, and sent back manufactured goods. Regional specialization was not confined to food grains, meat, and cotton. To provide tropical products like sugar, tea, coffee, or rubber in bulk, entire areas were turned into sugar, tea, rubber, or coffee plantations.

Rubber became the predominant industrial cash crop in Southeast Asia and characteristic of the mega-plantation model. Rubber seeds were brought from the Royal Botanic Gardens at Kew, London, after being stolen from Brazil (Jackson 2008). Rubber had

become a critically important plantation crop to supply Europe's second industrial revolution, essential for connecting and protecting the moving parts of machinery. A mere
345 acres were reported as planted with rubber in the Federated Malay States in 1897,
but within a quarter of a century, the Peninsula accounted for 53 percent of all rubber
planted in India, in Ceylon, and throughout Southeast Asia (Drabble 1973). The colonial
governments of the region supported the development of rubber by granting loans to
private developers, such as Malaysia's Loan to Planters Scheme of 1904, and by granting
lands at cheap prices. In Peninsular Malaysia, areas considered "wastelands"—sparsely
settled forestlands—were provided to rubber investors. In French Indochina, where the
rubber industry developed since the 1920s, concessions were practically handed out to
investors, which led to expansive land acquisitions that conflicted with upland ethnic
minorities (Byerlee 2014). Although rubber is an ideal crop for smallholders to produce,
colonial policies favored estate production while discouraging smallholders and initial
investments. Plus, larger planters were the only ones willing to take the technological and
financial risks of investing in a new crop to the region.

While rubber was the predominant plantation crop of the colonial period, it was by
no means the only one. Although oil palm did not become the dominant plantation crop
of the region until the second half of the twentieth century, the first commercial oil palm
plantations were established in Sumatra in 1911 and in Malaya in 1917[1] (Corley and
Tinker 2016). Ann Stoler (1995) writes of the *cultuurgebied* (plantation belt, in Dutch)
which emerged on Sumatra's east coast, also known as Deli, which included tea, tobacco,
rubber, oil palm, fiber (sisal), and coconut plantations, all butting against one another
(see Illustration 4.3). Plantation operations there became some of the most lucrative in
the Western colonial enterprise, and thus the area became known as the Dollar Land of
Deli. The Agrarian Land Law that the Dutch colonial government promulgated in 1870

Illustration 4.3. Sumatra's plantation belt (*cultuurgebied*), 1918 (adapted from Stoler 1995).

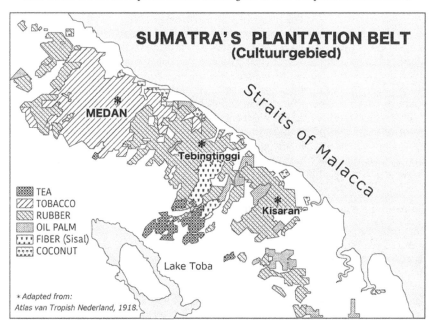

allowed multinational foreign investment, leading to a surge of not only Dutch investment but also British, American, and Franco-Belgian investments, among others. Some of the companies had rubber holdings in the area totaling up to 100,000 ha. The consolidation of foreign holdings in the area meant there was little land left for local use. The contemporary effect of this plantation history can be seen today, where 265 plantations cover an area of more than 700,000 hectares.

The profitability of plantation agriculture in Malaya and the Dutch East Indies inspired plantation development in French Indochina at the very beginning of the twentieth century. In addition to the emergence of a class of smallholding rubber producers, the colonial administration encouraged large-scale private investment in rubber plantations by granting huge tracts of land and using *corvée* labor to build a road network into more remote areas of Cochinchina (Southern Vietnam). By 1937, 127,000 ha of land had been planted with rubber in Indochina, 98,000 ha of which were in Cochinchina and 27,000 ha in Cambodia. Although approximately 70 percent of the rubber plantations were small (less than 40 ha), they accounted for only 6 percent of the total area planted. Most of the region's latex was produced by large-scale concession companies, typically between 1,000 and 5,000 ha, while a few companies, such as Michelin, owned plantations larger than 5,000 ha. By the late 1930s, Indochina was the fifth-largest producer of rubber in terms of area and fourth in terms of output (Murray 1992). The extensive coverage of rubber plantations across Cochinchina can be seen in Illustration 4.4.

Smaller companies and individual planters also played a role in the emergence of rubber plantations in colonial Southeast Asia. However, they were not always able to endure the volatility of global rubber prices. As early as the mid-1880s, when individual planters could not survive the economic crisis, 179 individual planters' estates in East Sumatra of the Dutch East Indies were consolidated and merged into four powerful companies, thus facilitating a trend of emerging mega-plantations (Stoler 1995: 16). Rubber prices slumped in the 1910s and 1930s, which many smaller planters could not tolerate, leading to a consolidation of their holdings and an emergence of large, vertically integrated firms, including major tire manufacturers such as Goodyear (Indonesia), Dunlop (Malaysia), and Michelin (Vietnam) (Barlow 1978; Bauer 1948).

The cash crop mega-plantations, especially rubber and oil palm, not only transformed the landscapes where they were developed but were also indirectly linked to the expansion of other agricultural areas, particularly for commercial rice production. Paul Kratoska has shown how the colonial period led to a transition from subsistence to commercial rice production, leading to the creation of larger, commercial rice fields into the marshy plains of Lower Burma, central Siam, and Cochinchina, requiring the creation of new waterways for transport and embankments for flood control. While most of this rice was exported to European destinations, a significant portion was also used to feed the laborers in plantation belts, particularly on the west coast of the Malay Peninsula and the east coast of Sumatra, which both had a food deficit, importing 50 to 70 percent of the rice consumed (Kratoska 2008: 78).

Postcolonial Plantations: Independence and Nationalism (1950s–1980s)

The plantation sector in Southeast Asia rapidly changed after World War II because of waves of postcolonial independence, nationalism, and socialism, in ways that paved the way for the expansion of contemporary mega-plantations. This happened in a bifurcated manner, however, in which the paths of plantation development were broadly divided by the front lines of the Cold War. Plantation development and expansion in zones of active conflict in Indochina were halted during the three decades of the Indochina Wars (1946–1975). Plantations were subsequently nationalized by socialist governments while

Illustration 4.4. Map of rubber plantations in Cochinchina, 1920s (adapted from Aso 2018: 11).

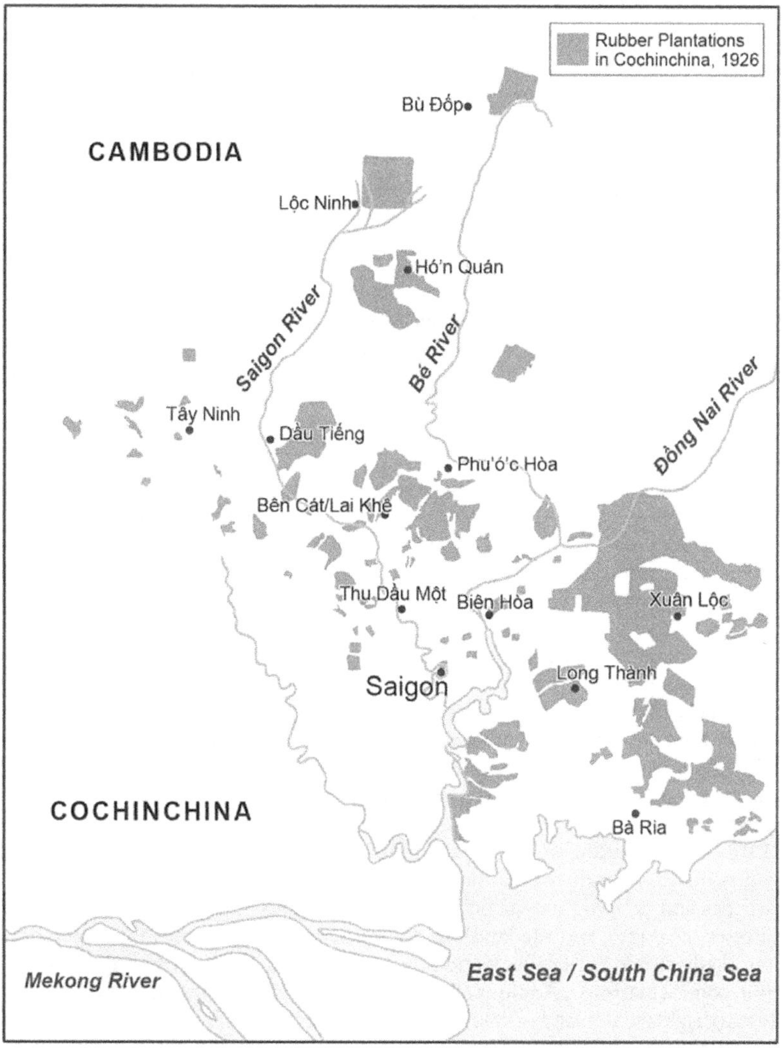

production and trade was limited due to economic sanctions by the Western Bloc. In contrast, the plantations of Thailand, the Philippines, Malaysia, and Indonesia could flourish outside of active zones of conflict and with the ability to trade commodities on the global economy, even when plantations were nationalized, such as in Malaysia and Indonesia.

In Malaysia and Indonesia, independence led to new forms of nationally driven plantation development that launched them into their greatest period of plantation expansion (Cramb and McCarthy 2016b). The European-owned plantation industry was nationalized, and a shift from rubber to oil palm proceeded concurrently. This led both countries to grant plantation concessions while also implementing nationally managed smallholder schemes or nucleus-estate arrangements, such as those by the Federal Land Development Authority (FELDA) in Malaysia and Perkebunan Inti Rakyat (PIR) in Indonesia. In Cambodia, Laos, Vietnam, and Myanmar (CLMV), in contrast, independence movements were hampered by war (two Indochina Wars, civil war in Myanmar) and closed socialist political-economic systems that stymied the expansion of plantations, even when they were nationalized (Byerlee 2014). Yet when these economies began opening up to market economies and foreign investment in the late 1980s, the powerful role of the state in controlling vast swathes of land in the country led to a rapid expansion of new mega-plantations not possible during the colonial era, as large amounts of state land could be granted to domestic and foreign companies (Hirsch and Scurrah 2015).

In Malaysia, nationalist concerns led to the emergence of managed smallholder schemes for the planting of oil palm, which have produced massive landscape transformation, despite smallholders being at the center of such changes. FELDA has played a critical role in mobilizing smallholder farmers to establish plantations across the country (Bissonnette and De Koninck 2017). FELDA is a government agency that was founded to resettle the rural poor into new areas and to organize cash crop production among smallholder farmers. Thus, the smallholder cash crop plantations that FELDA supported were also accompanied by large resettlement schemes and rural development projects. For example, the Jengka Project in Pahang included timber extraction, commercial plantations, and urban development in 24 settlement schemes and covered 121,700 ha. As of 1990, FELDA had settled 119,300 families and managed 475 schemes that covered a total crop area of 823,720 ha. Starting in the 1990s, FELDA began launching its own commercial plantations under FELDA Plantations Sdn Bhd, which eventually became a public company in 2003 and is now the largest palm oil producer in the world (Cramb and McCarthy 2016a). Thus, despite starting as a resettlement scheme of managed smallholders, its business model shifted to a model similar to plantation estates, therefore demonstrating the slippage between varying modes of production when pursuing megaplantation expansion.

The Indonesian government developed the PIR scheme, which is a nucleus estate and smallholder arrangement whereby an agribusiness firm establishes the core plantation estate and palm oil mill and then provides land to landless farmers, known as outgrowers or plasma, who plant oil palm trees whose fruit can be sold at the nearby mill. Initiated in the 1970s and supported by World Bank funding, the PIR scheme has been an important way in which new lands for plantation development have been opened, transforming landscapes and creating new plantation zones, bringing together state agencies, agribusinesses, peasants, and the landless. The nucleus estate provides inputs, credit, and technical advice and then collects and processes the fruit, thus resembling a type of production contract farming. Additionally, the smallholders are either local landholders with customary rights to the land or migrants from other regions of Indonesia, resettled out of densely populated areas via Indonesia's transmigration program.

Large-scale, capital-intensive plantation expansion was halted in Indochinese countries and Myanmar from the mid-1950s to the late 1980s during periods of war, land collectivization, agrarian reform, and restrictions on private capital and trade (Aso 2018; Byerlee 2014). In Vietnam, Cambodia, and Laos, two Indochinese wars that stretched from 1946 to 1975 economically devastated all three countries with field battles, insurgent warfare, bombing, and chemical defoliation. As the conflicts escalated, especially US bombing and chemical defoliation, plantation production was affected and halted. After the war, the socialist governments that came to power engaged in various forms of land and agricultural collectivization or nationalized plantations, which had detrimental effects on the plantation economy. In Myanmar (then Burma), the 1962 military coup led by General Ne Win led to a socialist military junta government, followed by economic deterioration. Myanmar went from a top rice exporter in the 1940s to a rice importer, demonstrating the impact of the economic transformation on plantation agriculture (Aung-Thwin and Aung-Thwin 2013).

However, the wars, revolutions, and socialist periods of Indochinese countries and Myanmar set the stage for rapid plantation expansion in the 1990s and 2000s (Hirsch and Scurrah 2015). This period led to greater state control over land and plantation industries. Thus, when these countries started to transition toward a market economy in the late 1990s, the government was able to offer large-scale concessions of state land to private investors, domestic and foreign, for the development of mega-plantations. Additionally, the socialist governments of the region had their own plans for large-scale plantation expansion, which set the stage for some forms of future plantation expansion. For example, the Myanmar government planned for the country to be a major exporter of agro-industrial crops such as oil palm.

Contemporary Displacements of Southeast Asia's Mega-Plantations

Multiple and layered historical drivers of mega-plantation development have firmly entrenched the plantation as a dominant economic system of the countryside across Southeast Asia. Throughout Southeast Asia, plantations are destroying and reformulating rural ecosystems for purposes of state building, internal colonization, and capital accumulation (Hall 2011; Li 2018), generating massive environmental transformations such as deforestation, loss of biodiversity, drought, and significant climate change emissions among others (Ahrends et al. 2015; Carlson et al. 2013; Fox et al. 2014). As contemporary forms of enclosure, plantations are inherently exclusionary, keeping out other forms of land use that do not fit within their monoculture logic (Hall et al. 2011). Mega-plantations are a key element of how land grabbing has operated in Southeast Asia, rapidly and extensively dispossessing various groups of peasants, indigenous peoples, and forest users of their lands and livelihoods (Bissonnette and De Koninck 2017; Schoenberger et al. 2017; White et al. 2012). In this section, we address the contemporary role of mega-plantations in Southeast Asia. We focus on the key dimensions that comprise mega-plantations today in the region: the scale and scope of the phenomenon, transnational linkages with the global economy, land displacement and dispossession, and environmental despoliation.

A key dimension of the trend of mega-plantations across Southeast Asia has been the scale and scope of plantation development since the colonial period but in particular over the past 20 to 40 years. The rapid and spectacular expansion of oil palm in insular Southeast Asia, particularly Malaysia and Indonesia, is characteristic of the mega-plantations that are emerging across the region. In Malaysia, more than 5 million ha of oil palm have been planted throughout the country (Cramb and McCarthy 2016b). In Indonesia, oil palm has rapidly expanded since 1970, when it covered only 100,000 ha of land, to 11 million ha as of 2015, equivalent to 40 percent of the country's area of arable land (Hawkins et al. 2016; Li 2018). Aiming to expand the coverage of oil palm plantations throughout the country, the government has planned for another 20 to 30 million ha to be planted (Li 2018). The largest plantation developer in the country has planted more than 380,000 ha of oil palm. Furthermore, during the downturn in palm oil prices in 2011, when many operators were struggling, major transnational corporations looked at the long run and bought up struggling plantations to increase their holdings, leading to consolidation within the sector (Hawkins et al. 2016). In Illustration 4.5, the distribution of mature, closed canopy oil palm across the lowlands of Peninsular Malaysia, Borneo, and Sumatra can be seen (as well as the distribution of peatland), showing distinctive belts of mega-plantation development in key regions of both countries as of 2010.

Illustration 4.5. Distribution of closed canopy oil palm and tropical peatland in the lowlands of Peninsular Malaysia, Borneo, and Sumatra. Provincial abbreviations in the figure (clockwise from top left): Peninsular Malaysia (PM), Sarawak (SW), Sabah (SB), Eastern Kalimantan (EK), Southern Kalimantan (SK), Central Kalimantan (CK), Western Kalimantan (WK), Lampung (LP), South Sumatra (SS), Bengkulu (BK), Jambi (JB), West Sumatra (WS), Riau (RI), North Sumatra (NS), Aceh (AC) (reprinted with permission from Koh et al. 2011).

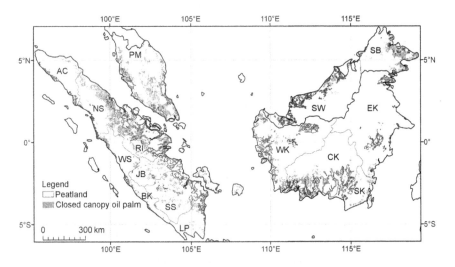

In the CLMV countries of the Lower Mekong, agricultural land has expanded by 9 million ha, or approximately 21 percent, from 1996 to 2015. An important driving force of this trend has been the granting of large-scale agriculture and tree plantation concessions that began in the late 1990s and accelerated around 2006. A total of 5.1 million ha of land have been granted for plantation development across the region, which in Cambodia, Laos, and Myanmar represents 66, 30, and 16 percent, respectively, of the amount of land that smallholder farmers cultivate. The boom crops of rubber, sugarcane, oil palm, cassava, and maize represent 76 percent of the concession areas in these countries (Ingalls et al. 2019).

Mega-plantation development across Southeast Asia has generated widespread displacement: of land uses, agrarian livelihoods, communities, and ecosystems. Such displacement occurs not only as a result of massive plantation estates that cover thousands of hectares at the plot level. Such displacement can even be generated by smallholders, especially when a wave of smallholders convert their agricultural and forest lands to a boom crop and transform the countryside. Thus, mega-plantation development has the potential to materialize via a wide range of production arrangements, all of which we consider here in Table 4.1. These include estate plantations established by government land concessions or outright land purchases, nucleus estate and smallholder arrangements, land-based contract farming, product-based contract farming, managed smallholders, and independent smallholders. In discussing the displacement of mega-plantations throughout the region, we reference the role that these various production forms can play in that process.

The dispossession of land and natural resources from rural land users, especially indigenous peoples, has been one of the most consistent critiques of plantation expansion in the region, especially in the literature on land grabbing, and is characteristic of mega-project development that displaces prior land uses and livelihoods. Much of the literature

Table 4.1. Description of Key Modes of Plantation Development and Their Relation to Mega-Plantations in Southeast Asia

Mode of production	Description	Relation to mega-plantation development
Estates	Private or state-owned enterprises own or exclusively lease large plantation areas with hired labor.	Estate plantations can cover large areas of land, including multiple plots that are thousands of hectares each. They can involve significant displacement of prior landscapes, including dispossession of peasant livelihoods and deforestation. They are often accompanied by multiple layers of infrastructure and are linked up to the global economy.
Nucleus estate and smallholder (NES) arrangements	Private or state-owned enterprises establish a "nucleus" estate, often including a processing facility and infrastructure, and then smallholders are supported to develop their own plantations nearby.	NES arrangements can cover areas larger than estate plantations, as they enroll smallholders into additional landscape conversion. They can create new plantation complexes or zones in rural areas where none previously existed.
Land-based contract farming	Private or state-owned enterprises develop plantations on community land and share control over the plantation or land with the community.	Land-based contract farming tends to involve smaller plots of land than estates, as the land comes from communities. In aggregate, however, these types of arrangements can cover large areas of a landscape, transforming its socio-environmental characteristics, especially when combined with other forms of plantation development.
Product-based contract farming	Private or state-owned enterprises enter into a production contract with a community or farmers in which production inputs are provided to farmers and a share of the product at harvest belongs to the enterprise.	Also involving small amounts of land at the individual plot level, product-based contract farming often involves many farmers entering contracts with a single company, thus leading to a coordinated transformation of a particular area into plantations.
Managed smallholders	The state organizes the development of smallholder plantations by providing land to farmers through leasing or resettlement.	Managed smallholder schemes are organized and led by the state and thus can lead to a significant displacement of rural areas, especially when settled with new migrants as in Malaysia.
Independent smallholders	Smallholders develop plantations using their own or borrowed inputs on their own or leased land.	In aggregate, independent smallholders planting a commercial plantation crop in response to policy incentives, and market signals can radically transform a whole landscape. Although producing independently, they can also be linked up with estate plantations and the processing facilities there, thus being tied into larger scales of mega-plantation development

has focused more on the impact of large-scale investments, especially estate plantations established through government land concessions and outright purchases. There has been a significant focus on such dispossession in Laos, Cambodia, and Myanmar, where the governments have granted concessions of so-called state land to domestic and foreign investors for plantation development, but such land was customarily used and managed for decades by peasants who are now dispossessed from it (Baird 2011; Beban and Work 2014; Kenney-Lazar 2012; Schoenberger et al. 2017; Suhardiman et al. 2015; Woods 2011). Estates are the dominant form of planted area in Malaysia and Indonesia, 61 and 56 percent, respectively (Cramb and McCarthy 2016a).

However, all the forms of plantation development we have described can include some element of dispossession. Even independent smallholders can be involved in developing plantations on contested land, ignoring the customary claims of marginalized groups. The marketization of land as a result of developing cash crops can lead to land sales and consolidation of land ownership, as Li (2018) has shown in the case of cacao plantations in Sulawesi, Indonesia. In Northern Laos, contract farming of rubber between Lao peasants and Chinese companies has become an alternative form of dispossession, even though it was pursued precisely to avoid this problem associated with large-scale concessions. In certain types of contracts, instead of dividing the produced latex among the two parties, they divided the management of land, putting up to 70 percent of land management in the companies' hands, leading to de facto dispossession (Dwyer 2013).

Oil palm plantations have attracted controversy for displacing tropical rainforests and replacing them with monoculture plantations: nearly half of oil palm planted has involved some forest destruction, and 70 percent of Indonesia's oil palm plantations are established on land that was part of the country's forest estate (Cramb and McCarthy 2016b). Not only are plantations across the region a major cause of deforestation; clearing forests and logging is oftentimes the primary motivation for plantation development. In Myanmar, the clearing of forests to make way for the expansion of commercial agriculture and tree plantations has become the leading cause of deforestation (Woods 2015). In many cases, large areas cleared are never planted with crops, or the crops planted are not tended to as the goal of logging timber has already been achieved. Plantations lead to significant carbon dioxide emissions by displacing carbon-rich environments, like primary forest areas and peatlands, and replacing them with monoculture plantations that absorb significantly less carbon (Carlson et al. 2013; Fox et al. 2014). Fifteen percent of oil palm in Malaysia and 25 percent in Indonesia has been established on peatland, which leads to carbon dioxide emissions (Cramb and McCarthy 2016b). The methods of displacement have their own environmental impacts: fire is often used in clearing land for oil palm plantations, especially in Indonesia, which leads to forest fires and air pollution (Cramb and McCarthy 2016b; Mizuno et al. 2016).

Mega-Plantation Politics

Despite the consistent expansion of mega-plantations across the region, their development has not gone uncontested. Instead, at just about every turn, mega-plantations have been subject to various forms of political reactions from customary land users, laborers, regulatory government agencies, and nongovernmental organizations, among others. Such politics range from everyday resistance, protests, strikes, and social movements to advocacy campaigns, regulatory reforms, and sustainability guidelines. Such political reactions have questioned the underlying logic of mega-plantations in their unrelenting displacement of rural landscapes, have limited the geographies of their expansion and which landscapes are displaced, or have transformed the socio-environmental dynamics of how mega-plantations are developed and operated. Mega-plantation politics operate across all of the varying political regimes of Southeast Asia, from single-party communist states to multiparty democracies, although in ways that are distinct to each geographical and historical political context. They have also operated during each historical period, from the colonial period to the present, but have amplified in the past few decades in response to the massive expansion faced.

Political reactions animated plantation expansion during the colonial period, largely in the form of labor politics on plantations (Stoler 1995). In Indochina, rubber tappers engaged in various forms of everyday resistance such as loafing, petty theft, sabotaging company property, self-mutilation, suicide, and desertion. They also organized eight large strikes between 1930 and 1937 that led to modest material gains and contributed to the growth of the Vietnam workers' movement in the 1930s (Murray 1992). The present period of plantation politics has been more animated by various dimensions of displacement: of customary lands, of forests, of carbon-rich ecological landscapes, and of small-holder uses of the land. Across the region, small-scale land and forest users have pursued a diverse set of political strategies for contesting the unjust displacement of their lands to make way for mega-plantation development (Ngidang 2005, 2008; Ramy Bulan 2006). Land displacement has sparked social movements in countries where freedom of political expression has recently emerged. In Myanmar, the political transition from a military junta to civilian government and then pluralistic democracy that began in 2010 has led to a flowering of social activism and movements to contest historical and contemporary land grabbing that has facilitated mega-plantation development (Mark 2016). Even in politically repressive contexts, creative forms of resistance have emerged to contest land expropriation. In Laos, the political repercussions for disruptive protest and other forms of contentious politics have led to creative forms of what several authors have termed "resisting with the state," putting significant pressure on state apparatuses to protect access to land (Kenney-Lazar et al. 2018; McAllister 2015).

Another set of politics has concerned the environmental displacements of mega-plantation development, led in particular by coalitions of local and international NGOs. These have been particularly pronounced in reaction to oil palm plantation development in the rainforests of Malaysia and Indonesia, building on the transnational advocacy campaigns against logging that began in the late 1980s. Such campaigns are produced transnationally by building links between indigenous peoples who customarily use the forests targeted for oil palm expansion, local activists and civil society organizations, and large international NGOs like the Worldwide Fund for Nature or Greenpeace. In Malaysia and Indonesia, such environmental conflicts are also land conflicts with local indigenous communities concerning whether the communities or the state have rights to the forests and the ability to make decisions concerning how they are used (Pye 2013a). The plight of orangutans whose habitats are being destroyed because of oil palm development has been particularly powerful in the media.

Finally, there have been political responses in the form of private regulation, particularly the development of voluntary guidelines, the most prominent of which has been the guidelines of the Roundtable on Sustainable Palm Oil (RSPO). Established in 2004, the RSPO aims to address critiques from activists and NGOs that oil palm is the cause of environmental and human rights abuses by developing a set of global standards that when followed would avoid such abuses. However, the RSPO has been heavily critiqued for not significantly altering the socio-environmental dynamics of oil palm plantation development and acting more as a tool of legitimacy for oil palm companies to protect their investments from critique and advocacy campaigns (Ruysschaert and Salles 2014). In the rubber sector, an RSPO-inspired set of standards, the Global Platform for Sustainable Natural Rubber, is under development by an association of the world's major tire companies.

Conclusion

Agro-industrial plantations have expanded across Southeast Asia since the colonial era, transforming vast swaths of rural landscapes into what Li (2018) has referred to as "plantation zones," playing a critical role in the progression of the Plantationocene in the region. Here, we conceptualize such plantation expansion through the lens of mega-projects—complex, expensive developments that have significant impacts on the economy, environment, and society through their creative destruction, radically displacing and transforming landscapes. They are developed through massive applications of state power and capital. Applied to the plantation sector, mega-plantations radically transform rural landscapes, displacing previously existing peasant communities and rural environments and producing in their place new landscapes of monoculture and mono-crop plantations, networks of road and electric infrastructure, processing facilities, and labor camps. Such transformations do not arise solely from the development of large-scale estate plantations with large plot sizes that constitute a megaproject in and of themselves. Mega-plantations are also produced when a complex array of plantation developments cohere in a particular landscape or region, which when combined lead to the same types of landscape transformations or at an even larger scale than single projects. Thus, mega-plantations develop through both rapid, intentional projects and a more spontaneous aggregation of smaller projects. In this article, we do not set a strict quantitative definition concerning what precisely constitutes a mega-plantation, as we believe they are better defined by qualitative parameters describing them as both a process and a particular type of landscape transformation.

Despite the essential role that mega-plantations have played in Southeast Asia's rural landscapes, their expansion has been restricted and shaped at times by political reactions from customary land users, smallholding peasants, laborers, civil society and NGOs, government regulators, and private industry organizations. Such reactions have strengthened over time, especially in the past two decades, as mega-plantations have expanded across a variety of frontiers, leaving few untouched landscapes for development. There are signs that the era of mega-plantation expansion in the region may be reaching its limits. CLMV countries have all put various types of limits on granting large-scale concessions for plantation development, although plantation capital may move into other arrangements as a result of contract farming and community or household land leasing. In Malaysia and Indonesia, oil palm expansion continues but under intense scrutiny from well-organized transnational advocacy campaigns. Even as the formations and arrangement of plantation development are altering, it is likely that large-scale displacement and transformation of entire landscapes will endure for some time.

▪ **ACKNOWLEDGMENTS**

We would like to thank Kim Thomas and Nate Badenoch for their sharp comments as discussants during the writing workshop "Contemporary Agrarian-Environmental Transformations across Southeast Asia," held at Kyoto University on 10 July 2018. Thank you to the two anonymous reviewers and journal editors for their insightful comments on the article. Any remaining errors or omissions are our own.

▪ **MILES KENNEY-LAZAR** is Assistant Professor in the Department of Geography at the National University of Singapore. He has been conducting research on the political, economic, and environmental geographies of large-scale Vietnamese and Chinese agro-industrial plantations in Laos over the past decade, particularly their threats to peasant claims on land and forested landscapes. He is currently expanding his research analyze the politics of land dispossession in peri-urban Laos and land rights restitution in Myanmar (Burma). He has written 13 peer-reviewed publications on these and related topics Email: geokmr@nus.edu.sg

▪ **NOBORU ISHIKAWA** is Professor of Anthropology at the Center for Southeast Asian Studies, Kyoto University. He earned his PhD in Anthropology from the Graduate Center, City University of New York. He has conducted fieldwork in Sarawak, Malaysia, exploring the construction of national space in the borderland, highland-lowland relations, the commodification of nature, and multispecies interactions in the tropics. His publications include *Between Frontiers: Nation and Identity in a Southeast Asian Borderland* (2010), *Transborder Governance of Forests, Rivers and Seas* (2010), *Flows and Movements in Southeast Asia* (2011) and *Anthropogenic Tropical Forests: Human-Nature Interfaces on the Plantation Frontier* (2019). Email: ishikawa@cseas.kyoto-u.ac.jp

▪ NOTE

1. Oil palm grows best in continuously wet, equatorial conditions within 10 degrees of the equator. Thus, it cannot be grown in many parts of mainland Southeast Asia.

▪ REFERENCES

Aso, Michitake. 2018. *Rubber and the Making of Vietnam: An Ecological History, 1897–1975.* Chapel Hill: University of North Carolina Press.

Ahrends, Antje, Peter M. Hollingsworth, Alan D. Ziegler, Jefferson M. Fox, Huafang Chen, Yufang Su, and Jianchu Xu. 2015. "Current Trends of Rubber Plantation Expansion May Threaten Biodiversity and Livelihoods." *Global Environmental Change* 34: 48–58.

Akram-Lodhi, A. Haroon, and Cristobal Kay. 2010. "Surveying the Agrarian Question (Part 2): Current Debates and Beyond." *Journal of Peasant Studies* 37 (2): 255–84.

Aung-Thwin, Michael, and Maitrii Aung-Thwin. 2013. *A History of Myanmar Since Ancient Times: Traditions and Transformations.* London: Reaktion Books.

Baird, Ian G. 2011. "Turning Land into Capital, Turning People into Labor: Primitive Accumulation and the Arrival of Large-Scale Economic Land Concessions in the Lao People's Democratic Republic." *New Proposals: Journal of Marxism and Interdisciplinary Inquiry* 5 (1): 10–26.

Baird, Ian G., William Noseworthy, Nghiem Phuong Tuyen, Le Thu Hua, and Jefferson Fox. 2019. "Land Grabs and Labour: Vietnamese Workers on Rubber Plantations in Southern Laos." *Singapore Journal of Tropical Geography* 40 (1): 50–70.

Bauer, Peter Thomas. 1948. *The Rubber Industry: A Study in Competition and Monopoly.* London: Longmans, Green & Co.

Barlow, Colin. 1978. *The Natural Rubber Industry, Its Development, Technology, and Economy in Malaysia.* Kuala Lumpur: Oxford University Press.

Beban, Alice, and Courtney Work. 2014. "The Spirits are Crying: Dispossessing Land and Possessing Bodies in Rural Cambodia." *Antipode* 46 (3): 593–610.

Bissonnette, Jean-François, and Rodolphe De Koninck. 2017. "The Return of the Plantation? Historical and Contemporary Trends in the Relation between Plantations and Smallholdings in Southeast Asia." *Journal of Peasant Studies* 44 (4): 918–938.

Borras, Saturnino M., and Jennifer C. Franco. 2012. "Global Land Grabbing and Trajectories of Agrarian Change: A Preliminary Analysis." *Journal of Agrarian Change* 12 (1): 34–59.

Brookes, Naomi J., and Giorgio Locatelli. 2015. "Power Plants as Megaprojects: Using Empirics to Shape Policy, Planning, and Construction Management." *Utilities Policy* 36: 57–66.

Bunker, Stephen G. 1985. *Underdeveloping the Amazon: Extraction, Unequal Exchange, and the Failure of the Modern State*. Chicago: University of Chicago Press.

Byerlee, Derek. 2014. "The Fall and Rise Again of Plantations in Tropical Asia: History Repeated?" *Land* 4 (3): 574–597.

Carlson, Kimberly M., Lisa M. Curran, Gregory P. Asner, Alice McDonald Pittman, Simon N. Trigg, and J. Marion Adeney. 2013. "Carbon Emissions from Forest Conversion by Kalimantan Oil Palm Plantations." *Nature Climate Change* 3: 283–287.

Corley, R. H. V., and P. B. Tinker. 2016. *The Oil Palm*. 5th ed. Hoboken, NJ: Wiley-Blackwell.

Cramb, Rob, and John F. McCarthy. 2016a. "Characterising Oil Palm Production in Indonesia and Malaysia." In Cramb and McCarthy 2016c: 27–77.

Cramb, Rob, and John F. McCarthy. 2016b. "Introduction." In Cramb and McCarthy 2016c: 1–26.

Cramb, Rob, and John F. McCarthy, eds. 2016c. *The Oil Palm Complex: Smallholders, Agribusiness and the State in Indonesia and Malaysia*. Singapore: National University of Singapore Press.

De Koninck, Rodolphe. 2011. "Southeast Asian Agricultural Expansion in Global Perspective." In *Borneo Transformed: Agricultural Expansion in Southeast Asia*, ed. Rodolphe De Koninck, Stéphane Bernard, and Jean-François Bissonnette, 1–9. Singapore: National University of Singapore Press.

De Schutter, Olivier. 2011. "How Not to Think of Land-Grabbing: Three Critiques of Large-Scale Investments in Farmland." *Journal of Peasant Studies* 38 (2): 249–279.

Drabble, John. 1973. *Rubber in Malay 1876–1922: The Genesis of the Industry*. Kuala Lumpur: Oxford University Press.

Dwyer, Michael B. 2013. "Building the Politics Machine: Tools for 'Resolving' the Global Land Grab." *Development and Change* 44 (2): 309–333.

FAO (Food and Agriculture Organization of the United Nations). 2016. FAOSTAT: Food and Agriculture Data. http://www.fao.org/faostat/en/?#home.

Feintrenie, Laurène, Wan Kian Chong, and Patrice Lavang. 2010. "Why Do Farmers Prefer Palm Oil? Lessons Learnt from Bungo District, Indonesia." *Small-Scale Forestry* 9 (3): 379–396.

Flyvbjerg, Bent. 2017. "Introduction: The Iron Law of Megaproject Management." In *The Oxford Handbook of Megaproject Management*, ed. Bent Flyvbjerg, 1–20. Oxford: Oxford University Press.

Fox, Jefferson, and Jean-Christophe Castella. 2013. "Expansion of Rubber *(Hevea brasiliensis)* in Mainland Southeast Asia: What are the Prospects for Smallholders?" *Journal of Peasant Studies* 40 (1): 155–170.

Fox, Jefferson, Jean-Christophe Castella, and Alan D. Ziegler. 2014. "Swidden, Rubber and Carbon: Can REDD+ Work for People and the Environment in Montane Mainland Southeast Asia." *Global Environmental Change* 29: 318–326.

Gellert, Paul K., and Barbara D. Lynch. 2003. "Mega-projects as Displacements." *International Social Science Journal* 55 (175): 15–25.

Goodman, David, and Michael Watts, eds. 1997. *Globalising Food: Agrarian Questions and Global Restructuring*. London: Routledge.

Hall, Derek. 2011. "Land Grabs, Land Control, and Southeast Asian Boom Crops." *Journal of Peasant Studies* 38 (4): 837–857.

Hall, Derek, Philip Hirsch, and Tania Murray Li. 2011. *Powers of Exclusion: Land Dilemmas in Southeast Asia*. Singapore: National University of Singapore Press.

Haraway, Donna. 2015. "Anthropocene, Capitalocene, Plantationocene, Chthulucene: Making Kin." *Environmental Humanities* 6 (1): 159–165.

Haraway, Donna, Noboru Ishikawa, Scott F. Gilbert, Kenneth Olwig, Anna L. Tsing, and Nils Bubandt. 2016. "Anthropologists Are Talking—About the Anthropocene." *Ethnos* 81 (3): 535–564.

Hawkins, Doug, Yingheng Chen, and Thomas Wigglesworth. 2016. *Indonesian Palm Oil Production Sector: A Wave of Consolidation to Come*. London: Hardman Agribusiness.

Hayami, Yujiro. 2010. "Plantations Agriculture." In *Handbook of Agricultural Economics*, eds. Robert Evenson and Prabhu Pingali, 3305–3321. Amsterdam: Elsevier.

Hirsch, Philip, and Natalia Scurrah. 2015. *The Political Economy of Land Governance in the Mekong Region*. Vientiane: Mekong Region Land Governance Project.

Ishikawa, Noboru. 2010. *Between Frontiers: Nation and Identity in a Southeast Asian Borderland*. Singapore: National University of Singapore Press.

Ishikawa, Noboru, and Ryoji Soda, eds. 2019. *Anthropogenic Tropical Forests: Human-Nature Interfaces on the Plantation Frontier*. Singapore: Springer Nature.

Ingalls, Micah, Jean-Christophe Diepart, Nhu Truong, Daniel Hayward, Tony Niel, Thol Sem, Chanthavone Phomphakdy, et al. 2019. *The Mekong State of Land*. Bern: Centre for Development and Environment, University of Bern and Mekong Region Land Governance.

Ito, Takeshi, Noer Fauzi Rachman, and Lakshmi A. Savitri. 2014. "Power to Make Land Dispossession Acceptable: A Policy Discourse Analysis of the Merauke Integrated Food and Energy Estate (MIFEE), Papua, Indonesia." *Journal of Peasant Studies* 41 (1): 29–50.

Jackson, Joe. 2008. *The Thief at the End of the World*. New York: Penguin.

Kautsky, Karl. (1899) 1988. *The Agrarian Question*. Vol 1. London: Zwan Publications.

Kenney-Lazar, Miles. 2012. "Plantation Rubber, Land Grabbing and Social-Property Transformation in Southern Laos." *Journal of Peasant Studies* 39 (3–4): 1017–1037.

Kenney-Lazar, Miles, Diana Suhardiman, and Michael B. Dwyer. 2018. "State Spaces of Resistance: Industrial Tree Plantations and the Struggle for Land in Laos." *Antipode* 50 (5): 1290–1310.

Kratoska, Paul H. 2008. "Commercial Rice Cultivation and the Regional Economy of Southeastern Asia, 1850–1950." In *Food and Globalization: Consumption, Markets, and Politics in the Modern World*, ed. Alexander Nützenadel and Frank Trentmann, 75–92. New York: Berg.

Koizumi, Yusuke. 2016. "Migration and its Impact in Riau Province, Indonesia: An Analysis of Population Census Data and Topographical Maps." *Journal of Asian Network for GIS-based Historical Studies* 4: 3–10.

Lee, Janice Ser Huay, Jaboury Ghazoul, Krystof Obidzinski, and Lian Pin Koh. 2014. "Oil Palm Smallholder Yields and Incomes Constrained by Harvesting Practices and Type of Smallholder Management in Indonesia." *Agronomy for Sustainable Development* 34 (2): 501–513.

Li, Tania M. 2018. "After the Land Grab: Infrastructural Violence and the 'Mafia System' in Indonesia's Oil Palm Plantation Zones." *Geoforum* 96: 328–337.

Li, Zhe, and Jefferson M. Fox. 2012. "Mapping Rubber Tree Growth in Mainland Southeast Asia Using Time-Series MODIS 250 m NDVI and Statistical Data." *Applied Geography* 32 (2): 420–432.

Mark, SiuSue. 2016. "Are the Odds of Justice 'Stacked' Against Them? Challenges and Opportunities for Securing Land Claims by Smallholder Farmers in Myanmar." *Critical Asian Studies* 48 (3): 443–460.

McAllister, Karen. 2015. "Rubber, Rights and Resistance: The Evolution of Local Struggles Against a Chinese Rubber Concession in Northern Laos." *Journal of Peasant Studies* 42 (3–4): 817–837.

McMichael, Philip. 1997. "Rethinking Globalization: The Agrarian Question Revisited." *Review of International Political Economy* 4 (4): 630–662.

McWilliams, Carey. 2000. *Factories in the Field: The Story of Migratory Farm Labor in California*. Berkeley, CA: University of California Press.

Mintz, Sidney W. 1985. *Sweetness and Power: The Place of Sugar in Modern History*. New York: Penguin.

Mizuno, Kousuke, Motoko Fujita, and Shuichi Kawai, eds. 2016. *Catastrophe and Regeneration in Indonesia's Peatlands: Ecology, Economy and Society*. Kyoto: Kyoto University Press.

Moore, Jason W. 2000. "Sugar and the Expansion of the Early Modern World-Economy: Commodity Frontiers, Ecological Transformation, and Industrialization." *Review (Fernand Braudel Center)* 23 (3): 409–433.

Murray, Martin J. 1992. "'White Gold' or 'White Blood'? The Rubber Plantations of Colonial Indochina, 1910–1940." *Journal of Peasant Studies* 19 (3–4): 41–67.

Ngidang, Dimbab. 2005. "Deconstruction and Reconstruction of Native Customary Land Tenure in Sarawak." *Southeast Asian Studies* 43 (1): 47–75.

Ngidang, Dimbab. 2008. "Contradictions in Land Development Schemes: The Case of Joint Ventures in Sarawak, Malaysia." *Asia Pacific Viewpoint* 43 (2): 157–180.

Orueta, Fernando Diaz, and Susan S. Fainstain. 2009. "The New Mega-Projects: Genesis and Impacts." *International Journal of Urban and Regional Research* 32 (4): 759–767.

Paige, Jeffrey M. 1997. *Coffee and Power: Revolution and the Rise of Democracy in Central America.* Cambridge, MA: Harvard University Press.

Pye, Oliver. 2013a. "An Analysis of Transnational Environmental Campaigning Around Palm Oil." In Pye and Bhattacharya 2013: 179–198.

Pye, Oliver. 2013b. "Introduction." In Pye and Bhattacharya 2013: 1–18.

Pye, Oliver, and Jayati Bhattacharya, eds. 2013. *The Palm Oil Controversy in Southeast Asia: A Transnational Perspective.* Singapore: ISEAS.

Pye, Oliver, Ramlah Daud, Yuyun Harmono, and Tatat. 2012. "Precarious Lives: Transnational Biographies of Oil Palm Workers." *Asia Pacific Viewpoint* 53 (3): 330–342.

Ramy Bulan. 2006. "Native Customary Land: The Trust as a Device for land Development in Sarawak." In *State, Communities and Forest in Contemporary Borneo*, ed. Fazilah Majid Cooke, 45–64. Canberra: ANU Press.

Riely, Jack. 2001. "Kalimantan's Peatland Disaster." *Inside Indonesia*, January–March.

Rist, Lucy, Laurène Feintrenie, and Patrice Levang. 2010. "The Livelihood Impacts of Oil Palm: Smallholders in Indonesia." *Biodiversity and Conservation* 19 (4): 1009–1024.

Ruysschaert, Denis, and Denis Salles. 2014. "Towards Global Voluntary Standards: Questioning the Effectiveness in Attaining Conservation Goals: The Case of Roundtable on Sustainable Palm Oil (RSPO)." *Ecological Economics* 107: 438–446.

Schoenberger, Laura, Derek Hall, and Peter Vandergeest. 2017. "What Happened When the Land Grab Came to Southeast Asia?" *Journal of Peasant Studies* 44 (4): 697–725.

Scott, James C. 1998. *Seeing Like a State: How Certain Schemes to Improve the Human Condition Have Failed.* New Haven, CT: Yale University Press.

Suhardiman, Diana, Mark Giordano, Oulavanh Keovilignavong, and Touleelor Sotoukee. 2015. "Revealing the Hidden Effects of Land Grabbing through Better Understanding of Farmers' Strategies in Dealing with Land Loss." *Land Use Policy* 49: 195–202.

Stoler, Ann L. 1995. *Capitalism and Confrontation in Sumatra's Plantation Belt, 1870–79.* Ann Arbor: University of Michigan Press.

Weinstein, Barbara. 1983. *The Amazon Rubber Boom, 1850–1920.* Stanford, CA: Stanford University Press.

White, Ben, Saturnino M. Borras, Ruth Hall, Ian Scoones, and Wendy Wolford. 2012. "The New Enclosures: Critical Perspectives on Corporate Land Deals." *Journal of Peasant Studies* 39 (3–4): 619–647.

Wolf, Eric. 1982. *Europe and the People Without History.* Berkeley: University of California Press.

Woods, Kevin. 2011. "Ceasefire Capitalism: Military-Private Partnerships, Resource Concessions and Military-State Building in the Burma-China Borderlands." *Journal of Peasant Studies* 38 (4): 747–770.

Woods, Kevin. 2015. *Commercial Agriculture Expansion in Myanmar: Links to Deforestation, Conversion Timber, and Land Conflicts.* Washington, DC: Forest Trends.

Zoomers, Annelies. 2010. "Globalisation and the Foreignisation of Space: Seven Processes Driving the Current Global Land Grab." *Journal of Peasant Studies* 37 (2): 429–447.

CHAPTER 5

—————◼—————

Becoming an Agricultural Growth Corridor
African Megaprojects at a Situated Scale

Serena Stein and Marc Kalina

Emerging agricultural growth corridors (AGCs) are often depicted by those who design, plan, and study them as actualized, existing spaces. However, on the ground, what exactly a corridor is, and how they are imagined conceptually and lived daily, is both subjective and changing. We can see this in the example of Malema, a district capital in northern Mozambique's Nampula Province, which straddles a recently renovated railway connecting coalfields in Tete Province to the sea at the Port of Nacala. As part of the Nacala Development Corridor (NDC), a multi-sectoral infrastructural megaproject linking Zambia, Malawi, and Mozambique, Malema sits at the nexus of regional developmental ambitions. Within its dusty and bustling central market, this contrast between imaginary and situated reality was repeatedly borne out in conversations among local residents during fieldwork in 2014 and 2015. "*Sou parte do corredor* [I am part of the corridor]," a peasant farmer, Ricardo, announced. Ricardo had traveled to town to sell a basket of *cebolas* (onions), a product the region is known for nationally. When prompted to reflect on what the corridor meant, if anything at all, to him, Ricardo thought for a moment. He pointed down to his shirt, which he had received at a recent fair to open the cotton-growing season. The shirt displayed the logo of a new agricultural investor who had distributed the shirts to the outgrower farmers who signed contracts with the company. Across the circle, Tavares, a local "market boy," shook his head, "That is not the corridor." He gestured across the market, toward the distant rail yard at the edge of town where a freshly painted green and white train emblazoned with the words Corridor de Desenvolvimento do Norte (Northern Development Corridor) and heavily laden with coal from Tete was slowly making its way toward the sea. Tavares replied, "That is the corridor." In both cases, the corridor as a development imaginary corresponds to partial views and many possible constituent parts.

The idea of development corridors as pathways to concentrated agricultural investment has been represented as a new trend in rural development strategy in the Global South. To international developmental organizations like the World Bank (Briceno-Garmendia and Foster 2010), AGCs are considered a novel way to coordinate simultaneous investments in commercial agribusiness and smallholder farmer livelihoods with various sectors, usually combining public and private investments, and built in landscapes of abundant natural resources. Deriving from the spatial development theories of the mid- to late twentieth century, corridor policy tends to propagate the belief that if the state provides the necessary inputs (i.e., transport logistics of roads, railway, ports, and inexpensive land), then the zone will naturally attract complementary private investments, fueling broad-based economic and social development (De Beer 2001; Priemus and Zonneveld 2003). In particular, AGCs increasingly entwine promises of improved food security and rural poverty reduction—even environmental sustainability and conservation goals—with energy development, natural resource extraction, and transport infrastructure through incoming capital by both long-standing investors and donors, such as Norway, and emerging ones, including China and Brazil (Bond 2017; Garcia et al. 2018; Scoones et al. 2013). Over the past decade, Africa's eastern seaboard has emerged as a laboratory for initiatives that attach agriculture objectives to infrastructure, mining, and energy in rising epicenters for investment. These include the Lamu Port and South Sudan Ethiopia Transport Corridor (LAPSSET) project of Kenya; the Southern Agricultural Growth Corridor (SAGCOT) of Tanzania; and the NDC across northern Mozambique, Malawi, and Zambia. These megaprojects have been hailed as a possible return to high modernist development while drawing on substantial private investment to realize transformative state agendas (Dye 2016; Mosley and Watson 2016; Scott 1998).

In a recent crop of literature, various researchers have shifted from prospective studies of AGCs to empirical investigations as policy implementation moves toward full force (Araghi 2009; Bakker et al. 2014; Chichava et al. 2013; Gonçalves 2017, 2019; Kalina and Scott 2018; Sloan et al. 2016; West and Haug 2017). This article reflects on a core problem studies encounter while attempting to trace megaproject imaginaries to the people, places, practices, and ecologies potentially affected by these schemes. That is, in contrast to the vast majority of academic studies that accept corridors as a given entity, grounded studies of AGCs must devise ways to interrogate their provisional *becoming*. Ultimately, we argue this entails a more situated research agenda that may help attribute experiences such as involuntary resettlement, conflict, new mobilities, and accumulations to the AGC megaprojects while continuing to question the ontology of the corridor and find appropriate sites, subjects, and methods to engage it. First, we argue AGCs derive from deeply rooted extractive logics and that continuities among contemporary and colonial corridors motivate concerns around land appropriation, new enclosures, and displacement over the past decade. Drawing from scholarship and our respective research, we illustrate the transition to AGCs through experimental attempts at attaching agricultural objectives to model economic corridor policy that moved from South Africa to Mozambique. Then, we critically reflect on recent studies that chart a more situated approach to AGCs in the context of Tanzania, Kenya, and Ethiopia. In doing so, we sketch a possible agenda of future research across landscapes and diffuse assemblages, attending to realities that often exceed and defy the envisioned "total projects" of corridor policy objectives.

The Development Corridor Agenda:
A Brief Genealogy and Colonial Antecedents

Corridors promise to enable flows of capital, commodities, and people to circulate with ease across space and between scales (Albrechts and Coppens 2003; Furundzic and Furundzic 2012). Comprised of conceptual and programmatic models for policy intervention, they are intended to facilitate access to markets, encourage the growth of trade and investment, boost productivity, and promote agglomeration effects (Ballard et al. 2017; De Vries and Priemus 2003; Priemus and Zonneveld 2003). As concentrated "bundles of infrastructure," they are pivotal in encouraging private investments in productive assets and create employment opportunities (De Beer 2001; Nogales 2014; Rogerson 2003). Furthermore, proponents tout the ability of corridors to facilitate inclusive growth by expanding economic opportunities in lagging regions and creating linkages between disparate—and often unequal—spaces (De and Iyengar 2014). Over the past decade, the spread of corridor projects has been noteworthy, particularly in Africa, where by some estimates 30 development corridors are taking shape (Browne 2015; Laurance et al. 2015; Letai and Tiampati 2015). If completed, these corridors will span more than 53,000, crisscrossing Africa and opening vast areas of land for investment in the process (Laurance et al. 2014, 2015).

Despite its recent popularity within twenty-first-century development narratives, the use of "corridor" as a concept of spatial planning has a long history, rooted in colonialism and extractive economy, and finally codified within the developmental state philosophy of the mid-twentieth century. Yet, within this trajectory, there have been few scholarly attempts[1] to trace the genealogy and evolution of the concept. The discourse of a "development corridor" was first coined by C. F. J. Whebell (1969), who observed that new generations of infrastructure are often located in the vicinity of older systems and sometimes, in cases of replacement, on top of older systems, naturally forming corridors between economically vital areas. As a consequence of this overlap, concentrated bundles of infrastructure exist, exerting a powerful influence on urbanization patterns and economic development. To Whebell, the logic behind corridor development in advanced and developing economies is to create these conditions where it has not occurred naturally, boosting competitive advantage and bringing investment to areas that have been previously neglected (Capello 2011; Priemus and Zonneveld 2003). "Gateways" create access to hinterland areas, which have historically not been prioritized by the state, through simultaneous development of seas ports, airports, teleports, and corridor infrastructure (roads, rail) (Capello 2011; Srivasta 2011). "Stages" of development are implicit in Whebell's (1969) interpretation of corridor development: initially, corridors exist for transport; then they become a logistics corridor, then a trade corridor, then an economic corridor, and finally a growth corridor (Nogales 2014; Srivasta 2011). Finally, within Southern Africa, corridor planning has also been used to address historic spatial inequalities. In post-apartheid South Africa, a variety of corridor forms featured heavily in planning for SDI programs designed to redress an apartheid legacy of racially dominated spatial socioeconomic structures, while AGCs have been used to drive land reform and the redistribution of agricultural land (Rogerson 2002, 2003).

While often taken as a recent invention in the age of megaprojects, development corridors predate scholarly attempts to describe them, and the corridor form emerging in Southern and East Africa today should be seen within a longer genealogy of spatial development. A reading of historical and geographical literature suggests corridors first emerged during the nineteenth century to facilitate the exploitation and control of subject territories by colonial nations, particularly in South Asia and Africa (Jedwab et al. 2016, 2017; Kalina 2017; Meleckey et al. 2018; Newitt 1981, 1995). For example, in the case of Mozambique, transport linkages were deeply rooted in the colonial envisioning of Mozambican territory not as a sovereign or settler state but as corridors linking British colonies to the Indian Ocean (Birmingham 1999; Henriksen 1979; Newitt 1995). In Mozambique, the notion of corridors, to the extent we can trace it, arose alongside Cecil Rhodes's dispute and the Rose-Colored Map, contested between Britain and Portugal. During the mid-1880s, Portugal sought to link its two colonies in Angola and Mozambique by way of an inland corridor (Birmingham 1999; Howes 2007; Nowell 1982). This ambition led to arguments with Germany and Britain over prospective boundaries, as Rhodes's efforts to expand his influence to what is today Zambia—along with massive pressure being exerted by the British government in London—forced Portuguese King Carlos to renounce any claims beyond Angola and Mozambique (Carneiro et al. 2000; Galbraith 1973; Nowell 1982). The final settlement, reached after the British ultimatum of 1890 resulted in Portuguese inland expansion but also deprived Rhodes of his personal African empire made access to the Indian Ocean through corridors (Birmingham 1999; Carneiro et al. 2000; Howes 2007). On reflection, it is possible that the early colonial preoccupation with corridors may be attributed to Rhodes, whose influence on the territory of Mozambique during the colonial era was considerable and who imagined a British Cape to Cairo corridor at the expense of Portuguese territorial ambitions (Galbraith 1973; Nowell 1982).

Once permanent borders had been delineated by the turn of the twentieth century, the corridor zones that emerged during Mozambique's late colonial period can be strongly attributed to colonial extraction and exploitation designed to benefit European companies and investments at the expense of native subjects (Birmingham 1999; Carneiro et al. 2000; Diogo 2018). Portuguese-controlled Lourenco Marques became the main harbor for the Transvaal, while Beira served as the gateway for Rhodesia. Britain's Nyasaland Protectorate, which later became Malawi, was connected to Beira and to the Port of Nacala in the north of Mozambique (Sequeira et al. 2014). This has led to predominantly east-west axis of transport, a pronounced and enduring geographic feature for a nation that consists of an abundant coastline that spans from the north to the south, with little hinterland of its own (Henriksen 1979; Kalina 2017). This remains evidence of British influence in Mozambique, while Portuguese presence was almost nonexistent throughout the territory until the 1940s (Newitt 1981). Before 1975, regional connections between Mozambique and its neighbors did not really exist outside these corridor links to apartheid Rhodesia and South Africa (Tate 2011). Furthermore, unlike Asia and Latin America—or perhaps even parts of Africa—the "DNA" of infrastructure works in Mozambique along the corridor path were not intended to connect to homegrown manufacturing industries. Rather, the notion of extraction, and export for neighboring countries (South Africa and Rhodesia/Zimbabwe in Mozambique's case), was always embedded in the corridor model (Bonfatti and Poelhekke 2017; Diogo 2018; Sequeira et al. 2014). Thus, it appears that corridors during Mozambique's colonial period existed not to connect or build nascent state form but rather to order and open up territory for colonial exploitation. This colonial antecedent for AGCs, and corridor pathways in general, is important because it laid the foundation for modern-day concerns about agro-extractivism, and the concentration of state resources in infrastructural investments that favor export markets over rural livelihoods.

The Rise of Agricultural Growth Corridors

Over the past decade AGCs, which focus on integrating infrastructure investment and agribusiness interventions across connected geographical territories, have proliferated across Africa (Kuhlmann et al. 2011; Nogales 2014; Paul and Steinbrecher 2013). The agro-corridor approach is said to offer the potential for policy makers and external actors to provide targeted support to low-income farmers to bring them to levels to benefit from the above potential opportunities offered by corridors, removing major barriers to impact, adoption, and scaling of agricultural research technologies and products (Paul and Steinbrecher 2013; Serraj et al. 2015). Corridors may offer better connected and supplied pilot areas to trigger transformational change of current agricultural production systems (Kuhlmann et al. 2011; Weng et al. 2013). The corridors agenda encourages more holistic approaches to policy issues by moving away from sectoral approaches (Byiers et al. 2016; Nogales 2014). This favors an integral focus on agricultural market failures, linking infrastructures, investment promotion tools, policy reforms, and multi-stakeholder partnerships, as well as access to finance and public services (Nogales 2014; Paul and Steinbrecher 2013; Serraj et al. 2015). Nonetheless, there is increasing concern about the potential negative environmental and social consequences of the AGC approach, despite its claim to champion more sustainable development (see Boye and Kaarhus 2011; Byiers et al. 2016; Kaarhus 2011; Paul and Steinbrecher 2013; Weng et al. 2013).

High-profile AGCs currently underway include SAGCOT; the Beira Agricultural Growth Corridor (BAGC) in Zambia, Zimbabwe, and Mozambique; and LAPSSET in Kenya (currently a transport corridor with imminent plans to incorporate agricultural expansion) (Picard et al. 2017; Serraj et al. 2015; Tate 2011). Where has this AGC model come from, why has it proliferated so seemingly fast, and how has it developed within an African context? AGCs can be read as an outgrowth of the interconnected triple crisis of food, fuel, and finance that struck the Global South in 2008. In 2007/2008, food price spikes plunged millions of people into food insecurity and subsequently catalyzed food-related conflict in at least 14 African nations (Berazneva and Lee 2013; Bush 2010; Scoones 2017). Concurrently, increasingly volatile oil prices, coupled with evidence of global peak oil created new incentives for non-oil-producing countries to invest in the production of agro-fuels (IEA 2011; Skarstein 2011). Finally, the global financial crisis created a desire to diversify investment portfolios, contributing to a "rediscovery" of agriculture within international investment circles, as well as a sighting of AGCs by international agribusiness companies as opportunities for market creation and expansion for proprietary agribusiness tech (Hall et al. 2017; Nogales 2014; Scoones 2017).

Since the triple crises of 2008, farmland investments have been viewed with greater curiosity and with a more favorable outlook for long-term profitability, especially in light of rising demand, and prices, for soft commodities (Cotula and Vermeulen 2009). Furthermore, as more than half of all agricultural land is in the world in Africa, the food crisis has been interpreted as an opportunity for the continent to capitalize on global economic trends (Hall 2011; McMichael and Schneider 2011). Eva Nogales (2014) describes the desire to coordinate private and public investment in agriculture as being central to the AGC model. For example, within the BAGC and SAGCOT, private and public investments have concentrated on the postharvest subsector (processing, storage, and packaging) of agricultural value chains (ACB 2015; Bergius 2014; Bergius et al. 2017; TNC 2017). These links are important in reducing food loss and can contribute to stability and availability of commodities across time and space (Bergius 2014; Serraj et al. 2015). Furthermore, both the BAGC and SAGCOT investment blueprints promote production clusters along the hinterland corridor (ACB 2015; Bergius et al. 2017; TNC 2017). Each cluster is envisaged with a nucleus farm and outgrower schemes, cold storage facilities, and infrastructure access, including roads, water, and energy (ACB 2015; Bergius 2014). They also envisage finance, as well as access to research, with public funds intended to finance catalytic funds (ACB 2015; Bergius et al. 2017). These types of multi-sectoral approaches continue to build on corridors as a backbone for investment.

Agglomeration lies at the heart of the emerging AGC model. For example, a "bread-basket approach" concentrates investment in a particular geographical area. "Breadbasket" regions are identified as being positioned for large productivity increases or on an infrastructure corridor. Countries could move sequentially, according to proponents, learning from success in one region or sector before spreading investments to others (Chui et al. 2012). Several African countries are adapting this model to existing agricultural areas and emphasizing smallholders (Koné 2012). Mali, for example, is considering a pilot bread-basket program for its Sikasso Region (Koné 2012; Sanghvi et al. 2011). The initiative aims to raise cereal production by 60 percent through a combination of yield increases and limited expansion onto new land (Sanghvi et al. 2011). There will also be strong support for export development, new roads and warehouses, and measures for climate mitigation and adaptation (such as water harvesting and locally adapted drought-resistant seed) (Sanghvi et al. 2011; Waldman and Richardson 2018).

In the case of the AGC development, commercial farms and facilities for storage and processing are often concentrated around major infrastructure projects (Picard et al. 2017; VCC 2011). Furthermore, AGCs are often built "atop" high-return investments in the mining sector (Kalina 2017; Weng et al. 2013). Private investors in mining and infrastructure provide the impetus, supported by governments that want to develop neglected regions of their countries (VCC 2011). This approach then recognizes the potential importance of extractive-based "anchor projects" to pay for infrastructure provision (Kunaka and Carruthers 2014; Le Roux 2004; Sequeira et al. 2014; Serraj et al. 2015). Such approaches might lead to what Philip Jourdan (2015, 2017) calls "densification" around corridors through cluster effects and expanding markets—the aforementioned agglomeration that has shown to be central to corridor ideology. Most agricultural-development plans focus on supply-side interventions, such as improved seed and fertilizers, and many pay too little attention to the demand side—the place where the increased production will ultimately go (Hall et al. 2017; Paul and Steinbrecher 2013). Once the subsistence requirements of the producers' families and local communities have been met, there are three main sources of demand: export markets (international and regional), domestic urban markets, and food processing (Kuhlmann et al. 2011; Lambert and MacNeil 2015).

As a result, land and dispossession has become a fundamental preoccupation in recent critical literature. By combining "marginal" land with the advanced knowledge and technologies of well-funded agribusiness corporations, it is expected that long-term goals of economic growth, poverty reduction, and food security can be accomplished. However, Bruce Byiers and Francesco Rampa (2013), among others, warn that AGCs may become "corridors of power" in which benefit streams are monopolized upward in the value chain. Key issues in this regard surround the terms on which smallholders are incorporated in global agricultural value chains, as well as land access.

The Mozambican Model: From Economic to Agricultural Corridors

In Mozambique, the emergence of an AGC model follows two decades of experimentation in various corridor forms across the South African Development Community (SADC) region (Kuhlmann et al. 2011; Tate 2011). The Maputo Development Corridor (MDC), Mozambique's first "development" corridor, and the precursor to all corridors in the region, has strongly influenced the corridors program and spatial planning across Southern Africa (Sequeira et al. 2014). Its design, investment structure, and regional frameworks have been adopted in most subsequent SADC projects (Sequeira et al. 2014; Tate 2011). However, the MDC's shortcomings have also been well documented, and scholars have criticized it for its failure to create employment opportunities, generate local development, and reduce poverty (see Castel-Branco 2007; Castel-Branco et al. 2005, 2015; Cunguara and Hanlon 2012; Rogerson 2002, 2003; Tate 2011). Investments in Mozambique's first AGC, the Beira Agricultural Growth Corridor, have been ongoing on since the 1960s, although much of the progress subsequently vanished during the civil war (Fair 1989; Meeuws 2004; Smith 1988). However, in the 2000s, with the help of donors and the private sector, the corridor reached a point where key infrastructure investments were again operational (ACB 2015; AgDevCo 2010). Nonetheless, the scope of investment remains far below initial expectations, with only $3 million being invested in the BAGC across 12 projects by 2013 (AgDevCo 2012; DFID 2013). Furthermore, the BAGC has recently been a site of controversy as the role of public-private partnerships in large-scale commercial agriculture has raised many questions around accountability, equity, and land tenure (Kaarhus 2018).

Following these experiences, as the promise for agricultural investment and infrastructure rehabilitation moved toward Mozambique's highly populated and agrarian northern provinces, the Nacala Development Corridor arguably has become Mozambique's most problematic corridor (Chichava et al. 2013; Gonçalves 2017, 2019; Kalina and Scott 2018; Shankland and Gonçalves 2016; Wolford and Nehring 2015). The NDC could be described as a further evolution of the corridor model in Mozambique to date, as it contains multiple corridor forms, including transport, development, and agricultural corridors, and represents a complex of development plans and public-private parternships alliances. Considered by many to have the greatest potential for commercial agriculture alongside vast coal deposits currently extracted by several global mining companies such as Brazil's Vale, the NDC has been marred by several controversies. Notably, this includes the ongoing ProSAVANA debacle: a trilateral agriculture development policy designed among Mozambican, Brazilian, and Japanese governments that sparked resistance from national and international environmental groups, criticizing it as a thinly veiled land grab for large-scale agribusiness interests (Bruna and Monjane 2018; Cotula and Vermeulen 2009; Deininger et al. 2011; Fairbairn 2013; Scoones et al. 2016; Shankland and Gonçalves 2016).

Thus, while Mozambique's corridors have been immense spaces of investment potential, we should ask what evidence supports continued promotion of the AGC approach in terms of inclusive agricultural development, and the diffusion of the corridor model elsewhere on the continent. The literature argues well-designed infrastructure development program can play a pivotal role in achieving human development (i.e., improving rural livelihoods by spreading economic activity and providing markets to isolated populations) (see Aschauer 1989; Auty 2008; Banerjee 2004; Calderón and Servén 2004; Christ and Ferrantino 2011; Gohou and Soumaré 2012; Hulten 1996; Jayne et al. 2010; Straub 2008; Straub and Terada-Hagiwara 2011). Yet, as a participatory and people-centered development strategy, the corridor remains largely inconclusive with respect to achieving these ends. Moreover, it is not only an issue that corridors have little evidence of "success" as intended objectives unravel. Rather, there is overwhelming evidence of incompletion (Kaarhus 2011) and considerable indications of undermining the intended welfare objectives. That is, an issue less often discussed is how corridors tend to never materialize (Cowen and Shenton 2005), and when they do, they bring increased land pressure, unfavorable terms of trade, and low-paying farm labor employment to agrarian populations.

Moreover, the skeptical view on the ground is that these projects do not simply fail to achieve ends, or unravel, but that they were never—by design—going to happen in the first place (Kalina 2017; Stein 2019). The "development corridor" therefore becomes a discursive device—and an imaginary—that shapes particular zones as the destination of foreign direct investment. This perhaps takes place so that state leaders can exact rents from potential investors, as has been the case in various contexts of spatial development schemes, to develop particular companies—and to do so, ultimately, without concern for a broader "cluster" or business environment (Byiers and Rampa 2013; Byiers and Vanheukelom 2014; Schiavoni et al. 2018; Sulle 2017a, 2017b; Weimer and Carrilho 2017). Again, little empirical evidence is thus far available regarding either the tendencies in or the effects of corridor investments with respect to Africa's AGCs. To properly unpack the legacy of the corridor model, scholars have acknowledged the need to examine a range of aspects, not limited to impacts on land use, including disruption to continuous areas of wildlife, outcomes of food (in)security with improved transportation and market access, and the relationship of investment to the developmental state. Each of these aspects require further scholarly investigation.

The Open Enclosure: Corridor Methodologies

For mainstream development economists and logistics specialists, it would seem that as corridor implementation takes full force, AGCs offer particularly compelling opportunities to measure welfare effects among agrarian populations by observing direct investments in agribusiness and smallholder commercialization, such as increased access to inputs and technologies. Compared to development corridor configurations that focus predominantly on transport logistics, resource extraction, or energy sectors, the effects of AGCs are perhaps more readily traceable to target populations and farming livelihoods, food security, and land tenure. In time, more assessments on ways in which AGCs meet and fall short of stated policy objectives will likely appear as part of policy evaluation and academic scholarship. However, mainstream studies are not obvious candidates for making creative inroads into key epistemological, ontological, and quotidian problems that corridor development poses for people, places, and broader ecologies.

Here we briefly feature a rising cohort of studies in which researchers have begun to probe consequences of AGCs at a situated scale. Many of these projects have been conducted by doctoral and early career scholars who are spending extended periods of fieldwork within anticipatory or early implementation phases of AGCs. Their research consists of interviews, focus groups, life histories, and ethnographic observation at single and multiple sites investigating the role corridor development plays in dynamic venues of everyday life, including customary councils, emerging boom towns, commercial agriculture fairs, contested borders, and along highways, railways, and feeder roads where farmers sell produce, pastoralists move livestock, informal and illicit economies thrive, and children play. Not long ago, scholars regularly questioned whether development corridors were more "hype" than substance and perhaps existed exclusively in the realm of discourse and imaginary (Elliott 2016: 518). Here, we explore how studies treat AGCs as "creative geographies" of mixed ontological status that require a constructivist approach to becoming (Biehl and Locke 2017; Cross 2014, 2015; Stewart 2014). Surprisingly, while grappling with problems of locating the corridor and gathering sociopolitical and economic implications for populations, few authors provide sustained reflection on their choice of sites and methods with respect to addressing concerns, namely how, when, and for whom AGCs become social facts.

Perhaps as expected, much of the recent literature revolves around questions of land, as the materialization of multiple investment projects in close proximity to one another limits prospects for smallholder farmers to be able to sustain and grow their operations, guarantee land access in the next generation, and ensure the right to food in the present and future. These investment clusters are also found to block access to shared productive resources for communities such as water and foraging areas, with a greater potential impact on women. This is the case in Clemens Greiner's (2016) study of land privatization and enclosure of space among Pokot pastoralists in Baringo County of northern Kenya. Here, the proliferation of fences, constructed with "enthusiasm," manifests the consolidation of new commitments to ownership. Similarly, Jevgeniy Bluwstein and colleagues (2018) attend to the problematic land squeeze, where the aggregation of "sectors, actors, institutions, time, and scales" fuels coinciding processes of land alienation. They describe the corridor not as a new entity but as an "amplification" of Tanzania's ongoing "scramble for land" continuing a two-decade trajectory of land intensification, alienation, and accumulation resulting from liberal economic reforms and government courtship of international investors. For such authors, AGCs describe landscapes of mutually reinforcing land pressure and should not be studied in isolation from historical and spatial continuities, as well as intervening factors like steep demographic growth rates, erosion of traditional power structures, and livelihood diversification (Chung 2017).

Amid land pressure, resistance and protest to the corridors help reify them as entities with real effects. For Hannah Elliott (2016: 518), LAPSSET is directly responsible for the surge in demand and price of land in a periphery of Isiolo. Previously described as a "'Turkana village," the boomtown has become an increasingly wealthy enclave drawing people from politically favored parts of Kenya. The town encompasses multiple overlapping political and moral projects of contestation, including deepening preexisting ethnic tensions, and is thus not simply the rolling out of a powerful center into its peripheries. To Zoe Cormack (2016) while in early field visits, LAPSSET was "at most a gesture, a wave of the arm in a northerly direction indicating where the road will pass," yet by 2015, there were attributable consequences as northern Kenyan residents of Kinna revived customary *dedha* councils to manage grazing land. In this way, resistance to appropriation of land is accompanied by a reconfiguration of cultural identity for pastoralists. Such observed effects are attributable to the development corridors but also inseparable from cumulative patterns in places that are socially and ecologically fluid and changeable. Alternatively, the act of defining, fixing, projecting, and legitimating corridor boundaries problematically relegates "smaller" geographical locations under study to the "outside" of broader landscapes and historical continuities (Corson 2011; Nalepa et al. 2017; Rocheleau 2005).

Other nodes of research push analysis beyond territory and toward space, memory, and affect. Charis Enns (2019) proposes a "mobilities" framework to bring focus to the ways people are moved by corridors and follows the leakage of information (symbolic mobility), capital (economic mobility), and networks (social mobility) beyond the corridor. Bluwstein et al. (2018) take a materialist approach, looking for "debris" (whether consultancy reports, maps, leftover equipment, and memories) of corridor projects that become grounded. Mobilities research has a growing literature that treats roads and roadsides not as non-places but as places of dwelling, selling, watching, and adapting to new rhythms and routines as road usage increases (Harvey and Knox 2015; Klaeger 2013; Mavhunga et al. 2016; Stewart 2014). This can accentuate social and class differences through divergent mobilities among pedestrians and automobile drivers, residents, and passersby. Furthermore, affect has emerged as a locus of various studies, referring to the intensity that seeps into experiences of infrastructure and investments. Greiner (2016) refers to the corridor as a "climate" rather than a territorial feature. The corridor spawns "economies of anticipation" that are lived and felt through speculation on future benefits and risks. Similarly, for Hassan Kochore (2016), the corridor extends to the "anxieties and enchantment" that accompanies construction of the Isiolo-Moyale Road, as the Kenyan state attempts to naturalize and legitimize its power and authority in regions distant from the political center. Finally, in northern Mozambique, Marc Kalina and Dianne Scott (2018) explore affect in relation to citizenship and "belonging" within the Nacala Development Corridor, reflecting on the ways citizens' marginal positionality, "relative" to the state, has been shaped by corridor development, as well as how Mozambican authoritarianism and paternalism impacts on this relationship.

Future corridor-related research can build on these situated approaches. Illicit economies that arise with large-scale investment may provide especially important counterpoints to intended objectives of AGC policy. With greater mobility, there are also new opportunities for economies of trafficking human organs, illegal timber, drugs, and poached game. Furthermore, the intersection of development corridors and conservation corridors, which provide linkages across landscapes for the benefit of biodiversity, could make productive multispecies contributions to the otherwise human-centered literature on AGCs (Goldman 2009). This is especially the case as greater human connectivity often undermines the unrestricted movement of wildlife and ecological continuity. Finally, the literature has yet to consider what might be deemed "rural cosmopolitan encounters" that occur amid AGC implementation: that is, the mixing and (dis)integration of diverse communities in both transient encounters and longer acts of dwelling (e.g., construction workers from other nations, agronomists and surveyors, settler homesteaders, agricultural intermediaries) (Stein 2019). This cosmopolitanism also extends to multispecies interactions, such as the arrival of new plant and animal varieties in the context of agriculture activities. These directions may allow for rich assessment of the "integrative promises" and "disintegrative threats" that may be attached to reconfigurations of space, land, heritage, and environment.

Conclusions

Visions of development along Africa's eastern seaboard increasingly link to agriculture objectives, by encouraging spatially targeted policies and investment to target agroecological or "underutilized" zones; producing and processing agricultural goods; and helping integrate smallholder farmers to national, regional, and international production networks. Throughout this article, we have grappled with and attempted to clarify conceptual ambiguity around emerging and evolving development corridors of various kinds, and specifically the potential benefits, costs, and situated experiences that may result as agricultural growth corridors unfold. Thus far, AGCs seem to differ considerably from large-scale development blueprints of high modernism, as described by James Scott (1998) two decades ago. In the introduction to the special issue of the *Journal of Eastern African Studies* on Kenyan and Ethiopian experiences with LAPSSET, Jason Mosley and Elizabeth Watson (2016) consider how current development corridors differ from the high modernist agenda. Namely, they identify that while modern corridor developments are state-promoted, they rely heavily on private investment. Rather than being met by anemic civil society response, the rising corridor megaprojects are met with keen interest in participatory planning and emboldened contestation among various nongovernmental organizations and citizen collectives. Furthermore, the aesthetic of confidence in positive social and environmental transformation that was described by Scott as integral to the high modernist typology seems to play out in a somewhat hesitant manner in today's climate of boom and bust global commodity markets and vicissitudes of interest among foreign investors attracted and repelled by high-risk frontier portfolios.

This article draws on emerging work toward offering several critical suggestions. First, we advocate for a better understanding of the history of corridors in future research. Today's corridors often overlay previous attempts to attract investment in agriculture on the same territory as colonial logistics, yet they repeatedly fail for reasons including state divestment, low private investment, and implementation challenges. Antecedent spatial projects highlight a deeply embedded logic of extraction that sets up expectations for potential social and environmental effects of contemporary projects. In the case of Mozambique, we see that corridor blueprints originated to link landlocked British colonies to the Indian Ocean were routed to resource-rich mineral zones and involved repeated and unsuccessful attempts to attach agricultural policies to infrastructure. Thus, in sedimented or layered landscapes of past and present investment, the ongoing failure and abandonment of agricultural objectives may serve as a powerful indication of future outcomes with respect to promises of inclusive growth and broad-based welfare impacts. Moreover, it will be important to track the ways agriculture continues as priority in development corridor megaproject as implementation advances or whether agricultural activities have only a nominal hold on projects and become sidelined as lucrative sectors, such as energy, take precedence. Already there are indications of agriculture's tenuous hold on some AGCs, as well as the secondary status of agricultural investments next to other sectors: for example, even though both Mozambique's Nacala Development Corridor and LAPSSET both contain significant agribusiness and irrigation components, the latter project is widely publicized and accepted as a transport corridor.

Finally, we encourage future studies to experiment with situated approaches to corridors that will enable nuanced comparisons between blueprints of rural transformation policy and everyday experiences that interact across diffuse, multi-scalar, and multi-sited assemblages named as "corridors" by re-emboldened high modernism. Ultimately, the article furthers conversation around the mixed ontological status of megaprojects as compositions of imaginary and matter, multi-scalar, multi-modal, and momentary and enduring composites of constituent parts (e.g., road infrastructure, conservation enclosures, towns, farmers, seeds)—none of which are naturally or necessarily integrated into the assemblage. It remains a challenge and requires careful consideration to observe and relate lived experiences to a corridor's creative geography. Nonetheless, the exercise of resisting the conception of megaprojects as manifest, territorialized containers leads, as the literature indicates, to productive observations of historical and spatial continuities of land, interpenetrating sectors, emerging forms of practice and affective engagement with space, and other concerns that are not simply macro or micro forces, or big (important) and small (off-register, invisible) concerns (Stewart 2014). In advocating for a constructivist approach, future studies may continue concerns around mobilities and stasis, affective arenas where futures collide with the present, and attention to rhythms and routines of dwelling along infrastructures and amid investments.

▪ **ACKNOWLEDGMENTS**

We would like to thank the anonymous referees, special issue coeditors, and journal editors for very helpful comments and critical suggestions on earlier versions of this article. We also acknowledge the individuals and institutions in Mozambique who facilitated the studies from which this article is derived. The staff at the Centro de Análise de Políticas at Universidade Eduardo Mondlane and the Instituto de Estudos Sociais e Económicos, in particular, have our gratitude.

■ SERENA STEIN is a PhD Candidate in the Department of Anthropology at Princeton University. Her research has been supported by the Wenner Gren Foundation, the National Science Foundation, the Fulbright-Hays Program, and Princeton University. Email: serenas@princeton.edu

■ MARC KALINA is Postdoctoral Research Fellow at the Durban University of Technology and has been conducting research projects in sub-Saharan Africa around infrastructural investment since 2011. Email: marc.kalina@gmail.com

■ NOTE

1. Important exceptions are the contributions by Capello (2011) and Priemus and Zonneveld (2003), who attempt to contextualize the emergence of corridors within their own studies but ultimately focus on issues such as governance or spatial inequalities, rather than constructing a broader genealogy of the term.

■ REFERENCES

ACB (African Centre for Biodiversity). 2015. *Agricultural Investment Activities in the Beira Corridor, Mozambique: Threats and Opportunities for Small-Scale Farmers*. Johannesburg: ACB.

AgDevCo. 2010. *Beira Agricultural Growth Corridor*. London: AgDevCo.

AgDevCo. 2012. *Agdevco: Developing Sustainable Agriculture in Africa*. London: AgDevCo.

Albrechts, Louis, and Tom Coppens. 2003. "Megacorridors: Striking a Balance between the Space of Flows and the Space of Places." *Journal of Transport Geography* 11 (3): 215–224.

Araghi, Farshad. 2009. "Accumulation by Displacement: Global Enclosures, Food Crisis, and the Ecological Contradictions of Capitalism." *Review (Fernand Braudel Center)* 32 (1): 113–146.

Aschauer, David A. 1989. "Is Public Expenditure Productive?" *Journal of Monetary Economics* 23 (2): 177–200.

Auty, Richard M. 2008. "Natural Resources and Development." In *International Handbook of Development Economics*, ed. Amitava Krishna Dutt and Jaime Ros, 388–403. Cheltenham: Edward Elgar.

Bakker, Karel A., Odiaua Ishanlosen, and George Abungu. 2014. *Heritage Impact Assessment for the Proposed Lamu Port-South Sudan-Ethiopia (LAPSSET) Corridor and the New Lamu Port and Metropolis Development Project, as Well as Related Development in the Lamu Archipelago, Kenya*. Paris: UNESCO.

Ballard, Richard, Romain Dittgen, Philip Harrison, and Alison Todes. 2017. "Megaprojects and Urban Visions: Johannesburg's Corridors of Freedom and Modderfontein." *Transformation: Critical Perspectives on Southern Africa* 95: 111–139.

Banerjee, Abhijit Vinayak. 2004. "Who Is Getting the Public Goods in India? Some Evidence and Some Speculation?" In *India's Emerging Economy: Performance and Prospects in the 1990s and Beyond*, ed. Kaushik Basu, 183–214. Cambridge, MA: MIT Press.

Berazneva, Julia, and David R. Lee. 2013. "Explaining the African Food Riots of 2007–2008: An Empirical Analysis." *Food Policy* 39: 28–39.

Bergius, Mikael, Tor A. Benjaminsen, and Mats Widren. 2017. "Green Economy, Scandinavian Investments and Agricultural Modernization in Tanzania." *Journal of Peasant Studies* 45 (4): 825–852.

Bergius, Mikael. 2014. "Expanding the Corporate Food Regime: The Southern Agricultural Growth Corridor of Tanzania." MA thesis, Norwegian University of Life Sciences.

Biehl, João, and Peter Locke, eds. 2017. *Unfinished: The Anthropology of Becoming*. Durham, NC: Duke University Press.

Birmingham, David. 1999. *Portugal in Africa*. London: Palgrave Macmillan.

Bluwstein, Jevgeniy, Jens Friis Lund, Kelly Askew, Howard Stein, Christine Noe, Rie Odgaard, Faustin Maganga, and Linda Engström. 2018. "Between Dependence and Deprivation: The Interlocking Nature of Land Alienation in Tanzania." *Journal of Agrarian Change* 18 (4): 806–830. https://doi.org/10.1111/joac.12271.

Bond, Patrick. 2017. "The BRICS Re-scramble Africa." In *The Political Economy of Emerging Markets: Varieties of BRICS in the Age of Global Crises and Austerity*, ed. Richard Westra. London: Routledge.

Bonfatti, Roberto, and Steven Poelhekke. 2017. "From Mine to Coast: Transport Infrastructure and the Direction of Trade in Developing Countries." *Journal of Development Economics* 127: 91–108.

Boye, Saafo Roba, and Randi Kaarhus. 2011. "Competing Claims and Contested Boundaries: Legitimating Land Rights in Isiolo District, Northern Kenya." *Africa Spectrum* 46 (2): 99–124.

Briceno-Garmendia, Cecilia M., and Vivien Foster. 2010. *Africa's Infrastructure: A Time for Transformation*. Washington, DC: World Bank.

Browne, Adrian. 2015. *LAPSSET: The History and Politics of an Eastern African Megaproject*. London: Rift Valley Institute.

Bruna, Natacha, and Boaventura Monjane. 2018. "Between Populist Rhetoric of Market-Oriented Agricultural Development and Rural Resistance in Mozambique." ERPI Conference Paper no. 56. Amsterdam: Transnational Institute.

Bush, Ray. 2010. "Food Riots: Poverty, Power, Protest." *Journal of Agrarian Change* 10 (1): 119–129.

Byiers, Bruce, and Francesco Rampa. 2013. "Corridors of Power or Plenty? Lessons from Tanzania and Mozambique and Implications for CAADP." ECDPM Discussion Paper no. 138. Maastricht: European Centre for Development Policy Management.

Byiers, Bruce, and Jan Vanheukelom. 2014. "What Drives Regional Economic Integration? Lessons from the Maputo Development Corridor and the North-South Corridor." ECDPM Discussion Paper no. 157: Maastricht: European Centre for Development Policy Management.

Byiers, Bruce, Paulina Bizzotto Molina, and Paul Engel. 2016. *Agricultural Growth Corridors: Mapping Potential Research Gaps on Impact, Implementation and Institutions*. Rome: Independent Science and Partnership Council | European Centre for Development and Policy Management.

Calderón, César, and Luis Servén. 2004. "The Effects of Infrastructure Development on Growth and Income Distribution." World Bank Policy Research Working Paper no. 3400. Washington, DC: World Bank.

Capello, Roberta. 2011. "Location, Regional Growth and Local Development Theories." *Aestimum* 58: 1–25.

Carneiro, Ana, Maria Paula Diogo, Ana Simões, and Manuel Troca. 2000. "Portuguese Engineering and the Colonial Project in the Nineteenth Century." *Icon* 6: 160–175.

Castel-Branco, Carlos Nuno. 2007. "Aid and Development: A Question of Ownership?" IESE Working Paper no. 01/2008. Maputo: Instituto de Estudos Sociais e Económicos.

Castel-Branco, Carlos Nuno, Nelsa Massingue, and Carlos Muianga, eds. 2015. *Questions on Productive Development in Mozambique*. Maputo: Instituto de Estudos Sociais e Económicos.

Castel-Branco, Carlos Nuno, José Sulemane, Francisco Fernandes, Amílcar Tivane, and Eugénio Paulo. 2005. "Macroeconomics of Scaling Up Aid Flows: Mozambique Case Study." Working paper, Maputo, 16 December.

Chichava, Sérgio, Jimena Duran, Lídia Cabral, Alex Shankland, Lila Buckley, Tang Lixia, and Zhang Yue. 2013. "Chinese and Brazilian Cooperation with African Agriculture: The Case of Mozambique." FAC Working Paper no. 49. Brighton: Future Agricultures Consortium.

Christ, Nannette, and Michael J. Ferrantino. 2011. "Land Transport for Export: The Effects of Cost, Time and Uncertainty in Sub-Saharan Africa." *World Development* 39 (10): 1749–1759.

Chui, Michael, James Manyika, Jacques Bughin, Richard Dobbs, Charles Roxburgh, Hugo Sarrazin, Geoffrey Sands, and Magdalena Westergren. 2012. *The Social Economy: Unlocking Value and Productivity through Social Technologies*. New York: McKinsey Global Institute.

Chung, Youjin Brigitte. 2017. "Engendering the New Enclosures: Development, Involuntary Resettlement and the Struggles for Social Reproduction in Coastal Tanzania: Engendering the New Enclosures in Tanzania." *Development and Change* 48 (1): 98–120.

Cormack, Zoe. 2016. "The Promotion of Pastoralist Heritage and Alternative 'Visions' for the Future of Northern Kenya." *Journal of Eastern African Studies* 10 (3): 548–567.

Corson, Catherine. 2011. "Territorialization, Enclosure and Neoliberalism: Non-state Influence in Struggles over Madagascar's Forests." *Journal of Peasant Studies* 38 (4): 703–726. https://doi.org/10.1080/03066150.2011.607696.

Cotula, Lorenzo, and Sonja Vermeulen. 2009. "Deal or No Deal: The Outlook for Agricultural Land Investment in Africa." *International Affairs* 85 (6): 1233–1247.

Cowen, Michael P., and Robert W. Shenton. 2005. *Doctrines of Development*. 2nd ed. New York: Routledge.

Cross, Jamie. 2014. *Dream Zones: Anticipating Capitalism and Development in India*. New York: Palgrave Macmillan.

Cross, Jamie. 2015. "The Economy of Anticipation: Hope, Infrastructure, and Economic Zones in South India." *Comparative Studies of South Asia, Africa, and the Middle East* 35 (3): 424–437.

Cunguara, Benedito, and Joseph Hanlon. 2012. "Whose Wealth Is It Anyway? Mozambique's Out-standing Economic Growth with Worsening Rural Poverty." *Development and Change* 43 (3): 623–647.

De Beer, Geoffrey R. M. 2001. "Regional Development Corridors and Spatial Development Initiatives: Some Current Perspectives on Potentials and Progress." Paper presented at the twentieth South African Transport Conference "Meeting the Transport Challenges in South Africa," CSIR International Convention Centre, Pretoria, 16–20 July.

De, Prabir, and Kavita Iyengar. 2014. *Developing Economic Corridors in South Asia*. India: Asian Development Bank.

De Vries, Jochem, and Hugo Priemus. 2003. "Megacorridors in North-West Europe: Issues for Transnational Spatial Governance." *Journal of Transport Geography* 11 (3): 225–233.

Deininger, Klaus, Derek Byerlee, Jonathan Lindsay, Andrew Norton, Harris Selod, and Mercedes Stickler. 2011. *Rising Global Interest in Farmland: Can It Yield Sustainable and Equitable Benefits?* Washington, DC: World Bank.

DFID (Department for International Development). 2013. *DFID's Trade Development Work in Southern Africa*. London: Independent Commission for Aid Impact.

Diogo, Maria Paula. 2018. "Re-Designing Africa: Railways and Globalization in the Era of the New Imperialism." In *Technology and Globalisation: Networks of Experts in World History*, ed. David Pretel and Lino Camprubi, 105–128. London: Palgrave Macmillan.

Dye, Barnaby. 2016. "The Return of 'High Modernism'? Exploring the Changing Development Paradigm through a Rwandan Case Study of Dam Construction." *Journal of Eastern African Studies* 10 (2): 303–324. https://doi.org/10.1080/17531055.2016.1181411.

Elliott, Hannah. 2016. "Planning, Property and Plots at the Gateway to Kenya's 'New Frontier.'" *Journal of Eastern African Studies* 10 (3): 511–529. https://doi.org/10.1080/17531055.2016.1266196.

Enns, Charis. 2019. "Infrastructure Projects and Rural Politics in Northern Kenya: The Use of Divergent Expertise to Negotiate the Terms of Land Deals for Transport Infrastructure." *Journal of Peasant Studies* 46 (2): 358–376. https://doi.org/10.1080/03066150.2017.1377185.

Fair, Denis. 1989. "Mozambique: The Beira, Maputo and Nacala corridors." *Africa Insight* 19 (1): 21–27.

Fairbairn, Madeleine. 2013. "Indirect Dispossession: Domestic Power Imbalances and Foreign Access to Land in Mozambique." *Development and Change* 44 (2): 335–356.

Furundzic, Danilo S., and Bozidar S. Furundzic. 2012. "Infrastructure Corridor as Linear City." Paper presented at the 1st International Conference on Architecture and Urban Design, Epoka University, 19–21 April.

Galbraith, John S. 1973. "Cecil Rhodes and His 'Cosmic Dreams': A Reassessment." *Journal of Imperial and Commonwealth History* 1 (2): 173–189.

Garcia, Ana, Yasmin Bitencourt, and Bárbara Dias. 2018. "Acordos de Protecção de Investimento dos BRICS na África: Mais do mesmo?" [BRICS investment protection agreements in Africa: More of the same?] In *Desafios para Moçambique 2018* [Challenges for Mozambique 2018], ed. Salvador Forquilha, 395–420. Maputo: Instituto de Estudos Sociais e Económicos.

Gohou, Gaston, and Issouf Soumaré. 2012. "Does Foreign Direct Investment Reduce Poverty in Africa and Are There Regional Differences?" *World Development* 40 (1): 75–95.

Goldman, Mara. 2009. "Constructing Connectivity: Conservation Corridors and Conservation Politics in East African Rangelands." *Annals of the Association of American Geographers* 99 (2): 335–359. https://doi.org/10.1080/00045600802708325.

Gonçalves, Euclides. 2017. "Nacala and Beira Agricultural Development Corridors: A View From the Centre." Paper presented at the IESE 5th International Academic Conference "Challenges of Social and Economic Research in Times of Crisis," Maputo, 19–21 September.

Gonçalves, Euclides. 2019. "Corridors Mini-Series: Agricultural Commercialisation along Mozambique's Growth Corridors." Future Agricultures, 14 February. https://www.future-agricultures. org/blog/corridors-mini-series-agricultural-commercialisation-along-mozambiques -growth-corridors/

Greiner, Clemens. 2016. "Land-Use Change, Territorial Restructuring, and Economies of Anticipation in Dryland Kenya." *Journal of Eastern African Studies* 10 (3): 530–547. https://doi.org/ 10.1080/17531055.2016.1266197.

Hall, Ruth. 2011. "Revisiting Unresolved Questions: Land, Food and Agriculture." *Transformation* 75: 81–94.

Hall, Ruth, Ian Scoones, and Dzodzi Tsikata. 2017. "Plantations, Outgrowers and Commercial Farming in Africa: Agricultural Commercialisation and Implications for Agrarian Change." *Journal of Peasant Studies* 44 (3): 515–537.

Harvey, Penny, and Hannah Knox. 2015. *Roads: An Anthropology of Infrastructure and Expertise.* Ithaca, NY: Cornell University Press.

Henriksen, Thomas H. 1979. *Mozambique: A History.* Totowa, NJ: Rowman & Littlefield.

Howes, Robert. 2007. "The British Press and Opposition to Lord Salisbury's Ultimatum of January 1890." *Portuguese Studies* 23 (2): 153–166.

Hulten, Charles R. 1996. "Infrastructure Capital and Economic Growth: How Well You Use it May be More Important Than How Much You Have." NBER Working Paper no. 5847. Washington DC: National Bureau of Economic Research.

IEA (International Energy Agency). 2011. *Technology Roadmap: Biofuels for Transport.* Paris: IEA.

Jayne, Thomas S., David Mather, and Elliot Mghenyi. 2010. "Principal Challenges Confronting Smallholder Agriculture in Sub-Saharan Africa." *World Development* 38 (10): 1384–1388.

Jedwab, Rémi, Edward Kerby, and Alexander Moradi. 2016. "History, Path Dependence and Development: Evidence from Colonial Railroads, Settlers and Cities in Kenya." *Economic Journal* 127 (603): 1467–1494.

Jedwab, Rémi, Edward Kerby, and Alexander Moradi. 2017. "How Colonial Railroads Defined Africa's Economic Geography." *CEPR Policy Portal*, 2 March. https://voxeu.org/article/ how-colonial-railroads-defined-africa-s-economic-geography.

Jourdan, Philip Paul. 2015. "Optimising the Development Impact of Mineral Resources Extraction in Zimbabwe." MA thesis, University of the Witwatersrand, Johannesburg.

Jourdan, Philip Paul. 2017. *Maximising South Africa's Mineral Endowment.* Tshwane: CSIR.

Kaarhus, Randi. 2011. "Agricultural Growth Corridors Equals Land-Grabbing? Models, Roles and Accountabilities in a Mozambican Case." Paper presented at the International Conference on Global Land Grabbing, University of Sussex, 6–8 April.

Kaarhus, Randi. 2018. "Land, Investments and Public-Private Partnerships: What Happened to the Beira Agricultural Growth Corridor in Mozambique?" *Journal of Modern African Studies* 56 (1): 87–112.

Kalina, Marc. 2017. "Citizen, State, and the Negotiation of Development: The Nacala Development Corridor and the N13 Highway Rehabilitation Programme." PhD diss., University of KwaZulu-Natal.

Kalina, Marc, and Dianne Scott. 2018. "'Governo Papa' and the 'Uncritical Citizen': Citizenship, Subjectness, and the State in Northern Mozambique." *Transformation: Critical Perspectives on Southern Africa* 98: 27–53.

Klaeger, Gabriel. 2013. "Dwelling on the Road: Routines, Rituals, and Roadblocks in Southern Ghana." *Africa: Journal of the International African Institute* 83 (3): 446–469.

Kochore, Hassan H. 2016. "The Road to Kenya? Visions, Expectations and Anxieties around New Infrastructure Development in Northern Kenya." *Journal of Eastern African Studies* 10 (3): 494–510. https://doi.org/10.1080/17531055.2016.1266198.

Koné, Oumar Sékou. 2012. "Agricultural Policy Making in Mali." TrustAfrica Working Paper.

Kuhlmann, Katrin, Susan Sechler, and Joe Guinan. 2011. "Africa's Development Corridors as Pathways to Agricultural Development, Regional Economic Integration and Food Security in Africa." Draft Working Paper, 15 June. Washington, DC: Aspen Institute.

Kunaka, Charles, and Robin Carruthers. 2014. *Trade and Transport Corridor Management Toolkit*. Washington, DC: World Bank.

Lambert, Melissa, and Marcia MacNeil. 2015. "Agricultural Growth Options for Poverty Reduciton in Mozambique." *ReSAKSS Issue Brief* 14.

Laurance, William F., Gopalsamay Reuben Clements, Sean Sloan, Christine S. O'Connell, Nathan D. Mueller, Miriam Goosem, Oscar Venter, et al. 2014. "A Global Strategy for Road Building." *Nature* 513 (7517): 229–232.

Laurance, William F., Sean Sloan, Lingfei Weng, and Jeffrey A. Sayer. 2015. "Estimating the Environmental Costs of Africa's Massive 'Development Corridors.'" *Current Biology* 25 (24): 3202–3208.

Le Roux, Helene. 2004. "Southern Africa Pursues Big Development-Corridor Plans." *Engineering News*, 16 July. https://www.engineeringnews.co.za/article/southern-africa-pursues-big-developmentcorridor-plans-2004-07-16/rep_id:4136.

Letai, John, and Michael Tiampati. 2015. "Capturing Benefits whilst Safeguarding Livelihoods: The Debate over LAPSSET." *Disaster Risk Reduction: East and Central Africa*. Rome: FAO.

Mavhunga, Clapperton, Jeroen Cuvelier, and Katrien Pype. 2016. "'Containers, Carriers, Vehicles': Three Views of Mobility from Africa." *Transfers* 6 (2): 43–53.

McMichael, Philip, and Mindi Schneider. 2011. "Food Security Politics and the Millennium Development Goals." *Third World Quarterly* 32 (1): 119–139.

Meeuws, Rene. 2004. *Mozambique: Trade and Transport Facilitation Audit*. Washington, DC: World Bank.

Melecky, Marin, Arjun Goswami, Akio Okamura, and Duncan Overfield. 2018. *The Web of Transport Corridors in South Asia*. Washington, DC: World Bank.

Mosley, Jason, and Elizabeth E. Watson. 2016. "Frontier Transformations: Development Visions, Spaces and Processes in Northern Kenya and Southern Ethiopia." *Journal of Eastern African Studies* 10 (3): 452–475. https://doi.org/10.1080/17531055.2016.1266199.

Nalepa, Rachel A., Anne G. Short Gianotti, and Dana M. Bauer. 2017. "Marginal Land and the Global Land Rush: A Spatial Exploration of Contested Lands and State-Directed Development in Contemporary Ethiopia." *Geoforum* 82: 237–251.

Newitt, Malyn. 1981. *Portugal in Africa: The Last Hundred Years*. London: C. Hurst & Co.

Newitt, Malyn. 1995. *A History of Mozambique*. Johannesburg: Wits University Press.

Nogales, Eva Gálvez. 2014. *Making Economic Corridors Work for the Agricultural Sector*. Agribusiness and Food Industries Series no. 4. Rome: FAO.

Nowell, Charles E. 1982. *The Rose-Colored Map: Portugal's Attempt to Build an African Empire from the Atlantic to the Indian Ocean*. Lisbon: Junta de Investigações Científicas do Ultramar.

Paul, Helena, and Ricarda Steinbrecher. 2013. "African Agricultural Growth Corridors and the New Alliance for Food Security and Nutrition: Who Benefits, Who Loses?" EcoNexus Report, June.

Picard, Francine, Mohamed Coulibaly, and Carin Smaller. 2017. "The Rise of Agricultural Growth Poles in Africa." Investment in Agriculture Policy Brief no. 6. Winnipeg: International Institute for Sustainable Dvelopment.

Priemus, Hugo, and Wil Zonneveld. 2003. "What Are Corridors and What Are the Issues? Introduction to Special Issue: The Governance of Corridors." *Journal of Transport Geography* 11 (3): 167–177.

Rocheleau, Dianne. 2005. "Maps as Power Tools: Locating Communities in Space or Situating People and Ecologies in Place?" In *Communities and Conservation: Histories and Politics of Community-Based Natural Resource Management*, ed. J. Peter Brosius, Anna Lowenhaupt Tsing, and Charles Zerner, 327–362. Walnut Creek, CA: AltraMira.

Rogerson, Christian M. 2002. "Spatial Development Initiatives in South Africa: Elements, Evolution and Evaluation." *Geography* 87 (1): 38–48.

Rogerson, Christian M. 2003. "Spatial Development Initiatives in Southern Africa: The Maputo Development Corridor." *Tijdschrift voor Economische en Sociale Geografie* 92 (3): 324–346.

Sanghvi, Sunil, Rupert Simons, and Roberto Uchoa De Paula. 2011. *Four Lessons for Transforming African Agriculture*. New York: McKinsey & Co.

Schiavoni, Christina M., Salena Tramel, Hannah Twomey, and Benedict S. Mongula. 2018. "Analysing Agricultural Investment from the Realities of Small-Scale Food Providers: Grounding the Debates." *Third World Quarterly* 39 (7): 1348–1366. https://doi.org/10.1080/01436597.2018.1460198.

Scoones, Ian. 2017. "Corridors, Commercializaton and Agricultural Change: Political Economy Dynamics." Paper presented at the 5th International Conference of the Mozambican Instituto de Estudos Sociais e Económicos, Maputo, 19–21 September.

Scoones, Ian, Kojo Amanor, Arilson Favareto, and Gubo Qi. 2016. "A New Politics of Development Cooperation? Chinese and Brazilian Engagements in African Agriculture." *World Development* 81: 1–12.

Scoones, Ian, Ruth Hall, Saturnino M. Borras, Ben White, and Wendy Wolford. 2013. "The Politics of Evidence: Methodologies for Understanding the Global Land Rush." *Journal of Peasant Studies* 40 (3): 469–483. https://doi.org/10.1080/03066150.2013.801341.

Scott, James C. 1998. *Seeing Like a State: How Certain Schemes to Improve the Human Condition Have Failed.* New Haven, CT: Yale University Press.

Sequeira, Sandra, Olivier Harmann, and Charles Kunaka. 2014. "Reviving Trade Routes: Evidence from the Maputo Corridor." SSATP Discussion Paper no. 14. Washington, DC: Africa Transport Policy Program.

Serraj, Rachid, Bruce Byers, Paul Engel, Paulina Bizzotto Molina, Francesco Rampa, and Jeffrey A. Sayer. 2015. "Agricultural Growth Corridors and Agricultural Transformation in Africa: Research Needs for Impact, Implementation and Institutions." Paper presented at the Global Forum for Innovations in Agriculture, Durban, South Africa, 1–2 December.

Shankland, Alex, and Euclides Gonçalves. 2016. "Imagining Agricultural Development in South-South Cooperation: The Contestation and Transformation of ProSAVANA." *World Development* 81: 35–46.

Skarstein, Rune. 2011. "Peak Oil and Climate Change: Triggers of the Drive for Biofuel Production." In *Biofuels, Land Grabbing and Food Security in Africa*, ed. Prosper B. Matondi, Kjell Havnevik, and Atakilte Beyene, 60–67. London: Zed Books.

Sloan, Sean, Bastian Bertzky, and William Laurance. 2016. "African Development Corridors Intersect Key Protected Areas." *African Journal of Ecology* 55: 731–737.

Smith, Jose. 1988. "The Beira Corridor Project." *Geography: Journal of the Geographical Association* 73 (3): 258–261.

Srivasta, Pradeep. 2011. "Regional Corridors Development in Regional Cooperation." ADB Economics Working Paper Series no. 258. Manila: Asian Development Bank.

Stewart, Kathleen. 2014. "Road Registers." *Cultural Geographies* 21 (4): 549–563. https://doi.org/10.1177/1474474014525053.

Straub, Stéphane. 2008. "Infrastructure and Development: A Critical Appraisal of the Macro Level Literature." Policy Research Working Paper no. 4590. Washington, DC: World Bank.

Straub, Stéphane, and Akiko Terada-Hagiwara. 2011. "Infrastructure and Growth in Developing Asia." *Asian Development Review* 28 (1): 119–156.

Sulle, Emmanuel. 2017a. "The Politics of Agricultural Growth Corridor of Tanzania." Paper presented at the IESE 5th International Academic Conference "Challenges of Social and Economic Research in Times of Crisis," Maputo, 19–21 September.

Sulle, Emmanuel. 2017b. "Social Differentiation and the Politics of Land: Sugar Cane Outgrowing in Kilombero, Tanzania." *Journal of Southern African Studies* 43 (3): 517–533. https://doi.org/10.1080/03057070.2016.1215171.

Stein, Serena. 2019. "Farmers, Donors, Settlers, Seeds: Extractivism and Convivial Ecologies in Mozambique's Agribusiness Frontier." PhD diss., Princeton University.

Tate, Rachel. 2011. "Can Development Corridors Now Produce Sustainable Domestic Outcomes in Mozambique?" Paper presented at the BISA Conference, London, 25–27 April.

TNC (The Nature Conservancy). 2017. "The Southern Agricultural Growth Corridor: Laying the Foundation for Smart Planning for Sustainable Agriculture in Tanzania." In *Growing Food in a Finite World: Case Studies of the Nature Conservancy's Key Agriculture Solutions.* Arlington, VA: TNC.

VCC (Vale Columbia Center on Sustainable International Investment). 2011. "Resource-Based Sustainable Development in the Lower Zambezi Basin." A Draft for Consultation, 1 June.

Waldman, Kurt B., and Robert B. Richardson. 2018. "Confronting Tradeoffs Between Agricultural Ecosystem Services and Adaptation to Climate Change in Mali." *Ecological Economics* 150: 184–193.

Weimer, Bernhard, and João Carrilho. 2017. *Political Economy of Decentralisation in Mozambique: Dynamics, Outcomes, Challenges.* Maputo: Instituto de Estudos Sociais e Económicos.

Weng, Lingfei, Agni Klintuni Boedhihartono, Paul H. G. M. Dirks, John Dixon, Muhammad Irfansyah Lubis, and Jeffrey A. Sayer. 2013. "Mineral Industries, Growth Corridors and Agricultural Development in Africa." *Global Food Security* 2 (3): 195–202. https://doi.org/10.1016/j.gfs.2013.07.003.

West, Jennifer, and Ruth Haug. 2017. "Polarised Narratives and Complex Realities in Tanzania's Southern Agricultural Growth Corridor." *Development in Practice* 27 (4): 418–431.

Whebell, C. F. J. 1969. "Corridors: A Theory of Urban Systems." *Annals of the Association of American Geographers* 59 (1): 1–25.

Wolford, Wendy, and Ryan Nehring. 2015. "Constructing Parallels: Brazilian Expertise and the Commodification of Land, Labour and Money in Mozambique." *Canadian Journal of Development Studies* 36 (2): 208–223.

CHAPTER 6

What Makes a Megaproject?
A Review of Global Hydropower Assemblages

Grant M. Gutierrez, Sarah Kelly, Joshua J. Cousins, and Christopher Sneddon

Introduction: Mega-Transformations of Hydropower

Few would question that early hydropower development represents a quintessential type of megaproject. Traditionally, a megaproject signified a massive, singular unit requiring extensive material and economic inputs (Flyvbjerg et al. 2003). Projects like the Aswan High Dam on the Nile or the Guri Dam in Venezuela, both towering more than one hundred meters, invoke such an image. Hydroelectric megaprojects are as impressive in scale as in scope. In 1950, large dams totaled around five thousand globally, with most of them located in Global North countries; 15 years later, that number jumped to 45,000, spanning more than 140 countries (ICOLD 1998), and this number now exceeds 59,000 (ICOLD 2019). This jump in dam development catalyzed the displacement of an estimated 40–80 million people, which prompted international organizations to seriously question the benefits versus costs of dams for local populations (WCD 2000). Indeed, the "concrete revolution" of large dam construction worldwide is one of the most notable trends in human-environment relations in the twentieth century (Sneddon 2015), contributing significant electricity and rapidly transforming human control over water resources.

Throughout the late twentieth century, large dams increasingly ignited opposition from networks of transnational social movements and nonprofit organizations on varying social and ecological grounds (Goldsmith and Hildyard 1984).[1] Yet financing for large dam development continues to increase (Ahlers et al. 2015; Richter et al. 2010), particularly in much of the Global South where nation-states and the global hydropower industry deem hydroelectric potential underdeveloped. Hydropower's "boom" is not only an artifact of the twentieth century but also a contemporary political challenge. Studies from the International Renewable Energy Agency (IRENA 2018) estimate that globally, hydropower jumped from producing 960,540 MW in 2008 to 1,270,496 MW in 2017; hydropower is currently undergoing a worldwide renaissance with capacity expected to grow 50 to 100 percent by 2050 (IHA 2015). Governments, international financers, and industry representatives successfully diffuse criticism by reframing hydroelectricity as renewable energy and now pitch hydropower projects as crucial to one hundred percent renewable energy goals.

Reframing hydropower as a viable renewable energy strategy currently manifests most prominently as the rapid development of small hydropower[2] and the resurgence of large hydropower. Many international developers and national governments push small hydropower because they consider it a lower-impact technology than large hydropower. As Christine Zarfl and coauthors (2015) show, there are 3,700 proposed dams worldwide, potentially increasing global hydropower by 73 percent. More than 2,700 will be small- to medium-scale hydropower (1 to 100 MW), with large dams supplying most of the electricity. At the international scale, climate change mitigation policies encourage adoption of both small and large hydropower, yet small hydropower tends to be more loosely regulated and often manifests as multiple, cascading projects in the same watershed. The global proliferation of small hydropower highlights the conceptual and political limitations of focusing on a single "project" or the size of the dam itself.

In this review, we emphasize how global hydropower assemblages help us understand the significance of socio-ecological change occurring in the world's rivers. We find that certain critical dimensions of hydropower development—sociotechnical imaginaries,[3] conflicts, and impacts—constitute a more holistic evaluation of the significance of megaprojects and global hydropower assemblages than the problematic labels "small" or "large." A focus on significance is not arbitrary. As a central feature of environmental impact assessments, significance is determined by the context and intensity of a proposed action. Considering hydropower projects as global assemblages (see Ogden et al. 2013) draws attention to the multiple scales, locations, and contingent relationships entangled with hydropower development.

We organize our review around three political elements that characterize global hydropower assemblages: large hydropower as symbolic of national development; hydropower as a locus of resistance that sparks transnational political activism; and small and large hydropower's ongoing alteration of river systems organized according to the purported logic of renewable energy transitions. We focus on the slippage and connections between large hydropower's history with small and large hydropower's present.[4] By questioning "mega," we also question what is labeled as small, demonstrating the need for analytical specificity and interdisciplinary inquiry for hydropower futures beyond the empirically loose category of "mega."

A Typology of Global Hydropower Assemblages

Hydropower's transformation of the world's rivers creates what Paul Robbins and Brian Marks (2010) term "assemblage geographies" that are both intimate and metabolic. They transform intimate human-nonhuman relationships in diverse socio-ecologies and produce profit in wide-reaching political-economic constellations. Analyzing hydropower as a global assemblage brings into sharp relief hydropower's multiplicity. As both river intervention and political-economic development endeavors, global hydropower assemblages consist of numerous financial, ideological, socio-ecological, and techno-political elements. Their geographies span World Bank boardrooms, concrete shipping routes, and subterranean mines where rare earth minerals for turbines are extracted. The hydropower industry employs typologies when categorizing different types of projects; these are often based on a dam's specific use type and operation status (IHA 2015). In this section, we provide a typology that maps the reach of global hydropower assemblages and reframes how we analyze their significance. Our typology suggests an alternative way to examine the significance of megaprojects in contrast to more traditional, or apolitical, approaches such as cost-benefit analyses. Evaluating small hydropower alongside large hydropower reveals the historically contingent, and politically linked, ways that "mega" is hegemonic in terms of how academics, activists, and practitioners analyze the significance of current hydropower assemblages. As we suggest, "megaprojects" are a limiting conceptual and political category for thinking about development.

When applied to dams and hydropower, "mega" can refer to several different properties: physical characteristics, the expenditures needed to complete the project, the associated megawatts, the length of time necessary for construction, and the socio-ecological impacts, among others (Ansar et al. 2017). A common way to think about megaprojects is through their spatial reach, as well as the role of public and private actors in designing, financing, and constructing dams. In Illustration 6.1, we mark these simplified attributes of megaprojects along two axes to designate their significance and allow for the comparison of different projects. The x-axis situates megaprojects horizontally along a spectrum from public to private and can refer to how megaprojects are financed, designed, and

Figure 6.1. Characteristics of hydropower development activities. The x-axis highlights the continuum from public to private, in terms of financing, implementation, and participation. The y-axis directs attention to the spatial reach and material characteristics of infrastructure. Neither axis is necessarily linear, but together they offer a useful typology to examine and compare across cases.

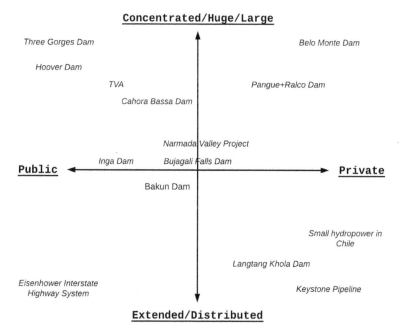

Concentrated/Huge/Large

Three Gorges Dam

Belo Monte Dam

Hoover Dam

TVA

Pangue+Ralco Dam

Cahora Bassa Dam

Narmada Valley Project

Inga Dam   Bujagali Falls Dam

Public ⟵   ⟶ Private

Bakun Dam

Small hydropower in Chile

Langtang Khola Dam

Eisenhower Interstate Highway System

Keystone Pipeline

Extended/Distributed

differentially beneficial to society. On the public side of the spectrum, megaprojects are marked by their symbolic importance for the public good. These projects receive public funds such as taxes or bonds for their construction, seek to include multiple stakeholders through the development process, and are owned and operated by governments or public utilities. In the United States, these public work projects represent about 32 percent of all dams (FEMA 2018). On the private end of the spectrum, megaprojects can take on similar development meanings among the public, but the infrastructures tend to serve private sector interests over the public good through their ownership and operations. For example, a hydropower project might power a local company or industry. Some projects that involve public-private endeavors do not easily chart on this axis; the center includes public-private endeavors that benefit each party.

The y-axis refers to the extent, spatial reach, and form of the megaproject. At one end of the pole, projects can be described as concentrated, huge, or large. This type of project is typically understood as a dense, large, and massive infrastructural agglomeration defined or scoped around a particular site. For example, these include large development projects in cities (e.g., Olympic grounds, stadiums, skyscrapers; see Fainstein 2008) or huge singular developments or structures with strong symbolic significance, such as the Three Gorges Dam in China. At the other end of the pole, megaprojects can be defined by their *extended* features and forms.[5] These are spatially distributed, far-reaching, and networked infrastructures and projects that span landscapes and territories and are part of larger development schemes characterized by their complexity, their heterogeneous components (e.g., interstate highways, submarine cables), and their near-to-distant impacts.

While Figure 1 offers a useful rubric to compare and orient megaprojects, we caution that these axes are neither static nor linear representations of megaprojects, but instead function as a simplified heuristic to show how projects emerge and exert influence. The matrix can help scope different components of the megaproject to be understood or studied (e.g., the transmission lines versus the dam). Our primary intent is to show how a simplified model of analysis that exclusively focuses on singular aspects of development, such as concentrated or extended features, is too narrow to understand how megaprojects produce social, technological, and ecological transformations and how their significance varies greatly by scale. Hydropower development, for example, exists along multiple continua that complicate the use of "mega" as a prefix, or its opposites of "micro," "mini," and "small," to describe projects.[6] Large or mega-hydropower projects typically involve large capital investments in the billions of dollars, take years to complete, enroll a complex set of actors, affect a large number of people, and pose major threats to terrestrial and freshwater biodiversity (Ansar et al. 2014; Benchimol and Peres 2015; Flyvbjerg 2007). Hydropower's resurgence foreshadows a massive increase in the number of hydroelectric dams, both large and small, and attendant socio-ecological impacts and transnational geopolitics.

Recent reports by the International Energy Agency (IEA 2010) and the World Bank (WB 2009) claim 70 percent of global hydropower potential remains untapped (1,330 gigawatts), primarily in regions of Africa and Asia-Pacific (Merme et al. 2014). A diverse array of nation-states—particularly those in regions with large segments of untapped hydropower potential such as West and East Africa, Central and Southeast Asia, and South America—garner multiple sources of financial and technical assistance to accelerate hydropower development (Zarfl et al. 2015). These activities are abetted by donor governments and their state-owned enterprises—prominently China, but also Iran and others—to establish advantageous economic relations and promote geopolitical aims (McDonald et al. 2009). Some of these projects, such as the series of Inga projects on the Congo River in Central Africa, are colossal and involve electricity transmission schemes on a continental scale (Showers 2011). In the Mekong and Himalaya regions, scholars argue international financial institutions now act as intermediaries in large hydro and small run-of-river projects for actors to make use of new financial instruments that disperse project funding with less transparency (Ahlers et al. 2015; Erlewein and Nüsser 2011; Merme et al. 2014). The complex political, economic, social, and ecological dimensions of global hydropower assemblages demand more holistic analyses.

We suggest the *significance* attributed to hydropower development by different actors is a more grounded way for social and physical scientists to measure the outcomes of a megaproject and the reach of its assemblage (Table 1). For example, incorporating how the residents of a site interpret project magnitude allows us to grapple with how massive infrastructural undertakings are remaking the world and how communities who live and hold interests near the site attach meaning to a project. The *extent* of a project in physical landscapes via road and transmission line infrastructure, and in networks of finance and resistance, is a key indicator to compare hydro-transformations. Significance also varies greatly based on scale, particularly from watersheds to state-making projects and geopolitical negotiations. The concept of significance shifts scholarly attention on hydropower to the work these projects do as assemblages in the world, and not just their material, or solely symbolic, components. In recognition of the politicized nature of hydropower development (Nüsser 2003), we suggest symbolism, conflicts, and impacts are perhaps more fruitful categories to capture significance than traditional ones such as size, spatio-temporalities, and functionality (Table 6.1).

Table 6.1. Categories of Significance for Hydropower Assemblages

Symbolism	Nationalism; mastering nature; renewable energy transitions; high modernism; scientism; sustainability
Conflicts	Geopolitical (e.g., transboundary rivers); international financing and ownership; grassroots resistance; Indigenous rights; transnational social movements; globalization
Impacts	Dispossession of local and Indigenous peoples; habitat fragmentation; altered stream flow and sediment disposition; inundating and harming sacred territory; affecting agricultural land and irrigation

Note: These categories and their associated examples are not exhaustive and not necessarily fixed outcomes. There is variation within the conflicts they generate, the types of symbolism underlying a project(s), and the social-ecological impacts of projects.

Next, we will expand on hydropower's significance by focusing on three political elements of global hydropower assemblages. Our emphasis focuses on how global assemblages and socio-ecological processes across sites transcend local, place-based dynamics (Ogden et al. 2013). Hydropower assemblages call in to effect multiplicity—of temporalities, of spatial scales, of political actors, and ecological relations (DeLanda 2006; Sneddon 2015).

Political Elements of Global Hydropower Assemblages

Global hydropower assemblages are multiple, and we focus on three of their characteristic features: hydropower as a vehicle for nation-state development, hydropower as a catalyst for social movements to organize against the proliferation of dams, and hydropower's central role in renewable energy development. Within each of these elements, the symbolism, conflicts, and impacts—our metrics for significance—associated with global hydropower assemblages call into question the efficacy of traditional metrics of "mega," like size, boundaries, inputs, and so on. We also contend the proliferation of small hydropower development in the era of renewable energy transitions captures contemporary reconfigurations of global hydropower assemblages.

Dams, Development, and the Project of Modernity

Interacting political-economic, geopolitical, and ideological forces combined to fuel the proliferation of hydroelectric generation systems across the planet over the past eight decades. For most of their history and continuing to the present, large hydropower projects have been bolstered by the hegemonic idea that "mastering" rivers was the most effective pathway toward using water resources to develop and modernize. Since their advent in the first half of the twentieth century, the dissemination of hydroelectric systems has become ensconced in national economic policies and state-driven ideologies of modernization (Isaacman and Isaacman 2013; Kaika 2006; Mitchell 2002; Sneddon 2015). This modernist project signifies the early history of global hydropower assemblages, as hydroelectric development activated global networks of techno-political power (Sneddon 2015).

The construction of Hoover Dam on the Colorado River in the 1930s and its attendant networks of water and electricity delivery across western US landscapes have rightly received intense scrutiny as seminal moments in the history of hydropower development (Hiltzik 2010; Worster 1985).[7] Additionally, Hoover construction established a model of mega-hydropower development that circulated throughout the world (Sneddon 2015). This style of exporting development also has antecedents in the Tennessee Valley Authority (TVA). Originally occurring in the name of "democratic" hydroelectric production (Ekbladh 2002), the transformation of the Tennessee Valley in the 1930s and 1940s offered an idealized framework for river basin development that rapidly proliferated across the planet in subsequent decades (Adas 2006; Baghel 2014; Barrow 1998; Klingensmith 2007; Molle 2009).

Both the Hoover Dam and the TVA cases underscore the geopolitical and imaginative aspects of hydropower development. Once the technological requirements of constructing massive structures and delivering electricity across vast distances were met, the dissemination of hydropower development to Asia, Africa, and Latin America was enveloped within Cold War geopolitics and the technological, political, and economic "sublimes" common to megaproject development (Flyvbjerg 2014). As in the United States, hydroelectric development in the USSR was a key component of its leaders' modernization and industrialization programs throughout the middle of the twentieth century, a period when the "display value" of megaprojects reached a zenith in the Soviet era (Josephson 1995). The foreign relations apparatuses of the US and Soviet states used hydroelectric dams as a means of maneuvering the leaders of emerging postcolonial nation-states into the defined ideological spheres of the Cold War. The leadership of many postcolonial regimes perceived the construction of hydroelectric projects as vital to both industrialization-led economic growth and as potent symbols of modernization (Sneddon 2015). India is a case in point, where the administration of Jawaharlal Nehru embraced damming, such as the Bhakra Dam for irrigation purposes in the context of the Green Revolution, as well as other hydroelectric endeavors to enhance their political legitimacy and stoke industrial activities. Dams, according to Nehru in a 1964 speech, were the "temples of the new age" (Klingensmith 2007).

As developers and governments promoted large dams around the world in the twentieth century, their implementation followed high-modernist ideals that placed an unquestioned faith in science and engineering—a vision that subordinated nature and people under state ideals of progress and development (Scott 1998). This scientism influenced

Franco's rhetoric of *regeneracionismo* in twentieth-century Spain (Swyngedouw 1999, 2007) as much as it did during India's postcolonial turn to nation-building (Klingensmith 2007). Hydropower as a state-making technology, however, is as current as ever. For instance, the Bhakra and Hirakud dams in India, the Volta Dam in Ghana, the Kariba Dam in Zambia, the Bhumibol Dam in Thailand, and the Aswan Dam in Egypt were all considered potent symbols of development by national and international organizations. Currently, scholars examine how hydropower and state-making require and generate new forms of subjectivity and citizenship, all bound to modernist understandings of the nation-state (Anand 2017; D. Hughes 2006; Lord 2014). While hydropower serves to bolster nation-building, multiple visions of the state emerge unevenly across state space, which complicate a universal nation-state imaginary (Akhter 2015; Harris 2012). Across cases, scale provides a key analytic for understanding the relationships between state-making, hydropower, and political negotiations.

Hydropower development relies on scalar narratives that entangle a suite of actors, both human and nonhuman within complex networks, to assert power or a particular worldview (Sneddon 2003). Dams are used as tools to govern and manage new geopolitical units, as well as biophysical units such as the basin and watershed (Bakker 1999). In his early environmental history of the damming the Columbia River, Richard White points out that dams, being "the same machines that masked labor also created new opportunities for labor . . . [and] this new work depended on precise organization of humans and nature, and this organization was spatial" (1995: 38). Oftentimes, the concept of river basin and watershed are used interchangeably (Barrow 1998; Molle 2009), and James Wescoat (2000) shows how the watershed concept becomes used within regional planning in the United States. Moreover, the notion of watershed often assumes the idea of a stakeholder within the bounds of the watershed, all of whom, it is assumed, seek common solutions because of their shared experiences in the watershed (Orlove and Caton 2010). Yet, the history of responding to watershed interventions demonstrates multiple configurations of problem solutions that are codified in different programs, legal documents, and government reports.

The United Nations Conference on the Human Environment in Stockholm in 1972 established the United Nations Environment Programme, whose creation exemplified the increasing calls from environmental scientists, anthropologists, dam-affected communities, and pro-poor development NGOs that even the most well-designed schemes generated negative social and ecological effects (see Farvar and Milton 1972). More recently, the comprehensive review of hydropower impacts carried out by the World Commission on Dams (WCD 2000) overwhelmingly found significant cost overruns and unmet promises of economic returns for many of the world's major dam projects. As Maria Kaika (2006) notes, large dams embody the geographical imaginations and material practices of modernization, as well as infrastructures that conquer nature and reconfigure spatial relationships. For example, Hoover Dam eventually became a potent symbol of both aesthetic achievement within civil engineering practices (Wilson 1985) and human domination over the natural and social worlds (Worster 1984). Slowly, physical and social scientists caught up with large hydro's trend in development, documenting the significant impacts across large swaths of space and long durations of time (McCully 2001).

In the Zambezi Valley of Mozambique, the massive Cahora Bassa Dam's meaning shifted over time in relation to nation-state and colonial politics and varying interpretations of the natural environment. Alan Isaacman and Barbara Isaacman (2013) uncover a politics of nature that involves differentiated understandings of the environment: one where the colonial regime viewed the dam as a technological marvel to control and regulate a wild and dangerous nature contrasted with the local worldviews of the Zambezi as a place that provides wealth and a multiplicity of lifeworlds. The transformation of the

Zambezi also touches on geopolitical and energy sovereignty, since more than 87 percent of the "displaced energy" is sold for export to South Africa. During the Portuguese colonial regime (1961–1974), guerilla and FRELIMO forces viewed the dam as an extension of white hegemony in the African continent because of its transnational energy regime. After colonial collapse, the FRELIMO government mobilized the dam as a technology of liberation. This discursive framing mobilized specific categories of nature, the state, and economy to dispossess people of the possibility of other worlds, displacing more than 30,000 residents dependent on the Zambezi River and its floodplains.

Overall, these development projects produced massive impacts. Large dams are likely to have significant, long-term social and ecological effects that frequently engender conflicts over displacement, the loss of cultural heritage sites, and competing uses (Chowdhury and Kipgen 2013; Huber and Joshi 2015; Scudder 1973; Sneddon and Fox 2008). The different functions of multipurpose dams (e.g., flood control, irrigation, electricity production) can also spark conflicts such as those between water suppliers and flood control managers (Cousins 2017). As large dam construction proliferated throughout the world, researchers interrogated the nature of hydropower impacts on upstream and downstream channel dynamics. Yet most of these studies were conducted in the Global North, where there is a longer track record of collecting consistent hydrological and ecosystem data. Large dams with artificial reservoirs impact a variety of processes and structures, from channel morphology (Brandt 2000; Chien 1985; Williams and Wolman 1984) to flow regulation and habitat fragmentation (Dynesius and Nilsson 1998; Nilsson et al. 2000) to floodplain morphology (Marren et al. 2014) to river and riparian ecology (Richter et al. 1996) through changes in the hydrology of rivers, such as the frequency of high and low flows, their magnitude and at what time of year and season they occur (Graf 1999; Power et al. 1995). For example, morphological changes in the river channel impact sediment load, creating "hungry waters" that erode the bed and banks of rivers to recapture the lost sediment load (McCully 2001). In general, the effects of dam impoundment on river processes are intimately linked to climate conditions, regional geography, types and operations of dams, and environmental conditions, though observed impacts tend toward homogenization and channelization of flow regime (Magilligan and Nislow 2005; Poff et al. 2007). Given this degree of physical intervention to the world's rivers, it is not surprising dams are connected to a noteworthy global example for networked grassroots resistance in defense of free-flowing rivers.

Dams and Their Discontents

In stark contrast to the imagining of dams as a potent modernizing force, hydropower also provokes enduring social conflicts across networks of locally disaffected peoples and their multiple global collaborators. These social movements draw attention to the multiple scales of impacts that hydropower intervention instigates in river systems and bring into sharp relief the widespread international alliance of anti-dam activists. Throughout the 1990s, roughly 640,000 MW of installed hydroelectric capacity provided almost 20 percent of the world's total electricity, revealing the scope to which large dams form part of the invisible infrastructure of everyday life for people across the planet (Gleick 1998). Recently, a diverse array of communities engaged in contentious politics began to invoke the phrase "water is life." For some, this rallying call against development interventions and dispossession reveals a powerful and complicated truth. These words, "water is life," bring to the fore the intersections between water and power, emphasizing that protecting water also protects life in its many forms. Water conflicts can also involve struggles for Indigenous self-determination and territorial sovereignty. Understanding the intersections between water and regimes of power is timely, yet long before this current moment, scholars of anti-dam social movements documented the ways water becomes a locus for political organizing.

While megaprojects such as large hydropower development have historically received pushback, it was not until the 1970s that directly affected people organized into formal movements to resist these projects in their territories (Garandeau et al. 2014; Omvedt 1987). Anti-dam movements rose parallel to the incipient environmental and conservation movements and gained traction as dams proliferated throughout the developing world (Cummings 1990; McCully 2001). These anti-dam social movements call attention to the variegated potential impacts from megaprojects, such as compromised Indigenous claims to land and territory (Athayde 2014; Ghosh 2006) or the social and economic impacts of resettlement and loss of livelihood (Katus et al. 2016; Nilsen 2008). These social movements are inspired by diverse sets of values for what constitute nature and society, such as the movement against hydropower in Patagonia, which produce geographic regions as exceptional "places of concern" (Schaeffer and Smits 2015).

Moreover, conflicts involving hydropower often involve conflicts in modes of development (Ahlers et al. 2014; Chowdhury and Kipgen 2013) and the politics of coloniality (Mitchell 2002). Early on, the World Bank was a major institution supporting hydropower (Omvedt 1987) and became a locus of anti-dam sentiments. For example, India's Narmada Valley project received World Bank support until it became a hotbed of political contestation in the early 1990s (Dwivedi 1998), at which point funding was partially retracted. The Narmada Valley became a focal point of international scrutiny because of a hotbed of issues: subversion of the environmental impact assessment process (McCully 2001), ties to state corruption (Omvedt 1992), and institutional epistemological bias (Erlewein 2013).[8] Over time, large dams also became embroiled in conflicts around water scarcity, and scholars have shown how the discourse of dams produces both the need for water supply and its perceived scarcity (Phadke 2002).

Indeed, increased environmental awareness at the international policy level over the Narmada projects in India helped spark what Gail Omvedt (1987) argues is the Third World's first "grassroots ecological movement." The anti-Narmada campaign Narmada Bachao Andolan (NBA), which arose to resist the displacement of people in the Narmada Valley because of large-scale dam development, is an exemplar of this organizing across scales (Dwivedi 1998; Nilsen 2008). Further, Omvedt (1993) argues this anti-dam campaign helped crystallize a formal environmental politics in India. Anti-dam social movements, as scholars show, become moments of knowledge brokering through different modes of political protest that incorporate science and other forms of knowledge in overlapping forms (Phadke 2005). These overlapping knowledges are part of an extensive circulation of local-global articulations as social movements gain size and momentum. Pablo Bose (2004) discusses the role of popular and public intellectuals in the rise of NBA, showing how activists like Medha Patkar and Arundhati Roy become embroiled in the conflict and garner mass media attention. Along similar lines, Jim Glassman (2002) analyzes the Thai Assembly of the Poor to demonstrate the global connections between anti-globalization protests following the WTO meeting in Seattle in 1999 and solidarity organizing with labor unions and communities resisting the Pak Mun Dam in Thailand.

Within Latin American water politics, few would dispute that the magnitude of the Ralco and Pangue dam projects (generating 690 MW and 450 MW, respectively) on the Upper Biobío River of south-central Chile was anything if not "mega."[9] For more than 10 years, a heated conflict involving the displacement of at least 42 Mapuche-Pehuenche Indigenous families and their sacred sites simmered alongside ecological and democratic concerns in post-dictatorial Chile. Under the Pinochet dictatorship (1973–1990), Chile's constitution and resource laws, including the Water Code (1981), were rewritten according to a neoliberal, pro-market ideology (Bauer 1998). Initially, the projects attracted the

World Bank's financing arm, the International Finance Corporation (IFC), continuing a history of World Bank investment in the country.[10] The Alto Biobío conflict in Chile embroiled actors at multiple scales (local, national, international) and crystallized a suite of inflecting concerns about development and the recognition of Indigenous rights in environmental assessments (Morales 1998).[11] Then, in 2007, Patagonia Sin Represas (Patagonia without Dams) famously cohered in protest of a proposed 1,912-kilometer transmission line and five hydropower projects (2,750 MW total) in southern Aysén, forming an international and transversal movement concentrated in Santiago and the Aysén region of Chile. The vast territory dragged into the conflict reflects in part the extent of the massive energetic undertaking. Popular imaginary of Patagonia as an untouched nature arguably motivated actors, as did the desire for democratic institutional proceedings (Borgias and Braun 2017; Schaeffer 2017). Conflicts involving hydropower, and water more broadly, proliferate throughout the country (Bauer 2015). How hydropower is imagined in Chile, and internationally, has shifted over time.

Small Hydropower in the Era of Renewable Energy Transitions

As we have discussed, large dams often served governments as symbols of national development and modernization. Today, governmental and industry actors promote hydropower generation in the name of renewable energy and mitigating the production of greenhouse gas emissions alongside economic development, despite the concerns of scientists, NGOs, and a variety of social movements that hydropower is neither renewable (because of reservoir emissions; see Deemer et al. 2016; Fearnside 2002) nor socially just (see Ahlers et al. 2015; Fletcher 2011; Maeck et al. 2013). In the past, the boosters of hydropower development in government, international finance, and business pointed out the sector's capacity to generate relatively cheap electricity to fuel industrialization.[12] An important discourse around hydropower as renewable energy—articulated across a range of geographical and political-economic contexts—emerged more recently through planetary concerns over global warming.

Overall, small and large hydropower are buoyed by the symbolism, and the discursive purchase, of a 100 percent renewable energy future (Ahlers et al. 2014; Frey and Linke 2002; Harlan 2018; Kelly-Richards et al. 2017). Small and micro-hydropower, for example, are often hailed as "green" or eco-friendly solutions, with limited environmental impacts, that can foster renewable energy transitions and provide rural electrification in less developed countries (Egré and Milewski 2002; Okot 2013; Paish 2002; Premalatha et al. 2014). The assumption that small hydropower is more benign is based on little evidence and runs the risk of repeating large hydropower's history to the detriment of affected populations (Premalatha et al. 2014).

Emergent literature on small hydropower identifies a variety of negative impacts and social conflicts across case studies (Couto and Olden 2018; Jumani et al. 2017; Kelly 2019; Kelly-Richards et al. 2017; Shaw et al. 2015; Silber-Coats 2017). This has major implications; an estimated 82,891 small hydropower projects are in phases of construction and operation in more than 150 countries (Couto and Olden 2018). In some cases—such as certain renewable energy portfolios like Chile's, cumulative impacts of cascade design in China, or Clean Development Mechanism (CDM) financing—small hydropower represents a contemporary articulation of global hydropower assemblages. As we demonstrate here, small hydro's current boom articulates with the past two political constellations of hydropower, particularly in terms of how its symbolism, conflicts, and impacts are framed and understood.

This point is made even more relevant by the reimagination of both small and large hydropower as integral to the transition to renewable energy. While small hydropower projects grow, climate change policies also promote the development of large hydropower (Moore et al. 2010). Climate change agreements like the Kyoto Protocol and the CDMs have spurred hydropower development to replace fossil fuel development (Erlewein and Nüsser 2011). Industry representatives encourage large hydropower as a means to transition into a renewable energy future by providing a less intermittent source of electricity than solar and wind while generating less carbon dioxide emissions per lifecycle than other sources (IHA 2018). Hydropower promotion as part of global climate change policy is evident in the CDM financing for hydropower, which funded large *and* small hydropower, producing a concentration of projects in the Himalayas of China and India, some of which did not meet CDM standards (Erlewein and Nüsser 2011).

Geographically, small hydropower's quick growth in mountainous regions worldwide concentrates projects in certain river basins as rural development schemes (Kelly-Richards et al. 2017). Thus, renewable energy development expresses locally as rapid socio-ecological change in mountainous rivers. As of 2014, China had roughly 48,000 small hydropower projects and 40 percent of the world's small hydropower installations (Couto and Olden 2018; Ptak 2014). Regionally, projects are boasted for their contribution to rural electrification and socioeconomic development, but minimal research documents the outcomes (Kibler and Tullos 2013; Ptak 2014, 2019). In the Yunnan Province, Tyler Harlan (2018) traces how interaction between government goals, private actor development, and climate mitigation funding have resulted in the regional transition from "rural utility to a low carbon industry," effectively shifting from micro hydro to "small" hydro installations (defined in China as generating 50 MW or less). A growing tendency in China to use the cascade design provokes considerable social and ecological impacts (Hennig and Harlan 2018). Scholars agree that small hydro's ecological and social impacts require more investigation (Couto and Olden 2018; Fung et al. 2019; Kelly-Richards et al. 2017; Kelly 2019; Lange et al. 2018). Currently, it appears that regulation for small hydropower stands to repeat the history of underestimating large hydro's impacts.

Within the discourses surrounding small hydropower, there tends to be a categorical conflation between "small" and "good," which leads decision makers to overlook negative impacts such as the cutting off of local access to water resources (Silber-Coats 2017). Confusion lingers regarding what actually constitutes small hydropower among policy makers and developers (Abbasi and Abbasi 2011; Kelly-Richards et al. 2017; Premalatha et al. 2014). This definition holds political implications: a persistent imaginary of small hydro as environmentally friendly (Premalatha et al. 2014) enables actors such as project developers to minimize the spatial extent and reporting of impacts. Here, hydropower's recasting as renewable energy interacts with its past: the emergent phenomenon of small hydro is regulated in relation to large hydropower, thus leading to inadequate regulation. In Chile, for example, operating up and downstream from the Pangue and Ralco dams on the Biobío River are multiple "nonconventional renewable energy" hydropower projects labeled as small hydropower. In Mapuche-Williche Indigenous territory of southern Chile, small hydropower's geographic preference for areas of cultural significance generates significant impacts, infringing on Mapuche-Williche territorial rights (Kelly 2019). In countries such as Chile and India, the cumulative socio-ecological change of these projects is not being considered in environmental impact assessments, in part because small hydropower is believed to be less invasive (Erlewein 2013; Kelly 2019).

Parallels exist in the imaginaries and discourses surrounding both small and large hydropower development, yet there are critical differences as well. For example, large hydropower's history has led to the transformation of the world's rivers—continuing to frame hydropower as green energy overlooks how hydropower's continued development substantially intervenes in the world's freshwater cycle (Nüsser and Baghel 2010). One of the most notable impacts of impoundment by dams is on a river's natural flow regime, or the diversity in magnitude, frequency, duration, rate of change and timing of discharge, and low and high flow events (Poff et al. 1997). The ecological integrity of a river system is dependent on heterogeneity in both process and form. Francis Magilligan and Keith Nislow (2005) analyzed pre- and post-impoundment data on dams across the United States, demonstrating a decrease in maximum flow and an increase in occurrence of minimum flows. More recently, scholarship has brought attention to hydropower's significant contribution to greenhouse gas emissions primarily through methane (and carbon dioxide) released in shallow and tropical reservoirs (Fearnside 2002; Guérin et al. 2006; Gunkel 2009; Steinhurst et al. 2012).

Small hydropower draws attention to a similar history of impacts, but one where symbolism in relation to size leads decision makers to overlook or downplay negative impacts. For example, the amount of megawatts generated is not directly proportional to hydropower's impacts (Bakken et al. 2014; Kelly-Richards et al. 2017; Kibler and Tullos 2013; Premalatha et al. 2014). To the contrary, megawatts can "mask impacts" for small hydropower projects that produce outsized impacts (Kelly 2019). Their disproportionate effect on biodiverse mountains streams and local landscapes can be severely detrimental in affected areas (Bakken et al. 2012; Pinho et al. 2007; Tang et al. 2012). Additionally, scholars are calling for examination of cumulative impacts of multiple small hydro projects at the watershed scale, particularly in terms of biodiversity (Couto and Olden 2018; Kelly-Richards et al. 2017; Kibler and Tullos 2013; Lange et al. 2018). Emphasis on size in hydropower projects, coupled with hydropower's looming history of megaprojects and simmering conflict, overlooks the significance and extent of hydropower's transformation of the world's rivers.

Conclusion: Hydropower Futures

In this article, we highlight the conflicts, impacts, and sociotechnical imaginaries entangled in hydropower development to draw analytic focus to how hydropower development activates global assemblages and networks of power, rather than being a singular infrastructure installation fixed by spatial and historical boundaries. The new global push for hydropower development following hydropower's recasting as renewable energy underscores the malleability of hydropower as a technological intervention and as a hegemonic notion for structuring hydro-social relations. Additionally, hydropower's history signals the vitality of water. Water is inextricably implicated in hydroelectric undertakings: its properties of flow invariably extend hydropower's reach. Tracking the materialities involved in megaprojects is critical to understanding the work each project does as an assemblage generating socio-ecological transformations.

"Mega" can be read in hydro-politics in multiple ways. Hydropower's historical interventions in the world's rivers are massive in scale and scope. Large conflicts and impacts left in hydro's wake do not necessarily correspond to one infrastructural project. All over the world, conflicts involving rivers run deep, typically involving human rights and significant costs. Conflicts over rivers present conflicts over life. A noteworthy portion of conflicts involve struggles for Indigenous self-determination. Despite its conflictive nature, hydropower projects are slated on development dockets all around the world. And it is ongoing river interventions that catalyze enduring socio-ecological change. This development occurs even amid uncertainty about hydropower's efficacy under changing precipitation regimes (Tarroja et. al. 2016).

Future research must trace hydropower's growth, particularly what appears to be the emergent trend of hydropower being developed with the 1–100 MW range. Scholars can address how environmental social movements against dam development, and alongside dam developers, become entangled in hydropower's emerging political economy as a renewable energy. Relatedly, scholarly examination could follow the ways hydropower as renewable energy resource gets bound up within contemporary nation-state politics and nation-building, which represents emergent geopolitics of the Anthropocene. Further, research on the ways rural people and people living at the margins of urban society come to understand alternative energy transition politics can shed light into the emerging subjectivities of hydroelectric development and climate change citizenship. A final direction for research, given the violent and colonial history of much of hydroelectric development, lies in continuing lines of research like Christine Folch's (2016) into movements toward energy sovereignty and the push for decolonizing energy politics through defending watersheds and waterways.

Hydropower's re-signification indicates how capitalism appropriates, and then re-interprets, its modes of resistance into new forms of encroachment and expansion (Gramsci 1971). Indeed, large and small hydropower continue to catalyze the transformation of the world's rivers, arguably diminishing resilience. Hydropower's history and current moment prompt us to think beyond megaprojects, to instead empirically assess the significance and reach of the assemblages that involve socio-ecological change, global environmental policy, and complex private-public arrangements. Transitions to renewable energy futures should not transpire at the expense of the world's river systems.

▪ **ACKNOWLEDGMENTS**

We would like to thank the journal editors and the editors of the special issue whose theme inspired our writing. A special thanks to Laura Ogden, who generously read earlier drafts of this article, as well as our three anonymous reviewers whose comments helped to hone our arguments.

▪ **GRANT M. GUTIERREZ** is a PhD Candidate in Ecology, Evolution, Ecosystems and Society at Dartmouth College. His research examines the relationships between climate change and watershed conservation politics in Chile.
Email: grant.m.gutierrez.gr@dartmouth.edu

▪ **SARAH KELLY** is a postdoctoral researcher in the Department of Anthropology at Dartmouth College. She is also a postdoctoral researcher associated with the Centro de Investigación para la Gestión Integrada del Riesgo de Desastres at the Universidad Católica de Chile in Santiago Chile. Her research addresses the intersection of hydropower development, Indigenous rights recognition, knowledge politics, and collaborative research methodologies. Email: sarah.kelly@cigiden.cl

▪ **JOSHUA J. COUSINS** is Assistant Professor in the Department of Environmental Studies at the State University of New York College of Environmental Science and Forestry. His teaching and research focus on issues of resource governance, sustainable urban systems, the political ecologies of water and energy, and the social dimensions of science and engineering. Email: jcousins@esf.edu

▪ **CHRISTOPHER SNEDDON** is Professor of Geography and Environmental Studies at Dartmouth College. His research examines how conflicts over water emerge at multiple scales and are linked to human alteration of river systems. His book *Concrete Revolution* (2015) explores the global geopolitical forces that contributed to the rapid spread of hydropower dams across the face of the planet throughout the twentieth century. Email: christopher.s.sneddon@dartmouth.edu

▪ NOTES

1. For an understanding of a river's natural flow regime, see Poff et al. (1997). For discussion of how hydropower disrupts ecosystem productivity and the impacts of sediment retention in rivers, among other social and ecological impacts, see Binger (1978), WCD (2000), Vörösmarty et al. (2003, 2004).
2. Definitions for the size of hydropower project vary by country and by reporting agency. A growing global consensus states that small hydropower generates 1 to 10 megawatts (MW), but the definition varies by country (Kelly-Richards et al. 2017; Lange et al. 2018). According to the International Commission on Large Dams, large dams are typically measured by the size of the concrete curtain (higher than 15 meters) and the amount of area inundated.
3. According to Jasanoff (2015: 4), socio-technical imaginaries are "collectively held, institutionally stabilized, and publicly performed visions of desirable futures, animated by shared understandings of forms of social life and social order attainable through, and supportive of, advances in science and technology." Within social and political theory, imaginaries have spanned from producing idealized political communities (Anderson 1983) to the intersubjective relations of individuals to broader networks (Taylor 2002). Nüsser and Baghel (2017) extend the sociotechnical imaginaries framework to hydropower through their framing of technological hydroscapes.
4. Our review does not address micro- or mini-hydropower because these are primarily low-impact projects that divert flows through pipes and bypass channels and have different turbine designs, costs, and efficiencies than small and large hydropower projects (Paish 2002).
5. The use of the terms extended and concentrated parallels theorizations of urbanization drawn from Lefebvre (2003) and further developed by Brenner (2014), Schmid (2018), and Soja (2013), among others.
6. In this article, we focus on small hydropower projects, since they are significantly larger than micro projects; Hoffken (2016) documents that some imagine micro-hydro a "beautiful" technology as they draw on different understandings of nature and science. These micro-hydropower projects, however, are context specific and entail different social and ecological impacts, maintenance needs, and exposure to extreme events (Arnaiz et al. 2018, Kusakana 2014).
7. Thomas Hughes (1983: 262–284) argues the coproduction of large-scale hydroelectric dams and long-range transmission lines in California during the late nineteenth and early twentieth centuries, made possible by a conjuncture of technological innovations, political, and economic interests, and the particular geographies of the region, was a similarly pivotal moment.
8. Other dam projects in India have been studied for both their connection to global flows of capital and exported/imported schemes of development (Biswas and Tortajada 2001) and for understanding the production of environmental subjects and subjectivity (Birkenholz 2009; Ghosh 2006).
9. Today, Ralco sits 30 kilometers upstream from the Pangue Dam. Built with a concrete curtain of 155 meters, the Ralco Dam meets the international agreed status of a mega-dam.
10. As read in WBG (2016): "The International Bank for Reconstruction and Development announced on March 25, 1948 that two loans were approved for Chile totaling $16 million (Loans 0005 and 0006); one for the development of electric power and water resources and the other for the importation of agricultural machinery and equipment. These were the Bank's first development loans and the first loans the Bank made to a country in Latin America."
11. These conflicts drew the attention of the Committee for Human Rights of the American Anthropological Association, whose "Pehuenche Report" denounced the IFC's suppression of anthropological knowledge detailing human rights violation and the forced resettlement of Indigenous communities (Johnston and Turner 1999).
12. This remains a crucial rationale for hydropower development and is often coupled to electric power targeted at specific industries such as mining. This is the case for the long-term plans to carry out hydropower development in the rivers basins of Sarawak, Malaysia—including the massive Bakun Dam—where nearly all the electricity produced is designated for the region's aluminum smelters (Sovacool and Bulan 2011).

▪ REFERENCES

Abbasi, Tasneem, and S. A. Abbasi. 2011. "Small Hydro and the Environmental Implications of Its Extensive Utilization." *Renewable and Sustainable Energy Reviews* 15 (4): 2134–2143.

Adas, Michael. 2006. *Dominance by Design: Technological Imperatives and America's Civilizing Mission.* Cambridge, MA: Belknap Press.

Ahlers, Rhodante, Luigia Brandimarte, Ineke Kleemans, and Said H. Sadat. 2014. "Ambitious Development on Fragile Foundations: Criticalities of Current Large Dam Construction in Afghanistan." *Geoforum* 54: 49–58.

Ahlers, Rhodante, Jessica Budds, Deepa Joshi, Vincent Merme, and Margreet Zwaantje Zwarteveen. 2015. "Framing Hydropower as Green Energy: Assessing Drivers, Risks and Tensions in the Eastern Himalayas." *Earth System Dynamics* 6 (1): 195–204.

Akhter, Majed. 2015. "Infrastructure Nation: State Space, Hegemony, and Hydraulic Regionalism in Pakistan." *Antipode* 47 (4): 849–870.

Anand, Nikhil. 2017. *Hydraulic City: Water and the Infrastructures of Citizenship in Mumbai.* Durham, NC: Duke University Press.

Ansar, Atif, Bent Flyvbjerg, Alexander Budzier, and Daniel Lunn. 2014. "Should We Build More Large Dams? The Actual Costs of Hydropower Megaproject Development." *Energy Policy* 69: 43–56.

Ansar, Atif, Bent Flyvbjerg, Alexander Budzier, and Daniel Lunn. 2017. "Big Is Fragile: An Attempt at Theorizing Scale." In *The Oxford Handbook of Megaproject Management,* ed. Bent Flyvbjerg, 60–95. Oxford: Oxford University Press.

Arnaiz, M., Thomas A. Cochrane, A. Calizaya, and Muskan Shrestha. 2018. "A Framework for Evaluating the Current Level of Success of Micro-Hydropower Schemes in Remote Communities of Developing Countries." *Energy for Sustainable Development* 44: 55–63.

Athayde, Simone. 2014. "Introduction: Indigenous Peoples, Dams, and Resistance." *Tipiti: Journal of the Society for the Anthropology of Lowland South America* 12 (2): 80–92.

Baghel, Ravi. 2014. *River Control in India: Spatial, Governmental and Subjective Dimensions.* New York: Springer

Bakken, Tor Haakon, Anne Guri Aase, Dagmar Hagen, Hakon Sundt, David N. Barton, and Päivi Lujala. 2014. "Demonstrating a New Framework for the Comparison of Environmental Impacts from Small-and Large-Scale Hydropower and Wind Power Projects." *Journal of Environmental Management* 140: 93–101.

Bakken, Tor Haakon, Hakon Sundt, Audun Ruud, and Atle Harby. 2012. "Development of Small versus Large Hydropower in Norway: Comparison of Environmental Impacts." *Energy Procedia* 20: 185–199.

Bakker, Karen. 1999. "The Politics of Hydropower: Developing the Mekong." *Political Geography* 18 (2): 209–232.

Barrow, Christopher J. 1998. "River Basin Development and Management: A Critical Review." *World Development* 26 (1): 171–186.

Bauer, Carl. 1998. *Against the Current: Privatization, Water Markets, and the State in Chile.* Boston: Kluwer Academic Publishers.

Bauer, Carl. 2015. "Water Conflicts and Entrenched Governance Problems in Chile's Market Model." *Water Alternatives* 8 (2): 147–172.

Benchimol, Maíra, and Carlos A. Peres. 2015. "Widespread Forest Vertebrate Extinctions Induced by a Mega Hydroelectric Dam in Lowland Amazonia." *PLOS ONE* 10 (7): e0129818.

Binger, Wilson V. 1978. *Environmental Effects of Large Dams.* New York: American Society of Civil Engineers.

Birkenholz, Trevor. 2009. "Groundwater Governmentality: Hegemony and Technologies of Resistance in Rajasthan's (India) Groundwater Governance." *Geographical Journal* 175 (3): 208–220.

Biswas, Asit K., and Cecilia Tortajada. 2001. "Development and Large Dams: A Global Perspective." *Water Resources Development* 17 (1): 9–21.

Borgias, Sophia L and Yvonne A. Braun. 2017. "From Dams to Democracy: Framing Processes and Political Opportunities in Chile's Patagonia Without Dams Movement." *Interface: A Journal on Social Movements* 9 (2): 300–328.

Bose, Pablo Shiladitya. 2004. "Critics and Experts, Activists and Academics: Intellectuals in the Fight for Social and Ecological Justice in the Narmada Valley, India." *International Review of Social History* 49 (S12): 133–157.

Brandt, S. Anders. 2000. "Classification of Geomorphological Effects Downstream of Dams." *Catena* 40 (4): 375–401.

Brenner, Neil. 2014. *Implosions/Explosions: Towards a Study of Planetary Urbanization*. Berlin: Jovis.

Chien, Ning. 1985. "Changes in River Regime after the Construction of Upstream Reservoirs." *Earth Surface Processes and Landforms* 10 (2): 143–159.

Chowdhury, Arnab Roy, and Ngamjahao Kipgen. 2013. "Deluge amidst Conflict: Hydropower Development and Displacement in the North-East Region of India." *Progress in Development Studies* 13 (3): 195–208.

Cousins, Joshua J. 2017. "Volume Control: Stormwater and the Politics of Urban Metabolism." *Geoforum* 85: 368–380.

Couto, Thiago B. A., and Julian D. Olden. 2018. "Global Proliferation of Small Hydropower Plants–Science and Policy." *Frontiers in Ecology and the Environment* 16 (2): 91–100.

Cummings, Barbara J. 1990. *Dam the Rivers, Damn the People: Development and Resistance in Amazonian Brazil*. London: Earthscan.

Deemer, Bridget R., John A. Harrison, Siyue Li, Jake J. Beaulieu, Tonya DelSontro, Nathan Barros, José F. Bezerra-Neto, et al. 2016. "Greenhouse Gas Emissions from Reservoir Water Surfaces: A New Global Synthesis." *BioScience* 66 (11): 949–964.

DeLanda, Manuel. 2006. *A New Philosophy of Society: Assemblage Theory and Social Complexity*. London: Continuum.

Dwivedi, Ranjit. 1998. "Resisting Dams and 'Development': Contemporary Significance of the Campaign against the Narmada Projects in India." *European Journal of Development Research* 10 (2): 135–183.

Dynesius, Matts, and Christer Nilsson. 1994. "Fragmentation and Flow Regulation of River Systems in the Northern Third of the World." *Science* 266 (5186): 753–762.

Egré, Dominique, and Joseph C Milewski. 2002. "The Diversity of Hydropower Projects." *Energy Policy* 30 (14): 1225–30.

Ekbladh, David. 2002. "'Mr. TVA': Grass-Roots Development, David Lilienthal, and the Rise and Fall of the Tennessee Valley Authority as a Symbol for U.S. Overseas Development, 1933–1973." *Diplomatic History* 26 (3): 335–374.

Erlewein, Alexander. 2013. "Disappearing Rivers: The Limits of Environmental Assessment for Hydropower in India." *Environmental Impact Assessment Review* 43: 135–143.

Erlewein, Alexander, and Nüsser, Marcus. 2011. "Offsetting Greenhouse Gas Emissions in the Himalaya? Clean Development Dams in Himachal Pradesh, India." *Mountain Research and Development* 31 (4): 293–304.

Fainstein, Susan S. 2008. "Mega-Projects in New York, London and Amsterdam." *International Journal of Urban and Regional Research* 32 (4): 768–785.

Farvar, M. Taghi, and John P. Milton, eds. 1972. *The Careless Technology: Ecology and International Development*. Garden City, NY: Natural History Press.

Fearnside, Philip. 2002. "Greenhouse Gas Emissions from a Hydroelectric Reservoir (Brazil's Tucuruí' Dam) and the Energy Policy Implications." *Water, Air and Soil Pollution* 133 (1–4): 69–96.

Fletcher, Robert. 2011. "When Environmental Issues Collide: Climate Change and the Shifting Political Ecology of Hydroelectric Power." *Peace and Conflict Monitor* 5 (1): 14–30.

Frey, Gary W., and Deborah M. Linke. 2002. "Hydropower as a Renewable and Sustainable Energy Resource: Meeting Global Energy Challenges in a Reasonable Way. *Energy Policy* 30 (14): 1261–1265.

Flyvbjerg, Bent. 2007. "Policy and Planning for Large-Infrastructure Projects: Problems, Causes, Cures." *Environment and Planning B: Planning and Design* 34 (4): 578–97.

Flyvbjerg, Bent. 2014. "What You Should Know about Megaprojects and Why: An Overview." *Project management journal* 45 (2): 6–19.

Flyvbjerg, Bent, Nils Bruzelius, and Werner Rothengatter. 2003. *Megaprojects and Risk: An Anatomy of Ambition*. Cambridge: Cambridge University Press.

Folch, Chrisinte. 2016. "The Nature of Sovereignty in the Anthropocene: Hydroelectric Lessons of Struggle, Otherness, and Economics from Paraguay." *Current Anthropology* 57 (5): 565–585.

Fung, Zali, Teerapong Pomun, Katrina J. Charles, and Julian Kirchherr. 2019. "Mapping the Social Impacts of Small Dams: The Case of Thailand's Ing River Basin." *Ambio* 48 (2): 180–191.

Garandeau, Regis, Stephen Edwards, and Mark Maslin. 2014. "Biophysical, Socioeconomic, and Geopolitical Impacts Assessments of Large Dams: An Overview." *Mega Dam Overview*, Hazard Centre, University College London.

Ghosh, Kaushik. 2006. "Between Global Flows and Local Dams: Indigenousness, Locality, and the Transnational Sphere in Jharkhand, India." *Cultural Anthropology* 21 (4): 501–534.

Glassman, Jim. 2002. "From Seattle (and Ubon) to Bangkok: the Scales of Resistance to Corporate Globalization." *Environment and Planning D: Society and Space* 20 (5): 513–533.

Gleick, Peter H. 1998. "The World's Water 1998–1999." *The Biannual Report on Freshwater Resources*. Washington, DC: Island Press.

Goldsmith, Edward, and Nicholas Hildyard, eds. 1984. *The Social and Environmental Effects of Large Dams*. San Francisco: Sierra Club Books.

Graf, William L. 1999. "Dam nation: a Geographic Census of American Dams and Their Large-Scale Hydrologic Impacts." *Water Resources Research* 35 (4): 1305–1311.

Gramsci, Antonio, Quintin Hoare, and Geoffrey Nowell-Smith. 1971. *Selections from the prison notebooks of Antonio Gramsci*. New York: International Publishers.

Guérin, Féderic, Gwenaël Abril, Sandrine Richard, Benoît Burban, Cécile Reynouard, Patrick Seyler, and Robert Delmas. 2006. "Methane and Carbon Dioxide Emissions from Tropical Reservoirs: Significance of Downstream Rivers." *Geophysical Research Letters* 33 (21): L21407.

Gunkel, Günter. 2009. "Hydropower: A Green Energy? Tropical Reservoirs and Greenhouse Gas Emissions." *CLEAN: Soil, Air, Water* 37 (9): 726–734.

Harlan, Tyler. 2018. "Rural Utility to Low-Carbon Industry: Small Hydropower and the Industrialization of Renewable Energy in China." *Geoforum* 95: 59–69.

Harris, Leila M. 2012. "State as Socionatural Effect: Variable and Emergent Geographies of the State in Southeastern Turkey." *Comparative Studies of South Asia, Africa and the Middle East* 32 (1): 25–39.

Hennig, Thomas, and Tyler Harlan 2018. "Shades of Green Energy: Geographies of Small Hydropower in Yunnan, China and the Challenges of Over-Development." *Global Environmental Change* 49: 116–128.

Hiltzik, Michael. 2010. *Colossus: Hoover Dam and the Making of the American Century*. New York: Simon & Schuster.

Hoffken, Johanna I. 2016. "Demystification and Localization in the Adoption of Micro-Hydro Technology: Insights from India." *Energy Research & Social Science* 22: 172–182.

Huber, Amelie, and Deepa Joshi. 2015. "Hydropower, Anti-politics, and the Opening of New Political Spaces in the Eastern Himalayas." *World Development* 76: 13–25.

Hughes, David. 2006. "Hydrology of Hope: Farm Dams, Conservation, and Whiteness in Zimbabwe." *American Ethnologist* 33 (2): 269–87

Hughes, Thomas. 1983. *Networks of Power: Electrification in Western Society 1880–1930*. Baltimore: John Hopkins University Press.

ICOLD (International Commission on Large Dams). 1998. *World Register of Dams*. Paris: ICOLD.

ICOLD (International Commission on Large Dams). 2019. *World Register of Dams*. Paris: ICOLD.

IEA (International Energy Agency) 2010. "Renewable Energy Essentials: Hydropower." http://www.iea.org/papers/2010/Hydropower_Essentials.pdf (accessed 17 June 2019).

IHA (International Hydropower Association). 2015. "Interview: What Is Driving the Hydropower Renaissance?" International Hydropower Association, 13 May. https://www.hydropower.org/blog/interview-what-is-driving-the-hydropower-renaissance.

IRENA (International Renewable Energy Agency). 2017. "Renewable Energy Capacity Statistics." Abu Dhabi: IRENA.

Isaacman, Allen F., and Barbara S. Isaacman. 2013. *Dams, Displacement and the Delusion of Development: Cahora Basa and Its Legacies in Mozambique, 1965–2007*. Athens: Ohio University Press.

Jasanoff, Sheila. 2015. "Future Imperfect: Science, Technology, and the Imaginations of Modernity." In *Dreamscapes of Modernity: Sociotechnical Imaginaries and the Fabrication of Power*, ed. Sheila Jasanoff and Sang-Hyun Kim, 1–33. Chicago: University of Chicago Press.

Johnston, Barbara Rose, and Terence Turner. 1999. "The Pehuenche: Human Rights, the Environment, and Hydrodevelopment on the Bío-Bío river, Chile." *Identities* 6 (2–3): 387–434.

Josephson, Paul R. 1995. "'Projects of the Century' in Soviet History: Large-Scale Technologies from Lenin to Gorbachev." *Technology and Culture* 36 (3): 519–559.

Jumani, Suman, Shishir Rao, Siddarth Machado, Anup Prakash. 2017. "Big Concerns with Small Projects: Evaluating the Socio-ecological Impacts of Small Hydropower Projects in India." *Ambio* 46 (4): 500–511.

Kaika, Maria. 2006. "Dams as Symbols of Modernization: The Urbanization of Nature Between Geographical Imagination and Materiality." *Annals of the Association of American Geographers* 96 (2): 276–301.

Katus, Susanne, Diana Suhardiman, and Senaratna Sellamutu, Sonali. 2016. "When Local Power Meets Hydropower: Reconceptualizing Resettlement Along the Nam Gnouang River in Laos." *Geoforum* 72: 6–15.

Kelly, Sarah. 2019. "Megawatts Mask Impacts: Small Hydropower and Knowledge Politics in the Puelwillimapu, Southern Chile." *Energy Research and Social Science* 54: 224–235.

Kelly-Richards, Sarah, Noah Silber-Coats, Arica Crootof, David Tecklin, and Carl Bauer. 2017. "Governing the Transition to Renewable Energy: A Review of Impacts and Policy Issues in the Small Hydropower Boom." *Energy Policy* 101: 251–264.

Kibler, Kelly M., and Desiree D. Tullos. 2013. "Cumulative Biophysical Impact of Small and Large Hydropower Development in Nu River, China." *Water Resources Research* 49 (6): 3104–3118.

Klingensmith, David. 2007. *"One Valley and a Thousand": Dams, Nationalism, and Development.* New Delhi: Oxford University Press.

Kusakana, Kanzumba. 2014. "A Survey of Innovative Technologies Increasing the Viability of Micro-Hydropower as a Cost Effective Rural Electrification Option in South Africa." *Renewable and Sustainable Energy Reviews* 37: 370–379.

Lange, Katharina, Phillip Meier, Clemens Trautwein, Martin Schmid, Christopher T. Robinson, Christine Weber, and Jakob Brodersen. 2018. "Basin-Scale Effects of Small Hydropower on Biodiversity Dynamics." *Frontiers in Ecology and the Environment* 16 (7): 397–404.

Lefebvre, Henri. 2003. *The Urban Revolution.* Minneapolis: University of Minnesota Press.

Lord, Austin. 2014. "Making a 'Hydropower Nation': Subjectivity, Mobility, and Work in a Nepalese Hydroscape." *Himalaya, the Journal of the Association for Nepal and Himalayan Studies* 34 (2): 111–121.

Maeck, Andreas, Tonya DelSontro, Daniel F. McGinnis, Helmut Fischer, Sabine Flury, Mark Schmidt, Peer Fietzek, and Andreas Lorke. 2013. "Sediment Trapping by Dams Creates Methane Emission Hot Spots." *Environmental Science & Technology* 47 (15): 8130–8137.

Magilligan, Francis J., and Keith H. Nislow 2005. "Changes in Hydrologic Regime by Dams." *Geomorphology* 71 (1–2): 61–78.

Marren, Philip M., James R. Grove, J. Angus Webb, and Michael J. Stewardson. 2014. "The Potential for Dams to Impact Lowland Meandering River Floodplain Geomorphology." *Scientific World Journal.* Published 22 January. http://dx.doi.org/10.1155/2014/309673

McCully, Patrick. 2001. *Silenced Rivers: The Ecology and Politics of Large Dams.* London: Zed Books

McDonald, Kristen, Peter Bosshard, and Nicole Brewer. 2009. "Exporting Dams: China's Hydropower Industry Goes Global." *Journal of Environmental Management* 90 (S3): S294–S302.

Merme, Vincent, Rhodante Ahlers, and Joyeeta Gupta. 2014. "Private Equity, Public Affair: Hydropower Financing in the Mekong Basin." *Global Environmental Change* 24: 20–29.

Mitchell, Timothy. 2002. *Rule of Experts: Egypt, Techno-politics, Modernity.* Berkeley: University of California Press.

Molle, Francois. 2009. "River-Basin Planning and Management: The Social Life of a Concept." *Geoforum* 40: 484–94.

Morales, Roberto, ed. 1998. *Ralco: Modernidad o Etnocidio en Territorio Mapuche* [Ralco: Modernity or ethnocide in Mapuche Territory]. Temuco: Instituto de Estudio Indígenas.

Nilsen, Alf Gunvald. 2008. "Political Economy, Social Movements, and State Power: A Marxian Perspective on Two Decades of Resistance to the Narmada Dam Projects." *Journal of Historical Sociology* 21 (2–3): 303–330.

Nilsson, Christer, Catherine A. Reidy, Mats Dynesius, and Carmen Ravenga. 2005. "Fragmentation and Flow Regulation of the World's Largest River Systems." *Science* 308 (5720): 405–408.

Nüsser, Marcus. 2003. "Political Ecology of Large Dams: A Critical Review." *Petermanns Geographische Mitteilungen* 147 (1): 20–27.

Nüsser, Marcus, and Ravi Baghel. 2017. "The Emergence of Technological Hydroscapes in the Anthropocene: Socio-Hydrology and Development Paradigms of Large Dams." In *Handbook on Geographies of Technology*, ed. Barney Warf, 287–301. Cheltenham: Edward Elgar.

Ogden, Laura A., Nik Heynen, Ulrich Oslender, Paige West, Karim-Aly S. Kassam, and Paul Robbins. 2013. "Global Assemblages, Resilience, and Earth Stewardship in the Anthropocene." *Frontiers in Ecology and the Environment* 11 (7): 341–347.

Okot, David Kilama. 2013. "Review of Small Hydropower Technology." *Renewable and Sustainable Energy Reviews* 26 (C): 515–520.

Omvedt, Gail. 1987. "India's Green Movements." *Race & Class* 28 (4): 29–38.

Omvedt, Gail. 1992. "Fount of Plenty or Bureaucratic Boondoggle? India's Narmada Project." *Capitalism Nature Socialism* 3 (4): 47–64.

Orlove, Ben, and Steve Caton. 2010. "Water Sustainability: Anthropological Approaches and Prospects." *Annual Review of Anthropology* 39: 401–415.

Paish, Oliver. 2002. "Small Hydro Power: Technology and Current Status." *Renewable and Sustainable Energy Reviews* 6 (5): 537–56.

Phadke, Roopali. 2002. "Assessing Water Scarcity and Watershed Development in Maharashtra, India: a Case Study of the Baliraja Memorial Dam." *Science, Technology, & Human Values* 27 (2): 236–261.

Phadke, Roopali. 2005. "People's Science in Action: the Politics of Protest and Knowledge Brokering in India." *Society and Natural Resources* 18 (4): 363–375.

Pinho, Paulo, Rodrigo Maia, and Ana Monterroso. 2007. "The Quality of Portuguese Environmental Impact Studies: The Case of Small Hydropower Projects." *Environmental Impact Assessment Review* 27 (3): 189–205.

Poff, N. LeRoy, J. David Allan, Mark B. Bain, James R. Karr, Karren L. Prestegaard, Brian D. Richter, Richard E. Sparks, and Julie C. Stromberg. 1997. "The Natural Flow Regime." *BioScience* 47 (11): 769–784.

Poff, N. LeRoy, Julian D. Olden, David M. Merritt, and David M. Pepin. 2007. "Homogenization of Regional River Dynamics by Dams and Global Biodiversity Implications." *PNAS* 104: 5732–5737.

Power, Mary E, Adrian Sun, Gary Parker, William E. Dietrich, and J. Timothy Wooton. 1995. "Hydraulic Food-Chain Models: an Approach to the Study of Food-Web Dynamics in Large Rivers." *BioScience* 45 (3): 159–67.

Premalatha, M., Tasneem Tabassum-Abbasi, and S.A. Abbasi. 2014. "A Critical View on the Eco-Friendliness of Small Hydroelectric Installations." *Science of the Total Environment* 481: 638–643.

Ptak, Thomas. 2014. "Dams and Development: Understanding Hydropower in Far Western Yunnan Province, China." *Focus on Geography* 57 (2): 43–53.

Ptak, Thomas. 2019. "Towards an Ethnography of Small Hydropower in China: Rural Electrification, Socioeconomic Development and Furtive Hydroscapes." *Energy Research & Social Science* 48: 116–130.

Richter, Brian D., Jeffrey V. Baumgartner, Jennifer Powell, David P. Braun. 1996. "A Method for Assessing Hydrologic Alteration within Ecosystems." *Conservation Biology* 10 (4): 1163–1174.

Richter, Brian D., Sandra Postel, Carmen Revenga, Thayer Scudder, Bernhard Lehner, Allegra Churchill, and Morgan Chow. 2010. "Lost in Development's Shadow: The Downstream Human Consequences of Dams." *Water Alternatives* 3 (2): 14–42.

Robbins, Paul, and Brian Marks. 2010. "Assemblage Geographies." In *The SAGE Handbook of Social Geographies*, ed. Susan J. Smith, Rachel Pain, Sallie A. Marston, and John Paul Jones III, 176–194. Thousand Oaks, CA: Sage.

Schaeffer, Colombina. 2017. "Democratizing the Flows of Democracy: Patagonia Sin Represas in the Awakening of Chile's Civil Society. In *Social Movements in Chile*, ed. Sofia Donosos and Marisa von Bülow, 131–159. New York: Palgrave Macmillan.

Schaeffer, Colombina, and Mattijs Smits. "2015. From Matters of Fact to Places of Concern? Energy, Environmental Movements and Place-Making in Chile and Thailand." *Geoforum* 65: 146–157.

Schmid, Christian. 2018. "Journeys through Planetary Urbanization: Decentering Perspectives on the Urban." *Environment and Planning D: Society and Space* 36 (3): 591–610.

Scott, James. 1998. *Seeing Like a State: How Certain Schemes to Improve the Human Condition Have Failed.* New Haven, CT: Yale University Press.

Scudder, Thayer. 1973. "The Human Ecology of Big Projects: River Basin Development and Re-settlement." *Annual Review of Anthropology* 2: 45–55.

Shaw, Karena, Stephen D. Hill, Amanda D. Boyd, Lindsay Monk, Joanna Reid, Edna F. Einsiedel. 2015. "Conflicted or Constructive? Exploring Community Responses to New Energy Developments in Canada." *Energy Research and Social Science* 8: 41–51.

Showers, Kate B. 2011. "Electrifying Africa: An Environmental History with Policy Implications." *Geografiska Annaler: Series B, Human Geography* 93 (3): 193–221.

Silber-Coats, Noah. 2017. "Clean Energy and Water conflicts: Contested Narratives of Small Hydropower in Mexico's Sierra Madre Oriental." *Water Alternatives* 10 (2): 578–601.

Sneddon, Christopher. 2003. "Reconfiguring Scale and Power: the Khong-Chi-Mun Project in Northeast Thailand." *Environment and Planning A* 35 (12): 2229–2250.

Sneddon, Christopher. 2015. *Concrete Revolution: Large Dams, Cold War Geopolitics, and the US Bureau of Reclamation.* Chicago: University of Chicago Press

Sneddon, Christopher, and Coleen Fox. 2008. "Struggles over Dams as Struggles for Justice: The World Commission on Dams (WCD) and Anti-Dam Campaigns in Thailand and Mozambique." *Society & Natural Resources: An International Journal* 21 (7): 625–640.

Soja, Edward. 2013. "Regional Urbanization and the End of the Metropolis Era." In *The New Blackwell Companion to the City*, ed. Gary Bridge and Sophie Watson, 679–689. Malden, MA: John Wiley & Sons.

Sovacool, Benjamin K., and L.C. Bulan. 2011. "Behind an Ambitious Megaproject in Asia: The History and Implications of the Bakun Hydroelectric Dam in Borneo." *Energy Policy* 39 (9): 4842–4859.

Steinhurst, William, Patrick Knight, and Melissa Schultz. 2012. "Hydropower Greenhouse Gas Emissions." Report on State of the Research, Synapse Energy Economics, Inc., Cambridge, MA.

Swyngedouw Erik. 1999. "Modernity and Hybridity: Nature, *Regeneracionismo*, and the Production of the Spanish Waterscape, 1890–1930." *Annals of the American Association of Geographers* 89 (3): 443–465

Swyngedouw Erik. 2007. "Technonatural Revolutions: The Scalar Politics of Franco's Hydro-social Dream for Spain, 1939–1975." *Transactions of the Institute of British Geographers* 32 (1): 9–28.

Tang Xianqiang, Qingyun Li, Min Wu, Wenjian Tang, Feng Jin, Jonathan Haynes, and Miklas Scholz. 2012. "Ecological Environment Protection in Chinese Rural Hydropower Development Practices: A Review." *Water Air Soil Pollution* 223 (6): 3033–3048.

Tarroja, Brian, Amir AghaKouchak, and Scott Samuelsen. 2016. "Quantifying Climate Change Impacts on Hydropower Generation and Implications on Electric Grid Greenhouse Gas Emissions and Operation." *Energy* 11: 295–305.

Vörösmarty, Charles, D. Lettenmaier, Christian Leveque, Michel Meybeck, Claudia Pahl-Wostl, Joseph Alcamo, William Cosgrove, H. Grassl, Holger Hoff, and Pavel Kabat. 2004. "Humans Transforming the Global Water System." *Eos Transactions American Geophysical Union* 85 (48): 509–520.

Vörösmarty, Charles, Michel Meybeck, Balazs Fekete, Keshav Sharma, Pamela Green, and James Syvitski. 2003. "Anthropogenic Sediment Retention: Major Global Impact from Registered River Impoundments." *Global and Planetary Change* 39 (1–2): 169–190.

Wescoat, James. 2000. "'Watersheds' in Regional Planning." In *The American Planning Tradition: Culture and Policy*, ed. Robert Fishman, 147–172. Washington, DC: Wilson Center, Smithsonian Institution.

White, Richard. 1995. *The Organic Machine: The Remaking of the Columbia River.* New York: Hill & Wang.

Williams, Garnett P., and M. Gordon Wolman. 1984. "Downstream Effects of Dams on Alluvial Rivers." US Geological Survey, Professional Paper 1286.

Wilson, Richard Guy. 1985. "Machine-Age Iconography in the American West: the Design of Hoover Dam." *Pacific Historical Review* 54 (4): 463–493.

WB (World Bank). 2009. "Directions in Hydropower." http://siteresources.worldban-k.org/INTWAT/Resources/Directions_in_Hydropower_FINAL.pdf (accessed 19 June 2019).

WBG (World Bank Group). 2016. "World Bank's First Development Loans to Chile, 1948." World Bank Group Archives Exhibit Series no. 057. Originally published January 2007. http://documents1.worldbank.org/curated/en/308691468185347709/pdf/104690-WP-PUBLIC-2007-01-World-Banks-First-Development-Loans-to-Chile.pdf

WCD (World Commission on Dams). 2000. *Dams and Development: A New Framework for Decision Making: A report of the World Commission on Dams.* London: Earthscan.

Worster, Donald. 1984. "The Hoover Dam: a Study in Domination." In *Social and Environmental Impacts of Large Dams, Volume 2: Case Studies*, ed. Edward Goldsmith and Nicholas Hildyard, 17–24. Cornwall: Wadebridge Ecological Centre.

Worster, Donald. 1985. *Rivers of Empire: Water, Aridity, and the Growth of the American West.* New York: Pantheon Books.

Zarfl, Christiane, Alexander Lumsdon, Juergen Berlekamp, Laura Tydecks, and Klement Tockner. 2015. "A Global Boom in Hydropower Dam Construction." *Aquatic Sciences* 77 (1): 161–170.

CHAPTER 7

Remaking Oceans Governance
Critical Perspectives on Marine Spatial Planning

Luke Fairbanks, Noëlle Boucquey, Lisa M. Campbell, and Sarah Wise

Introduction

New marine spatial planning (MSP) projects are being carried out in ocean spaces across the world. Since the early 2000s, state, NGO, and intergovernmental actors have promoted MSP, and the academic literature has followed these movements. Rather than focus on managing individual sectors such as fishing, shipping, or marine protected areas, MSP seeks to integrate those traditionally disconnected management arrangements through a vision of rational and comprehensive governance. Achieving this vision necessarily involves creating new databases, maps, and planning strategies to aid decision-making for coastal nations. Currently, MSP is used by more than 70 countries and covers nearly 10 percent of the world's national ocean jurisdictions (IOC and DG MARE 2017; IOC-UNESCO 2019), while ongoing efforts to reform fragmented high seas governance may present new opportunities to develop MSP for international waters (Wright et al. 2019).[1] MSP projects thus span large geographies and jurisdictions but also comprise "mega-projects" in how they collectively represent a fundamental shift in the theory and practice of oceans governance worldwide.

The framing of MSP demonstrates the ambitiousness of the idea. Most descriptions of MSP suggest a state of social-ecological harmony is possible through comprehensive governance. The idea is that by mapping ocean space and enhancing stakeholder participation in planning, MSP can "encourage compatible uses, reduce conflicts among uses, and reduce conflicts between human uses and the environment" (Ehler 2008: 841). Further, MSP projects are often entwined with broader visions of ecosystem-based management (EBM) and sustainable development. Some projects emphasize achieving balance between extractive, recreational, and conservation activities (e.g., Douvere et al. 2007; Kyriazi et al. 2013), while others focus on developing frameworks for new "blue" or "sustainable" industries like wind energy or aquaculture (e.g., Jongbloed et al. 2014; Lester et al. 2018). Underlying most projects is the perspective that "by providing a co-ordinated, cross-sectoral and future-oriented approach to marine management, [MSP] offers the potential of establishing more harmonious and rational spatial patterns of sea use" (Jay et al. 2012: 2).

The broad MSP literature has been largely driven by the natural sciences. However, an important portion of MSP research has been conducted in policy and social science disciplines. Understandably for an emerging phenomenon, much of this literature has focused on applied policy questions through case studies of MSP projects (e.g., Gunton and Joseph 2010; Smythe 2017); efforts to operationalize MSP's aims of EBM, participatory governance, and legal harmony offshore (e.g., Frazão Santos et al. 2015; Gopnik et al. 2012; Halpern et al. 2008); and the development of ideal models for MSP (e.g., Ansong et al. 2017; McCreary et al. 2016). Where critical, this literature has primarily examined what lessons can be learned from MSP processes and how the concept of MSP can be better applied in practice, most often regarding improved stakeholder participation or environmental protection.

Since about 2010, a critical MSP literature has emerged that goes beyond "lessons learned" or specific "ways and means" critiques to interrogate MSP projects from critical theoretical perspectives. Using social theory largely from planning, geography, and critical policy studies, these authors have begun to articulate the implications of "doing MSP" in terms of ideas such as the organization of marine space, the power of assembled actors in those spaces, and the ontological implications of planning and its support tools (e.g., ocean data infrastructures). In this article, we identify and explore four key elements of MSP that are receiving—and, we suggest, need additional—attention in the critical MSP literature: (1) planning discourse and narrative; (2) ocean economies and equity; (3) online ocean data and new digital ontologies; and (4) new and broad networks of ocean actors. In identifying these elements, we explore insights gained from the critical literature and highlight additional avenues of research for the field.[2] Afterward, we draw on our own work examining MSP in the United States to briefly illustrate and discuss how the four elements operate and may be critiqued. Together, these elements and MSP overall are remaking oceans governance; they are producing a vision of large-scale comprehensive and collaborative action across ocean spaces, actors, and institutions. Moreover, they constitute four separate but linked "mega" elements of a broader assemblage of MSP megaprojects that has emerged. Collectively, these megaprojects represent a significant shift in the scale and scope of oceans governance worldwide. We explore what this shift means for human-ocean relationships and futures, and we elucidate how it might support or foreclose possibilities for human and environmental well-being.

In conducting this review, we distinguish our definition of megaprojects as both more comprehensive and more nuanced than commonly used definitions. Currently, much of the literature on megaprojects explores specific large and expensive terrestrial initiatives such as mining compounds, airport, rail, or freeway construction, urban redevelopment schemes, or focused projects like space exploration or the Olympics (Flyvbjerg 2014; Gellert and Lynch 2003; Lehrer and Laidley 2008; Orueta and Fainstein 2008; Sanderson 2012; Wray 2014). Megaprojects are defined implicitly or explicitly as "projects which transform landscapes rapidly, intentionally, and profoundly in very visible ways, and require coordinated applications of capital and state power" (Gellert and Lynch 2003: 15).

While recognizing the importance of analyzing such projects, we argue for a definition of megaprojects that incorporates both the possibility of large-scale landscape and seascape change, as well as substantial changes to digital spaces, discourses, and modes of governance in likewise profound but perhaps less visible (and less rapid) ways. Moreover, while state and private capital might infuse such projects, power can also be produced through diverse associations within and among megaprojects.

While there exists a global assemblage of MSP projects that conceptually links together the underlying assumptions, practices, and goals of MSP, it is realized through projects at regional and national scales that can emerge differently in practice. In this way, the global MSP trend is not only remaking oceans governance generally but also, in its multiple forms, is producing multiple *remakings* across contexts. Indeed, we discuss the extent to which MSP differs from classic megaprojects in terms of its variability, physical infrastructure, effects on human communities, and political and social visibility. In considering MSP in this light, we contribute to broader conversations about the role of new megaprojects in shaping socionatural relationships across scales, spaces, and places, and we explore how the governing ethos and technologies associated with these projects might together shape the physical, discursive, and digital spaces of the future.

Four Elements of Marine Spatial Planning

Planning Discourse and Narrative

Similar to our efforts in the introduction, most MSP articles—critical and otherwise—begin by framing MSP in terms of why it has arisen, what it is, and what it can accomplish. Though there are minor variations in emphasis and tone, there is an MSP narrative: a "story" with a beginning, middle, and end (Roe 1991). In it, MSP, first, has arisen in response to the complicated "marine problem" of oceans and their governance, including declining environmental quality and resource overextraction exacerbated by growing human populations, increased interest in oceans resources and spaces to support economic growth across a range of sectors and scales, and inadequate and uncoordinated institutions for management. Second, in response to this problem, MSP offers "a public process of analyzing and allocating the spatial and temporal distribution of human activities in marine areas to achieve ecological, economic, and social objectives" (Ehler and Douvere 2009: 18). MSP ideally is adaptive, ecosystem- and area-based, integrated across sectors and institutions, and participatory (Ehler and Douvere 2009). Third, supported by scientific data and geospatial technologies, MSP done "right" can balance development and environmental protection, and social and economic goals, thus reducing conflict among stakeholders. It is the multifaceted promise of MSP that has led to its rapid expansion throughout a number of maritime jurisdictions (Jay 2010).

We begin our review of the critical MSP literature with efforts to deconstruct and/or problematize the MSP narrative and its assumptions. Some of the earliest work in this vein was done by Deborah Peel and M. Greg Loyd (2004). Using John Hannigan's (1995) framework for understanding how environmental issues gain traction in society, the authors trace how factors ranging from scientific authority to the media coalesced to support a "social reconstruction" of the marine problem with MSP situated as its potential solution. While the authors were uncertain whether the reconstruction would hold, Stephen Jay (2010), writing six years later, is more certain of MSP's longevity. He shares Peel and Lloyd's (2004) interest in the origins of MSP, tracing its evolution through traditions of marine management and promoted by the marine community (i.e., ocean scientists, managers, etc.). Having identified key themes in MSP similar to those in the aforementioned narrative, Jay (2010) expresses two concerns. First, MSP has developed in isolation and consequently learned little from the longer tradition of terrestrial spatial planning (TSP) (for a recent review of MSP in relation to planning, see Retzlaff and LeBleu 2018), and second, MSP has been driven primarily by the marine community with a rational epistemology that places scientific data as foremost to decision-making.

In a sentiment echoed by researchers including Paola Gazzola and colleagues (2015) and Sue Kidd and Geraint Ellis (2012), Jay and colleagues (2012: 2) argue "a wider disciplinary exchange [between TSP and MSP] would strengthen the emergence of a robust theory and practice of marine planning." In the history of TSP, a rational scientific approach was ultimately displaced, as it demanded too much of limited time and resources, belied the complexity of planning problems that made complete "knowledge" impossible, and was increasingly challenged for its assumed impartiality. As Geraint Ellis and Wesley Flannery (2016: 124) note, this early phase of TSP's history generally served elite interests at the expense of others. However, TSP has since shifted to a more processual or communicative understanding of planning (Kidd and Ellis 2012), whereas a parallel transition largely has not occurred within MSP.

In critiques of the rational epistemology underlying the MSP narrative, a first and central concern of critical scholars is not about science per se but rather how the narrative of a science- and ecosystem-based process diverges from real-world MSP practice. For example, Jay et al. (2016) examine the tensions in German MSP as its rational vision encountered a more relativist approach that placed the environment as just one among a suite of planning considerations. Differences in discursive emphasis could not be sustained on implementation, and the same marine community that originally pushed for MSP felt as if their ecological interests were overlooked in practice. Similar findings have been reflected in research on other marine planning practices, even if not fully MSP. In their study of aquaculture expansion in New Zealand, Michael McGinnis and Meghan Collins (2013) find not one but three visions of science and suggest the distinctions among them are not easily reconciled and lie at the heart of spatial allocation conflicts. Ultimately, agreement that MSP should be science-based does not mean there is agreement on what science tells us. Moreover, if science is uncertain—and it often is—then its role in resolving (rather than inflaming) disputes among competing interests becomes problematic. If MSP is ideally science driven, then lack of scientific certainty can be used to undermine its legitimacy (Fleming and Jones 2012).

A second concern about the MSP narrative relates to the role of stakeholder participation. In the common narrative, broad participation in MSP is the means by which conflict can be reconciled and "win-win-win" solutions can be found. However, several authors have critiqued the "unsettling assumption that participation among broad stakeholder groups can lead to equitable and consensual decisions" (Tafon 2017: 2). Some scholars are concerned participation alone will be inadequate to resolving conflicts in MSP; D. M. Fleming and Peter Jones (2012) argue the participatory emphasis in MSP be combined with more government leadership and statutory power. For others, the concern is more fundamental. Svein Jentoft (2017) problematizes participation by describing how stakeholders possess different knowledges, access, and incentives; different stakes in particular outcomes; and differing abilities to influence whose stakes are prioritized in MSP. With its emphasis on spatial allocation, MSP is a system of governing by inclusion and exclusion (Flannery et al. 2018), but the participatory narrative belies this, with its suggestion that all interests can be met with compromise and consensus.

In light of these findings, Ralph Tafon (2017: 2) argues MSP has been shoved "into the domain of the post-political, where rational consensus, rather than antagonism and power relations, is assumed to characterize MSP social relations." Heather Ritchie illustrates the post-political nature of MSP in her textual analysis of a succession of MSP documents produced under different UK governments, in which broad stroke consensual terms displaced "antagonism, conflict and disagreement" (2014: 674). At its worst, stakeholder participation is a "technique of government" that can co-opt genuine desire for democratic participation in decision-making. The emphasis on rational decision-making combined with participation and consensus can leave little (but not no) room for a radical rethinking of governance possibilities through MSP (Tafon 2017).

Whether focused on the MSP narrative's commitment to rational decision-making or broad stakeholder participation, these authors share a concern with how the MSP narrative masks questions of power and politics. Similarly, they are critical of existing research that adopts the MSP narrative and assesses it on its own terms, in effect reproducing the problematic assumptions, structures, and governance practices implicit in "rational" MSP megaprojects (and divorced from the lessons of TSP). The research needs identified by critical scholars include questions related to the distributional outcomes of MSP, the impacts of MSP on existing rights regimes, how participation is enacted in MSP, how MSP processes vary in different institutional contexts, and whether possibilities exist for a radical reorientation of MSP that foregrounds concerns like community, equity, and difference. Attention to power is essential given the speed at which MSP is advancing, and each of these questions is mediated by power in different forms—including discursive, institutional, and procedural power (Jentoft 2017). As Ellis and Flannery (2016: 124) argue in reference to MSP in the United Kingdom, without an explicit acknowledgment of power in MSP, "we can assume that the process will simply reflect existing power structures," including, most notably, "the market logic that dominates virtually all other realms of public policy."

Ocean Economies and Equity

The alignment of MSP with market logic and capitalist expansion is an emerging concern in the critical MSP literature. In step with the global proliferation of MSP has been a renewed attention to the economic potential of the oceans, perhaps best exemplified by the post-Rio+20 expansion of the Blue Economy (BE). The BE term has been articulated in different ways and by different actors ranging from Small Island Developing States to the World Bank. It is used to variously refer to the natural capital of the sea, the economic contributions of ocean industries to global wealth, the development of new oceans innovations and technologies, or the key role the oceans play in fisher and island livelihoods (Silver et al. 2015; Voyer et al. 2018). In some articulations, BE manifests as the concept of Blue Growth, which is most closely tied to the development ocean industries—ranging from aquaculture to deep-sea mining—and their contributions to large-scale economic development (Barbesgaard 2018). The all-encompassing nature of BE hides many of its internal and discursive contradictions (e.g., incompatibilities between economic sectors, ecosystem priorities, and/or stakeholders; lack of clarity over rights and equity), but its common (and rhetorically attractive) focus on sustainable development and oceans management holds it together.

Critical MSP scholars have explored the interactions between MSP and new economic concepts like BE, including attention to the distributional and equity impacts of broadscale economic reorganization at sea. At a fundamental level, the rational economic logic that underlies BE appears to have found its governance companion in MSP, whose own epistemological foundations ostensibly provide the applied framework needed to translate the BE concept to practice (Kerr et al. 2015). Discursive and conceptual attention to techno-scientific practice, quantification and valuation, and rational EBM, for example, are common across MSP and many BE articulations. In the European sphere, MSP is considered "central to the EU's Blue Growth strategies" (Jentoft 2017: 275), and "blue growth is the dominant overall priority" across many of the region's MSP programs (Jones et al. 2016: 256). More generally, calling to mind the comprehensive vision of MSP, Michelle Voyer and colleagues (2018: 6) explain, "the focus of the Blue Economy is on integrated management, which aims to manage across sectors, across geographical scales and across the land-ocean interface" (see also Barbesgaard 2018: 131). Necessarily, this scope and scale can be addressed only through the similarly broad "universal tool" of MSP (Voyer et al. 2018: 17), which itself is typically enacted at national or regional scales similar to BE.

Given the potential for the convergence of MSP and new economic practice like BE to dramatically remake ocean economies, scholars have begun to critically examine the economic relationships between MSP and its stakeholders, including coastal communities. Whereas Kidd and Ellis (2012: 62) noted in 2012 that "the distributional impacts of MSP are largely unknown," scholars in the few intervening years have leveled important critiques of MSP, asking, who benefits from these new oceans governance projects (Flannery et al. 2016)? Ellis and Flannery (2016: 126) warn that the common MSP narrative falsely removes planning from "the dirty world of power, wealth and exploitation" that can underlie neoliberal projects like BE. Consequently, without critical reflection on its practice, "MSP, and the Blue Growth which it aims to facilitate, may turn into a zero-sum game rather than a win for all" (Jentoft 2017: 270). Indeed, Nathan Bennett and colleagues (2015) and Mads Barbesgaard (2018) write that MSP and Blue Growth projects, respectively, can amount to "ocean grabbing," or the dispossession of marine spaces and resources from coastal users and communities. In some cases, supposed participatory and cross-sectoral MSP comprises (or devolves into) little more than what might be termed "strategic sectoral planning" driven by powerful actors like offshore energy firms or existing government bodies (Jones et al. 2016; see also Flannery and Ó Cinnéide 2012). The results can be real and perceived exclusionary processes (and inequitable economic outcomes) for already marginalized actors (Kerr et al. 2015; Flannery et al. 2018; Tafon et al. 2018). This research upends the supposed "win-win-win" scenario found in the typical MSP narrative and shows that MSP may simply serve to bolster neoliberal structures and cement existing power and wealth differentials.

Underlying these distributional impacts are not only applied governance shortfalls but also more conceptual questions about the nature of MSP and its economic implications. In their effort to develop a relational conception of BE, for instance, Gordon Winder and Richard Le Heron (2017: 21) assert BE initiatives "are all territorial projects as well as economic projects." In the Chinese context, Young Choi (2017: 39) similarly argues BE "is more than an economy-making project; it is necessarily a governmental project through spatial interventions, opening up new 'governable spaces.'" While these governable spaces in China are filled by a state-led functional zoning program, the implications for MSP generally are clear: at sea, economic aspirations are intimately entwined with spatial reorganization and reallocation. Through this, we see the conceptual and discursive overlaps between MSP and BE: MSP is not only compatible with many popular articulations of BE but also necessitated by it.

Critical MSP scholars are now examining the interplay between MSP and new trends in ocean economies. The full range of processual and material outcomes for communities, environments, and economies remain to be seen. However, critical analysts have raised caution about the role MSP plays in reshaping economic practices and relations. At the same time, it is important to be open to and interrogate the alternative economic arrangements that may be impacted by—or arise from—MSP projects. In such cases, we might find economies that run counter to BE or conventional neoliberal expectations, both problematizing supposedly rational economic and ecosystem-based MSP and offering new lines of inquiry for critical research (Fairbanks et al. 2018; Jentoft and Knol 2014). As a result, in addition to tracking how MSP and BE continue to converge and shape one another, moving forward, researchers might ask, how can MSP offer venues for seemingly marginalized actors to assert material economic claims (e.g., fishing grounds), new knowledges and ontologies of ocean environments, and alternative concerns of equity and economic outcomes? Approaching these questions does not mean issues such as incomplete stakeholder participation, exclusion, or inequitable planning have been "solved," but it does provide new avenues to problematize the assumption that MSP (particularly when linked to neoliberal projects like BE) is an inherently disempowering management process (i.e., an "ocean grab"). Indeed, the BE concept itself leaves room for concerns related to fishing communities and livelihoods, suggesting alternative iterations of BE and MSP practice can exist (Silver et al. 2015). As the next section describes, one way these complications, contradictions, and opportunities can arise is within the digital infrastructures that underlie MSP megaprojects.

Online Ocean Data and New Digital Ontologies

To meet the goals of EBM and rational allocation of ocean spaces, resources, and uses, large-scale mapping projects and online ocean data collections have been implemented to support MSP. These data practices are producing new digital ontologies of ocean environments. As databases and maps have proliferated, critical MSP scholars have interrogated the practical, political, and ontological implications of the production and consumption of these data programs. Scholars have examined the lack of complexity in depictions of human relationships with ocean space as MSP projects began to map human activities (e.g., shipping, oil exploration, fishing) and ecosystem characteristics (e.g., marine mammals, temperature gradients, seagrass beds) (Flannery and Ellis 2016; St. Martin and Hall-Arber 2008), as well as the consequences that particular practices of oceans mapping and visualization might have for how marine spaces are imagined and governed (Boucquey et al. 2016, 2019; Smith 2015).

Mapping processes appear to have become "obligatory passing point[s]" for governing ocean spaces (Smith and Brennan 2012: 214) and are essential to the performance of MSP projects. Mappings allow marine space to become "known" as information is inscribed in databases and displayed in public data portals, meetings, and documents. At the same time, maps "can produce reality as much as represent it," as the mapping process necessarily simplifies and categorizes ocean data in particular ways (211). Though such is the nature of all maps, the magnitude of ocean space available for management via MSP raises concerns that these spaces—along with the actors, environments, and activities within them—will be "engineered" to be amenable to map-based management (Smith and Brennan 2012; Smith 2015). Moreover, as human and nonhuman actors of all kinds are funneled through MSP mapping processes—participatory or otherwise—there are important questions as to how their roles might change.

In her analysis of spatial management for the New England scallop fishery, for example, Julia Olson observes that bio-economic models created by fisheries managers depicted fishers and ocean environments in ways that prioritized simpler management over nuanced understandings of human-ocean relationships. The models emphasized percentages of ocean floor open to fishing and concentrated on the highest-grossing operations, rather than assessing the importance of various (specific) locations to different fishing operations. Such models changed the ontological focus of management and led to a shift in the conceptualization of scallop fishing as something more akin to farming, marginalizing traditional fishing knowledge in the process. Ultimately, as Olson (2010: 301) notes, "mapping the seabed can be easily allied to the commoditization of knowledge through the material and cultural power of groups" seeking to manage resources in more rational, neoliberal ways.

Others have similarly traced the ontological outcomes of particular technologies and mapping processes. What these critical observations make clear is the importance of mapping processes in defining categories that condition possibilities for ocean spaces. In her study of government-sponsored mapmaking focused on identifying ecologically "valuable" and "vulnerable" regions of the Barents Sea, Maikke Knol (2011: 990) finds that "the process determined the problems." Controversies over oil and gas exploration were diminished and redirected as areas outside the new valuable and vulnerable regions became viewed as available for development. The mapmaking process also shifted the governance focus from an EBM ideal to a stakeholder debate; "the zoning system became organized around questions such as what is allowed, where, and when," rather than how proposed activities might interact with broader socionatural systems.

Consequently, while "stakeholders" (a complex designation in itself) are often called upon to channel their knowledge through MSP mapping processes, these efforts are themselves fraught and necessitate critical examination. As Arielle Levine and Christine Feinholz (2015: 65) report, participatory GIS workshops in Hawaii were helpful for mapping coastal human activities, but a category of "culturally significant uses" proved problematic. While participants agreed the category was important, they said they could speak only for their own families' areas, each family had a story, and some significant sites could not be represented via the workshop process. Others opted not to map spaces at all rather than risk misrepresenting the significance of Hawaiian cultural uses. The authors conclude that attempting to map such uses "challenges the epistemological limits of conventional GIS." First, participants' mental maps contained more information than is possible to fit into a GIS data layer, and second, a danger exists in mapmaking of "reifying boundaries" that are in fact changeable and dynamic—particularly at sea.

These examples demonstrate reason for caution as governing bodies respond to calls to increase sociocultural representation in MSP maps and databases. More generally, they suggest research into large-scale mapping practices should interrogate how maps are assembled in the first place, and the decision-making that elevates their importance in managing the "contested geographical and moral spaces" of the sea (Knol 2011: 983). As MSP mappings become ubiquitous, researchers are recognizing the inherent tensions associated with ever-increasing amounts of ocean data in terms of decision-making about how (and which) data are used and displayed. For instance, Francisco Ascui and colleagues examine the role of ocean-based "environmental Big Data" (collected by underwater sensors) as an actor in controversies over salmon aquaculture in an Australian harbor. They argue the role of data has been under-theorized and that particular sets of data have the power to dramatically shift the discourse and practice of environmental governance. In their case, differences between modeled and physically sensed water quality, and controversies over who could access the data, were central to public narratives, industry practices, and government decision-making regarding how to regulate aquaculture in the harbor. As they note, "it no longer makes sense to regard data as a mere intermediary, but rather as a key mediator in social relations" (2018: 18). This suggests future critical MSP work could further examine how data of all kinds—big or small—take on their own agency and affect how other actors come to be known and managed.

As these studies illustrate, critical insights are being be made about every aspect of the data collection, mapping, and display that support MSP megaprojects. They suggest some key threads of research to push further. In terms of data collection, more work is needed to investigate how different datasets arise and how they affect our understandings of marine ecosystems. Beyond datasets, models are increasingly used to make educated assumptions about such systems. How do these simulations interact with more traditional data collections, and what types of ocean imaginaries do they construct? The role of data and their influence on the direction of governance decisions is a related concern (Smith 2015). In terms of mapping, these studies hint that many important decisions occur in collating and storing original data, creating metadata, constructing categories, drawing boundaries, and editing maps (Boucquey et al. 2019). Questions remain about how these decisions are made and what actors are involved in making them. As "obligatory passing points" (Smith and Brennan 2012), the importance of maps in MSP is firmly established, but additional work examining what role maps play in potential ocean enclosure and control by powerful actors is needed. Finally, useful work is being done in terms of applying more relational perspectives to MSP, and this could be pushed further by incorporating complementary theory (such as ontological politics) to more carefully examine the relationships between ocean data, visualization, and planning outcomes.

New and Broad Networks of Ocean Actors

Early literature on MSP tended to simplify the networks of actors enrolled in MSP with broad descriptors, referring to, for example, human actors as "stakeholders" and non-human or environmental actors as "ecosystems" (Boucquey et al. 2016). This language reproduced the common MSP narrative and provided a way to discursively simplify MSP networks into traceable and navigable systems of actors, activities, and user rights. In reality, however, these categories do not address the dynamic relationships, interactions, and reach of heterogeneous MSP actors at sea (Boucquey et al. 2016; Fairbanks et al. 2018). They further simplify the (possible) relationships between enrolled actors—often limiting them to already well-described, visible, or data-driven activities like human uses or environmental protection. As a result, the promise of MSP to be a collaborative planning method that "achieve[s] consensus among all sectors operating in a particular area" (Pomeroy and Douvere 2008: 816) has proved far more inexact in practice. While the possibility of consensus is put forth for (and within) MSP networks, MSP is often fragmented and emergent. It involves complex assemblages of human and nonhuman actors that hold a diversity of competing, overlapping, and associated interests (Fairbanks et al. 2018). These networks may reach well beyond the stakeholders or ecosystems typically engaged in planning (to include, e.g., marginalized coastal communities, overlooked species or offshore uses, etc.), further illustrating a fundamental and "mega" scale and scope in MSP projects that can be obscured in planning practice.

Critical MSP scholars have problematized simple conceptualizations of MSP networks, and several key points emerge within the literature. First, research has explored the evolving nature of MSP as a social process and examined how MSP both requires myriad actors to be enacted while simultaneously generating new networks of actors through its practice. Second, critical scholars have moved beyond the primarily operational concerns of engagement in MSP to interrogate the complexity of human and nonhuman actors enrolled in planning. As MSP has been implemented differentially across the globe, scholars have highlighted the limits of the common stakeholder/ecosystem binary, demonstrating that it fractures under closer examination to reveal MSP networks comprised of a multiplicity of actors, processes, and associations across space and scales. Third, as power remains central in MSP, the literature explores the role—and emergent properties—of power and equity in the structure of MSP networks and the practice of MSP itself.

Drawing on innovation theory, Andrew Merrie and Per Olsson trace the emergence and spread of MSP as an idea and technology. The authors identify what they call "institutional entrepreneurs"—a key network of global actors in the marine community involved in knowledge exchange and promotion of MSP. This group is attributed with spreading "a common understanding of MSP and its recognition as a tool for managing cumulative impacts, conflicting human uses, and . . . for integrated ecosystem-based management"

(2014: 372). Although informal, the group shared institutional authority and power and was well positioned to leverage scientific knowledge to encourage the uptake of MSP, helping shape and cohere a global assemblage of MSP efforts. The literature emerging from this network remains foundational to MSP (see, e.g., Halpern et al. 2008; Douvere et al. 2007; Ehler 2008) and has informed the trajectory of planning innovation, at times reproducing the aforementioned (problematic) MSP narrative in the process. More recently, Paola Gazzola and Vincent Onyango describe how shared social values about the marine environment encapsulated by the MSP narrative and marine community inform the practice of MSP: "The role that institutions, practitioners and stakeholders play in producing or reproducing societal values, professional norms, ideas or discourses are also important in explaining how and why planning is practiced in a certain way" (2018: 10). Consequently, people, organizations, and institutions are not simply participating in the planning process but also shaping, reconfiguring, and often reproducing what marine space and spatial planning means through their own emergent networks.

Through implementation, MSP projects also create and mobilize new networks of actors. Mark Dubois and colleagues, for example, show how marine policy has encouraged alliances among sectors (including fishers and scientists), leading to the emergence of "a new type of scientifically literate fisherman." The authors suggest this new fisherman was formed through their participation in UK MSP processes. Through collaboration and shared planning experiences, "an opportunity to shift fishers' participation in the knowledge production and management decision-making process from knowledge holders/data collectors to knowledge agents became possible" (2016: 53). These newly minted actors are products of MSP in the same way as new mapping technologies, datasets, and planning bodies, but can also find new measures of power or autonomy by working within the MSP process itself.

Extending these findings beyond human actors, Jay (2018) writes in favor of considering the dynamism and fluidity of "the sea's materiality" when planning marine spaces. This mirrors similar calls by Christopher Bear (2013, 2017) to better attend to the active roles of nonhuman actors in marine governance; fish, for instance, are not only represented through data practice and MSP discourse, but themselves affect human use and management practices through their physical movements, migrations, and life cycles. This conceptualization moves MSP into a realm of dynamic networks and entanglements, which "introduce[s] a new level of interaction, energy and change to the sense of space-being-planned" (Jay 2018: 14). In other words, networks of heterogeneous actors create new spaces of meaning and placemaking; further, power may be emergent within the broader MSP assemblage, as new "interactions, energy and change" coalesce to upend or reshape existing planning structures. This is echoed in other examinations of the role of nonhuman actors in MSP that have interrogated how they are produced in planning and how their material and representational actions can reshape planning networks and trajectories (Boucquey et al. 2016; Fairbanks et al. 2018).

Critical MSP scholars raise questions about how MSP networks form, change, and shift over time and space. As a broad and multifaceted management scheme, MSP—and its various iterations at national and regional scales—is necessarily comprised of a diversity of actors. While at a basic level these networks are expansive and heterogeneous, pointing to the difficulties that can come with characterizing MSP to begin with, it is also important to ask questions such as the following: How do such networks or assemblages form and stabilize? Where is power centered within them? How can (and do) seemingly marginalized actors (including nonhuman actors) intervene in planning processes and (re-)form their own networks, and with what effects? In the following section, we examine these and other questions in relation to the case of US MSP and identify additional lines of inquiry for future critical MSP studies.

Discussion: Critical Insights from US MSP

In this section, we briefly illustrate how the four broad elements of MSP discussed in the critical literature operate in the context of US marine spatial planning. We do this to show how these themes matter in real-world settings, explain more specifically how each element contributes to an overall shift in the scale and scope of oceans governance, and illustrate how they are intertwined and can be analyzed through critical theory. Through this case, we explore what this broad shift in oceans governance might mean for human-ocean relationships and futures not just in the US but also around the globe. At the same time, we emphasize that MSP takes many forms in different places, and it will be important for future research to interrogate these forms and their differential effects on human and environmental actors.

US MSP arrived somewhat late in the development of global MSP projects. It was formally introduced in 2010 as a primary component of President Barack Obama's National Ocean Policy (NOP; Executive Order 13547) to develop "comprehensive, adaptive, integrated, ecosystem-based, and transparent" spatial management in US waters. Though US MSP soon discursively shifted to the more politically palatable term of "US ocean planning," it largely followed the typical MSP narrative as outlined in this article. In particular, it featured a strong "salvation" (Campbell et al. 2008) component to the story that placed MSP as a solution to "siloed" sectoral US oceans management and longstanding controversies over fisheries collapses, renewable energy development, protected areas, and other issues (Fairbanks et al. 2018). In contrast to other nations (and early NOP drafts), US MSP has evolved as federally supported but regionally led efforts, with "[US] states, tribes, and Regional Fishery Management Councils" given the option to "choose to participate on regional planning bodies" (RPBs) and craft their own regional ocean plans (NOC 2013). Currently, four US regions have developed RPBs: the West Coast, Pacific Islands, Northeast, and Mid-Atlantic. These continue to operate with the social and regulatory networks and geospatial infrastructures initiated during the Obama years (Boucquey et al. 2019), despite the Trump administration's rescinding of Executive Order 13547 in 2018.

The US MSP narrative has had material implications for the way digital geospatial infrastructures have developed. The vocabulary of EBM—species, populations, ecosystems—and of global MSP (e.g., "engaged stakeholders") shapes data collection, organization, and visualization in the US regional online ocean data portals (Boucquey et al. 2016, 2019). In this regard, we can see how discourse and narrative—the "reconstruction" of MSP (cf. Peel and Lloyd 2004) and its rational epistemologies (Jay et al. 2012; Ritchie 2010)—are intricately and inherently linked with geospatial practice. Ocean data and digital ontologies reproduce and strengthen the MSP narrative and vice versa. But what is hidden by the narrative—and its associated logics and data practices—are the uncertainties, contingencies, and subtle politics involved in determining who or what counts as a stakeholder in US oceans governance, what data are included or excluded from data portals and displays, and how the portals are connected to (and shape) networks of MSP actors.

While the material agencies of human and nonhuman actors are often obscured in discourse and practice, US MSP shows this is not an inevitable outcome of planning. For example, the formal inclusion of Native American tribes in RPBs has presented opportunities for those actors to resist or destabilize some of the dominant and taken-for-granted aspects of MSP. Tribal representatives have sometimes halted planning proceedings to interrogate terms such as "stakeholder," characterizing their tribe's relationship to the ocean as very different from what stakeholder connotes and sparking debate about the epistemological and ontological assumptions of MSP (e.g., how do we capture and understand sociocultural or relational values in data and planning?) (Boucquey et al 2016;

Fairbanks et al. 2018). In other cases, previously "invisible" or overlooked oceans users (e.g., recreational kayakers or pleasure boaters) have been able to assert their interests through new planning forums or participatory mapping initiatives. Among nonhuman actors, there is a growing recognition of the challenges posed by the fluidity of ocean environments and organisms themselves, with ongoing debates about how to account for climate change, animal migrations, and stochastic events in US ocean data portals and planning documents (Fairbanks et al. 2018). Practitioners deeply involved with data portal development have spoken frankly about how they are in "uncharted territory" as they struggle to coherently assemble data, metadata, and maps in understandable and useful ways (Boucquey et al. 2016, 2019).

These cases of uncertainty, resistance, or counter-narrative remind us MSP projects are young and still emergent. Even though a dominant MSP narrative persists, possibilities for difference through a variety of visions of MSP remain in play. The "winners" and "losers" of MSP are not necessarily determined by preexisting power (and capital) relations. Indeed, while US MSP may risk being an exclusionary process (Flannery et al. 2018) and some of its motivations trace to powerful offshore capital reminiscent of BE (e.g., wind energy interests), various "practices of assemblage," such as engagement and mapping opportunities, provide avenues for different actors to assert themselves in planning and craft alternative futures beyond marginalizing oceans enclosures (Fairbanks et al. 2018).

As Melissa Nursey-Bray (2016: 129) writes, while MSP is "based on managing multiple uses, this is not the same as reconciling the multiple cultures and knowledge domains within those groups." Even within a seemingly coherent MSP project, there exists a diversity of conflicting views on economic practice and ocean use (Boucquey et al. 2016; Fairbanks et al. 2018). However, "the lurking presence of conflict should not be a cause for despair" but rather serve to remind us that even supposedly rational or post-political projects like MSP "are not immunized from politics" (Tafon et al. 2018: 19). Instead, the politics present within MSP can offer openings for something other than a rational and neoliberal economic agenda to emerge. Jentoft and Knol (2014: 10), for example, explain how MSP presents both risk and opportunity for North Sea small-scale actors, as it can "help protect fishers against the intrusion of other user-group" and provide ways to assert spatial claims to the sea. This mirrors recent work by Paul Foley and Charles Mather (2018), who argue "ocean grabbing" may, in some cases, be a tool of communities rather than powerful actors; a way for them to assert resource claims through a form of "terraqueous territoriality" onto adjacent seas. Consequently—and perhaps paradoxically—local actors and others often overlooked in oceans governance may in turn be empowered through MSP (Johnsen and Hersoug 2014), with their own community economies and alternative economic practices legitimized and strengthened. Indeed, this is often part of the participatory promise of MSP and its narrative in the United States and elsewhere, even if its "success" is variable in practice (Fairbanks et al. 2018).

Through this discussion, we can see how the four elements of MSP discussed earlier are inextricably linked in reality (here, through the US MSP case). This necessitates theoretical development to better understand the full scale and scope of MSP actors, networks, practices, and relationships, including those that are unexpected, emergent, or often marginalized in oceans governance processes. To attend to these concerns and elucidate different possibilities and alternative futures for MSP, critical scholars might continue to turn their attention to relational understandings of space and governance. As described earlier, work led by Jay and colleagues is pushing this strand of research forward (e.g., Jay 2010, 2012, 2018; Jay and Toonen 2015; Jay et al. 2012). Jay (2018: 6) suggests a framework for incorporating a relational notion of "lively space" (Massey 2005) into MSP processes, denoted by the categories of "flexing, teeming, integrating, connecting, reconfiguring, and anticipating."

In the United States, these relational categories represent a substantial shift from the ones that often guide MSP (e.g., "stakeholders," "ecosystems," existing jurisdictional boundaries). Yet we have seen their material implications in practice as, for instance, human-nonhuman encounters between protected species and offshore uses have shaped both RPB planning decisions and activities on the sea itself (Fairbanks et al. 2018), in effect "forming an [MSP] assemblage of entangled interactions" (Jay 2018: 13). In this way, we see evidence that MSP can be practiced differently, even given its existing tools. While it is important to identify and analyze where MSP is enacted as post-political or hegemonic megaprojects, it is equally important to identify where the politics remain, where power may be dis- and reassembled through new actors and relationships, and how those actors can work through (or resist) MSP to craft new futures that improve human and environmental well-being. For example, MSP tools and practices including participatory GIS, engagement with traditionally marginalized actors, enrollment in new conservation and development opportunities (e.g., marine protected areas or offshore aquaculture), or—as seen in the United States—the development of "story maps" that showcase diverse and relational interactions between people, culture, and ocean space, all present possibilities for difference and for exploring the lively spaces of MSP.

In this regard, although critical scholars should continue to analyze and critique the marginalizing and disempowering implications of MSP, there also exist research avenues to explore the converse: difference and opportunity. MSP is not uniformly remaking oceans governance into a post-political seascape (though this may occur through some MSP projects) but is a collection of multiple *remakings* with different dynamics, actors, and possibilities—albeit tied together by the conceptual elements identified in this paper. Rather than examining MSP on its own terms, integrating new critical ideas and theory can help researchers remain open to the fluidity of the human-ocean relationships, outcomes, and alternative futures for those enrolled in MSP. In this way, we can highlight how MSP (or other megaprojects) might—perhaps surprisingly—provide avenues to improve human and environmental well-being, through resistance, participation, or efforts to remake the assemblage itself.

Conclusions

Marine spatial planning is a relatively new but significant oceans governance strategy worldwide. Through geospatial practices and participatory management, it promises a rational and comprehensive way to unify traditionally disconnected oceans governance arrangements, sectors, actors, and uses under the umbrella of ecosystem-based management. In this review of the critical MSP literature, we aimed to go beyond the practical and operational concerns of MSP to better synthesize the conceptual, discursive, and theoretical critiques that have been leveled at the governance project. These critiques have largely (but not exclusively) been related to four key elements we identify in the global spread of MSP: (1) planning discourse and narrative; (2) ocean economies and equity; (3) online ocean data and new digital ontologies; and (4) new and broad networks of ocean actors. Beyond conceptually linking MSP projects together and serving as ways to characterize planning efforts, these four elements can be key avenues for scholars to engage in productive critiques and contribute to steering MSP in diverse directions. Thus, we reiterate our call for continued work on critical MSP using new and emergent critical thought including relational theory, ontological politics, critical GIS, and political ecology, among others. By incorporating these concepts, critical scholars might be better equipped to interrogate the dynamic and large-scale nature of MSP assemblages, including bringing greater attention to the material actions of nonhuman actors and their concomitant consequences for shaping power, decision-making, and governance (Ascui et al. 2018; Bear 2017). Here we echo Flannery and Ellis's (2016) call for a more "radical" reorientation of MSP practice and research that foregrounds concerns of equity, and also draw inspiration from Jay (2018), Philip Steinberg and Kimberley Peters (2015), and others who have called for more "lively" or "wet" ontologies of oceans spaces and governance processes. We suggest that by drawing on these diverse and interdisciplinary ideas, we might better get a "hold" on the scale, scope, and dynamics of megaprojects like MSP.

While we have called MSP initiatives "megaprojects" throughout this article, it is worth considering how MSP differs from classic megaprojects. Though the digital footprint of MSP is ever expanding (via portals and databases) along with its scope of oceanic surveillance (via ship and animal tracking devices, satellite imagery, and physical sensors), the physical infrastructures of MSP megaprojects do not always visibly transform seascapes in the dramatic manner that has traditionally defined megaprojects. This is context-dependent, as MSP can enable aquaculture, wind energy, and other visible uses in new spaces. However, even in these cases physical development is often much slower and more deliberate than may be observed in terrestrial analogs. Without such (rapid) visible transformations—and the displacement of human communities often associated with terrestrial megaprojects—social and political engagement with MSP has been arguably less contentious, at least outside of obvious stakeholder groups such as fishers or shipping interests. Discussions and disagreements are typically focused around spatial management priorities rather than imminent physical development. Thus, MSP has sometimes progressed without broad public scrutiny, even as certain actors actively and earnestly engage in planning processes. We argue, however, none of these characteristics should disqualify MSP efforts from being conceptualized as megaprojects. Indeed, we suggest it is not necessarily the visible (or rapid) changes in landscapes or seascapes that best defines megaprojects, but also the discursive, digital, ontological, and governance practices that such projects might entail. Together, these elements can have similarly far-reaching and significant impacts on social, economic, or environmental reorganization, even where visible changes are difficult to discern. At sea, material changes are often not clearly seen or known; rather, they are discovered, portrayed, and communicated through scientific and geospatial technologies and governance assemblages like MSP.

Consequently, as MSP megaprojects remake social and material oceanic relationships, we must be attentive to their differential implementations and manifestations across socio-spatial contexts. We suggest critical MSP scholars should both continue to investigate these cases but also put them in conversation with one another so that we may better grasp the reach of this modern remaking of oceans governance—including its differential processes and effects across spaces (i.e., multiple MSP megaprojects and multiple *remakings*) and its consequences for future human and environmental well-being. Lastly, while not all these insights will be relevant across the range of megaproject studies, we hope the land/sea divide does not dissuade critical scholars on either side. Although our own present review focuses on oceans research, in truth this "divide" is often more uncertain and liminal than often described (much like megaprojects themselves). Moving forward, lessons, theory, and insights can and should be shared across geographies and disciplines if we hope to grasp the true measure of megaprojects and their implications for environment and society.

▪ **ACKNOWLEDGMENTS**

This review was a collaborative effort. Luke Fairbanks and Noëlle Boucquey share lead authorship, and each author reviewed and wrote about an element of the critical MSP literature as follows: planning discourse and narrative (Campbell), ocean economies and equity (Fairbanks), online ocean data and new digital ontologies (Boucquey), and new and broad networks of ocean actors (Wise). We also thank Kevin St. Martin for his contributions to our US MSP research project, as well as two anonymous reviewers for constructive feedback on the original manuscript. The research that informed this review was supported by the US National Science Foundation (award nos. 1359943 and 1359805).

▪ **LUKE FAIRBANKS** is a Research Scientist at the Duke University Marine Laboratory in the Nicholas School of the Environment at Duke University. His research interests include human-environment interactions in ocean and coastal spaces, as well as geographic approaches to understanding environmental policy and management. Email: luke.fairbanks@duke.edu

▪ **NOËLLE BOUCQUEY** is Assistant Professor of Environmental Studies at Eckerd College. She studies the social, political, and spatial dimensions of marine resource use and governance, with particular attention to how physical and virtual infrastructures mediate knowledge, resource access, and governance practices. Email: boucqun@eckerd.edu

▪ **LISA M. CAMPBELL** is the Rachel Carson Professor of Marine Affairs and Policy at the Duke University Marine Laboratory in the Nicholas School of the Environment at Duke University. Her research interests include oceans governance and how science and non-state actors inform governance processes and outcomes. Email: lisa.m.campbell@duke.edu

▪ **SARAH WISE** is an anthropologist with the National Oceanic and Atmospheric Administration National Marine Fisheries Service. Her research explores the intersection between science and policy and the cross-scale effects on coastal communities, and particularly focuses on informational pathways and decision-making under conditions of rapid social and environmental change. Email: sarah.wise@noaa.gov

▪ **NOTES**

1. National ocean jurisdictions include 12-mile territorial seas and 200-mile exclusive economic zones, as delineated by the UN Law of the Sea. International waters, or the high seas, are all ocean areas beyond national jurisdiction.
2. Reviewed studies were identified as follows: (1) We conducted searches in Web of Science (WOS) and Scopus for articles published between 2006 and 2018 using the terms: "marine spatial planning" OR "marine planning" OR "maritime planning" OR "ocean planning" OR "ocean zoning" OR "marine zoning." This produced 1,225 articles. (2) We limited our search by social science disciplines, producing 524 articles. (3) We selected articles based on their titles, keywords, abstracts, and our own familiarity with their content and authors to determine a subset of critical MSP scholarship. (4) We supplemented these results with targeted searches in Google Scholar for specific authors and using Step 1's search terms to find additional articles written shortly before or after our initial search frame or not indexed by WOS or Scopus. Our final review sample included 73 articles of critical MSP scholarship. An additional 82 articles that addressed, but did not focus on, critical themes, theory, and/or spatial oceans governance practices were also used to complement our review.

▪ REFERENCES

Ansong, Joseph, Elena Gissi, and Helena Calado. 2017. "An Approach to Ecosystem-Based Management in Maritime Spatial Planning Process." *Ocean & Coastal Management* 141: 65–81.

Ascui, Francisco, Marcus Haward, and Heather Lovell. 2018. "Salmon, Sensors, and Translation: The Agency of Big Data in Environmental Governance." *Environment and Planning D: Society and Space* 36 (5): 905–925.

Barbesgaard, Mads. 2018. "Blue Growth: Savior or Ocean Grabbing?" *Journal of Peasant Studies* 45 (1): 130–149.

Bear, Christopher. 2013. "Assembling the Sea: Materiality, Movement and Regulatory Practices in the Cardigan Bay Scallop Fishery." *Cultural Geographies* 20 (1): 21–41.

Bear, Christopher. 2017. "Assembling Ocean Life: More-Than-Human Entanglements in the Blue Economy." *Dialogues in Human Geography* 7 (1): 27–31.

Bennett, Nathan J., Hugh Govan, and Terre Satterfield. 2015. "Ocean Grabbing." *Marine Policy* 57: 61–68.

Boucquey, Noëlle, Luke Fairbanks, Kevin St. Martin, Lisa M. Campbell, and Bonnie McCay. 2016. "The Ontological Politics of Marine Spatial Planning: Assembling the Ocean and Shaping the Capacities of 'Community' and 'Environment.'" *Geoforum* 75: 1–11.

Boucquey, Noëlle, Kevin St. Martin, Luke Fairbanks, Lisa M. Campbell, and Sarah Wise. 2019. "Ocean Data Portals: Performing a New Infrastructure for Oceans Governance." *Environment and Planning D: Society and Space* 37 (3): 484–503. https://doi.org/10.1177/0263775818822829.

Campbell, Lisa. M., Noella J. Gray, and Zoe A. Meletis. 2008. "Political Ecology Perspectives on Ecotourism to Parks and Protected Areas." In *Transforming Parks and Protected Areas*, ed. Kevin S. Hanna, Douglas A. Clark, and D. Scott Slocombe, 111–120. London: Routledge

Choi, Young Rae. 2017. "The Blue Economy as Governmentality and the Making of New Spatial Rationalities." *Dialogues in Human Geography* 7 (1): 37–41.

Douvere, Fanny, Frank Maes, A. Vanhulle, and Jan Schrijvers. 2007. "The Role of Marine Spatial Planning in Sea Use Management: The Belgian Case." *Marine Policy* 31 (2): 182–191.

Dubois, Mark, Maria Hadjimichael, and Jesper Raakjær. 2016. "The Rise of the Scientific Fisherman: Mobilising Knowledge and Negotiating User Rights in the Devon Inshore Brown Crab Fishery, UK." *Marine Policy* 65: 48–55.

Ehler, Charles. 2008. "Conclusions: Benefits, Lessons Learned, and Future Challenges of Marine Spatial Planning." *Marine Policy* 32 (5): 840–843.

Ehler, Charles, and Fanny Douvere. 2009. *Marine Spatial Planning: A Step-by-Step Approach toward Ecosystem-Based Management.* Intergovernmental Oceanographic Commission Manual and Guides No. 53, ICAM Dossier No. 6. Paris: UNESCO.

Fairbanks, Luke, Lisa M. Campbell, Noëlle Boucquey, and Kevin St. Martin. 2018. "Assembling Enclosure: Reading Marine Spatial Planning for Alternatives." *Annals of the American Association of Geographers* 108 (1): 144–161.

Flannery, Wesley, and Geraint Ellis. 2016. "Marine Spatial Planning: Cui Bono?" *Planning Theory & Practice* 17 (1): 122–128.

Flannery, Wesley, and Micheál Ó Cinnéide. 2012. "A Roadmap for Marine Spatial Planning: A Critical Examination of the European Commission's Guiding Principles Based on Their Application in the Clyde MSP Pilot Project." *Marine Policy* 36 (1): 265–271.

Flannery, Wesley, Geraint Ellis, Melissa Nursey-Bray, Jan P. M. van Tatenhove, Christina Kelly, Scott Coffen-Smouth, Rhona Fairgrieve, et al. 2016. "Exploring the Winners and Losers of Marine Environmental Governance/Marine Spatial Planning: *Cui Bono?*/'More than Fishy Business': Epistemology, Integration and Conflict in Marine Spatial Planning/Marine Spatial Planning: Power and Scaping/Surely Not All Planning Is Evil?/Marine Spatial Planning: A Canadian Perspective/Maritime Spatial Planning—'Ad Utilitatem Omnium'/Marine Spatial Planning: 'It Is Better to Be on the Train than Being Hit by It'/Reflections from the Perspective of Recreational Anglers and Boats for Hire/Maritime Spatial Planning and Marine Renewable Energy." *Planning Theory and Practice* 17 (1): 121–151.

Flannery, Wesley, Noel Healy, and Marcos Luna. 2018. "Exclusion and Non-participation in Marine Spatial Planning." *Marine Policy* 88: 32–40.

Fleming, D. M., and Peter J. S. Jones. 2012. "Challenges to Achieving Greater and Fairer Stake-holder Involvement in Marine Spatial Planning as Illustrated by the Lyme Bay Scallop Dredg-ing Closure." *Marine Policy* 36 (2): 370–377.

Flyvbjerg, Bent. 2014. "What You Should Know about Megaprojects and Why: An Overview." *Project Management Journal* 45 (2): 6–19.

Foley, Paul, and Charles Mather. 2018. "Ocean Grabbing, Terraqueous Territoriality and Social Development." *Territory, Politics, Governance* Early Online, https://doi.org/10.1080/21622671 .2018.1442245.

Frazão Santos, Catarina, Michael Orbach, Helena Calado, and Francisco Andrade. 2015. "Chal-lenges in Implementing Sustainable Marine Spatial Planning: The New Portuguese Legal Framework Case." *Marine Policy* 61: 196–206.

Gazzola, Paola, and Vincent Onyango. 2018. "Shared Values for the Marine Environment: Devel-oping a Culture of Practice for Marine Spatial Planning." *Journal of Environmental Policy & Planning* 20 (4): 468–481.

Gazzola, Paola, Maggie H. Roe, and Paul J. Cowie. 2015. "Marine Spatial Planning and Terrestrial Spatial Planning: Reflecting on New Agendas." *Environment and Planning C: Government and Policy* 33 (5): 1156–1172.

Gellert, Paul K., and Barbara D. Lynch. 2003. "Mega-Projects as Displacements." *International Social Science Journal* 55 (175): 15–25.

Gopnik, Morgan, Claire Fieseler, Laura Cantral, Kate McClellan, Linwood Pendleton, and Larry Crowder. 2012. "Coming to the Table: Early Stakeholder Engagement in Marine Spatial Plan-ning." *Marine Policy* 36 (5): 1139–1149.

Gunton, Thomas, and Chris Joseph. 2010. "Economic and Environmental Values in Marine Plan-ning: A Case Study of Canada's West Coast." *Environments* 37 (3): 111–127.

Halpern, Benjamin S., Karen L. McLeod, Andrew A. Rosenberg, and Larry B. Crowder. 2008. "Managing for Cumulative Impacts in Ecosystem-Based Management through Ocean Zoning." *Ocean & Coastal Management* 51 (3): 203–211.

Hannigan, John A. 1995. *Environmental Sociology: A Social Constructionist Perspective*. London: Routledge.

IOC (Intergovernmental Geographic Commission) and DG MARE (Directorate-General for Maritime Affairs and Fisheries). 2017. *2nd International Conference on Marine/Maritime Spatial Planning, 15–17 March 2017, Paris, France*. IOC Workshop Reports Series no. 279. Paris: UNESCO.

IOC-UNESCO. 2019. "Marine Spatial Planning Programme." http://msp.ioc-unesco.org.

Jay, Stephen A. 2010. "Marine Management and the Construction of Marine Spatial Planning." *Town Planning Review* 81 (2): 173–192.

Jay, Stephen A. 2012. "Marine Space: Manoeuvring towards a Relational Understanding." *Journal of Environmental Policy & Planning* 14 (1): 81–96.

Jay, Stephen A. 2018. "The Shifting Sea: From Soft Space to Lively Space." *Journal of Environmental Policy & Planning* 20 (4): 450–467.

Jay, Stephen A., and Hilde M. Toonen. 2015. "The Power of the Offshore (Super-) Grid in Ad-vancing Marine Regionalization." *Ocean & Coastal Management* 117: 32–42.

Jay, Stephen A., Geraint Ellis, and Sue Kidd. 2012. "Marine Spatial Planning: A New Frontier?" *Journal of Environmental Policy & Planning* 14 (1): 1–5.

Jay, Stephen A., Thomas Klenke, and Holger Janßen. 2016. "Consensus and Variance in the Eco-system Approach to Marine Spatial Planning: German Perspectives and Multi-actor Implica-tions." *Land Use Policy* 54: 129–138.

Jentoft, Svein. 2017. "Small-Scale Fisheries within Maritime Spatial Planning: Knowledge Integra-tion and Power." *Journal of Environmental Policy & Planning* 19 (3): 266–278.

Jentoft, Svein, and Maikke Knol. 2014. "Marine Spatial Planning: Risk or Opportunity for Fisheries in the North Sea?" *Maritime Studies* 13 (1): 1–16.

Johnsen, Jahn Petter, and Bjorn Hersoug. 2014. "Local Empowerment through the Creation of Coastal Space?" *Ecology and Society* 19 (2): https://doi.org/10.5751/ES-06465-190260.

Jones, Peter J. S., Louise M. Lieberknecht, and Wanfei Qiu. 2016. "Marine Spatial Planning in Real-ity: Introduction to Case Studies and Discussion of Findings." *Marine Policy* 71: 256–264.

Jongbloed, Ruud H., Jan T. van der Wal, and Han J. Lindeboom. 2014. "Identifying Space for Offshore Wind Energy in the North Sea. Consequences of Scenario Calculations for Interactions with Other Marine Uses." *Energy Policy* 68: 320–333.

Kerr, Sandy, John Colton, Kate Johnson, and Glen Wright. 2015. "Rights and Ownership in Sea Country: Implications of Marine Renewable Energy for Indigenous and Local Communities." *Marine Policy* 52: 108–115.

Kidd, Sue, and Geraint Ellis. 2012. "From the Land to Sea and Back Again? Using Terrestrial Planning to Understand the Process of Marine Spatial Planning." *Journal of Environmental Policy & Planning* 14 (1): 49–66.

Knol, Maikke. 2011. "Mapping Ocean Governance: From Ecological Values to Policy Instrumentation." *Journal of Environmental Planning and Management* 54 (7): 979–995.

Kyriazi, Zacharoula, Frank Maes, Marijn Rabaut, Magda Vincx, and Steven Degraer. 2013. "The Integration of Nature Conservation into the Marine Spatial Planning Process." *Marine Policy* 38: 133–139.

Lehrer, Ute, and Jennefer Laidley. 2008. "Old Mega-Projects Newly Packaged? Waterfront Redevelopment in Toronto." *International Journal of Urban and Regional Research* 32 (4): 786–803.

Lester, S. E., J. M. Stevens, R. R. Gentry, C. V. Kappel, T. W. Bell, C. J. Costello, S. D. Gaines, et al. 2018. "Marine Spatial Planning Makes Room for Offshore Aquaculture in Crowded Coastal Waters." *Nature Communications* 9 (1): 945.

Levine, Arielle S., and Christine L. Feinholz. 2015. "Participatory GIS to Inform Coral Reef Ecosystem Management: Mapping Human Coastal and Ocean Uses in Hawaii." *Applied Geography* 59: 60–69.

Massey, Doreen. 2005. *For Space*. London: Sage.

Merrie, Andrew, and Per Olsson. 2014. "An Innovation and Agency Perspective on the Emergence and Spread of Marine Spatial Planning." *Marine Policy* 44: 366–374.

McCreary, Scott, Phyllis Grifman, and Meredith Cowart. 2016. "Creating Stable Agreements in Marine Policy: Learning from the California South Coast Marine Life Protection Act Initiative." *Negotiation Journal* 32 (1): 23–48.

McGinnis, Michael V., and Meghan Collins. 2013. "A Race for Marine Space: Science, Values, and Aquaculture Planning in New Zealand." *Coastal Management* 41 (5): 401–419.

NOC (National Ocean Council). 2013. *National Ocean Policy Final Implementation Plan*. Washington, DC: NOC.

Nursey-Bray, Melissa. 2016. "'More than Fishy Business': Epistemology, Integration and Conflict in Marine Spatial Planning." *Planning Theory & Practice* 17 (1): 129–132.

Olson, Julia. 2010. "Seeding Nature, Ceding Culture: Redefining the Boundaries of the Marine Commons through Spatial Management and GIS." *Geoforum* 41 (2): 293–303.

Orueta, Fernando Diaz, and Susan S. Fainstein. 2008. "The New Mega-Projects: Genesis and Impacts." *International Journal of Urban and Regional Research* 32 (4): 759–767.

Peel, Deborah, and M. Greg Lloyd. 2004. "The Social Reconstruction of the Marine Environment: Towards Marine Spatial Planning?" *Town Planning Review* 75 (3): 359–378.

Pomeroy, Robert, and Fanny Douvere. 2008. "The Engagement of Stakeholders in the Marine Spatial Planning Process." *Marine Policy* 32 (5): 816–822.

Retzlaff, Rebecca, and Charlene LeBleu. 2018. "Marine Spatial Planning: Exploring the Role of Planning Practice and Research." *Journal of Planning Literature* 33 (4): 466–491.

Ritchie, Heather. 2014. "Understanding Emerging Discourses of Marine Spatial Planning in the UK." *Land Use Policy* 38: 666–675.

Roe, Emery M. 1991. "Development Narratives, or Making the Best of Blueprint Development." *World Development* 19 (4): 287–300.

Sanderson, Joe. 2012. "Risk, Uncertainty and Governance in Megaprojects: A Critical Discussion of Alternative Explanations." *International Journal of Project Management* 30 (4): 432–443.

Silver, Jennifer J., Noella J. Gray, Lisa M. Campbell, Luke W. Fairbanks, and Rebecca L. Gruby. 2015. "Blue Economy and Competing Discourses in International Oceans Governance." *The Journal of Environment & Development* 24 (2): 135–160.

Smith, Glen. 2015. "Creating the Spaces, Filling Them up. Marine Spatial Planning in the Pentland Firth and Orkney Waters." *Ocean & Coastal Management* 116: 132–142.

Smith, Glen, and Ruth E. Brennan. 2012. "Losing Our Way with Mapping: Thinking Critically about Marine Spatial Planning in Scotland." *Ocean & Coastal Management* 69: 210–216.

Smythe, Tiffany C. 2017. "Marine Spatial Planning as a Tool for Regional Ocean Governance? An Analysis of the New England Ocean Planning Network." *Ocean & Coastal Management* 135: 11–24.

St. Martin, Kevin, and Madeleine Hall-Arber. 2008. "The Missing Layer: Geo-Technologies, Communities, and Implications for Marine Spatial Planning." *Marine Policy* 32 (5): 779–786.

Steinberg, Philip, and Kimberley Peters. 2015. "Wet Ontologies, Fluid Spaces: Giving Depth to Volume through Oceanic Thinking." *Environment and Planning D: Society and Space* 33 (2): 247–264.

Tafon, Ralph V. 2018. "Taking Power to Sea: Towards a Post-Structuralist Discourse Theoretical Critique of Marine Spatial Planning." *Environment and Planning C: Politics and Space* 36 (2): 258–273.

Tafon, Ralph, David Howarth, and Steven Griggs. 2018. "The Politics of Estonia's Offshore Wind Energy Programme: Discourse, Power and Marine Spatial Planning." *Environment and Planning C: Politics and Space* 37 (1): 157–176.

Voyer, Michelle, Genevieve Quirk, Alistair McIlgorm, and Kamal Azmi. 2018. "Shades of Blue: What Do Competing Interpretations of the Blue Economy Mean for Oceans Governance?" *Journal of Environmental Policy & Planning* 20 (5): 595–616.

Winder, Gordon M., and Richard Le Heron. 2017. "Assembling a Blue Economy Moment? Geographic Engagement with Globalizing Biological-Economic Relations in Multi-Use Marine Environments." *Dialogues in Human Geography* 7 (1): 3–26.

Wray, Ian. 2014. "Mega Projects and Regional Revival: Comparing Proposals for Atlantic Gateway and High Speed Rail in Northern England." *Town Planning Review* 85 (6): 731–751.

Wright, Glen, Kristina M. Gjerde, David E. Johnson, Aria Finkelstein, Maria Adelaide Ferreira, Daniel C. Dunn, Mariamalia Rodriguez Chaves, and Anthony Grehan. 2019. "Marine Spatial Planning in Areas beyond National Jurisdiction." *Marine Policy*. Published online 12 February. https://doi.org/10.1016/j.marpol.2018.12.003.

CHAPTER 8

(Un)seen Seas
Technological Mediation, Oceanic Imaginaries, and Future Depths

Stephanie Ratté

Remote ways of seeing and imagining the oceans—through technologies like geographic information systems, robotics, and artificial intelligence—are aiding an expansion of human influence over vast oceanic spaces. This article investigates how oceans are becoming known remotely and digitally, reviewing the literature on the mobilization of technologies and methodologies aimed at translating immense marine spaces into functional, measurable, or geographically specific knowledge. These technologies are becoming one principal means through which we understand spaces that exist at scales that make them nearly unfathomable and in places that render them largely invisible. The application of such technological developments parallel international deliberations around the need for more comprehensive regulation of the exploration and exploitation of the high seas, spaces beyond the jurisdiction of any one nation.

In presenting this literature, I attempt to offer three interrelated points: First, I suggest that while the application of remote modes of envisioning the oceans significantly expands human reach, they simultaneously obscure the presence of the human figure specifically and that of life more generally. Second, I reflect on how the oceans are increasingly a place of future imaginings, a site in which visions of the wild encounter technological abstractions to conjure novel possibilities for laying claim to a new frontier. Finally, building on a tradition of critically examining the use of geographic technologies in producing particular expressions of spatial thinking, this article seeks to understand what "seeing" large oceanic spaces means for proponents of marine sustainability and extraction—who seemingly have embraced the promise of spatial and explorative technologies, despite diverging aspirations.

I hope to expose some of the threads that bring together a multitude of scholarly efforts—both academic and gray—drawn from literature in the social sciences, natural sciences, and engineering. Together, these works produce particular fields of vision through which people come to "see" and understand the oceans. I specifically emphasize "see" to draw attention to the assumptions made in the processes of envisioning, and imagining, through technological and digital mediation. What does it mean to think we can envision vast spaces that are otherwise remote and disconnected? What does "seeing" mean for spatial and scalar understandings of unseen places, and—for the oceans—places that are materially fluid? Where and how do we place ourselves when we are distanced from envisioned spaces? The ocean spaces pursued by technical and digital efforts appear "unimaginably enormous relative to human scale" (Rozwadowski 2010: 521). It is in part this enormity that generates new and valuable questions about how we imagine the "unimaginable."

Mediation and Translation: Technology in the Sea

Until quite recently, the sea was an "often forgotten portion of the planet" for scholars, which, when studied, was characterized by a strong orientation toward policy-relevant literature (Steinberg 1999: 368). The geographer Philip Steinberg notes that difficulty accessing deep-sea areas contributed to an emphasis by physical geographers on studying coastal waters (1999: 372). On mapping more specifically, Dawn Wright suggests geographers were, for much time, "largely absent from the push to map the final frontier of the planet: the oceans." This changed, in part, as increasing interest and sponsorship of globe-spanning research into "Earth systems" emerged (1999: 427), although many argue human geographers continue to "under-study" ocean spaces (Cardwell and Thornton 2015; Gibbs and Warren 2014; Hasty and Peters 2012).

As spatial technologies and techniques, including geographic information systems (GIS) and visual and acoustic remote sensing, have advanced, deep and distant sea spaces have become more accessible and the focus of greater scholarly and public attention (Steinberg 1999: 372). This growing attention to the oceans suggests why it is not uncommon now to hear scholars, advocates, and devotees of the oceans assert that Earth is poorly named. Rather, we should call this "Blue Marble" by the name of the majority material surfacing the planet: Ocean (Grevsmühl 2016; Helmreich 2009: 3). So frequently is this championed, or perhaps so self-evident it appears now that images of a suspended globe digitally proliferate and attest to the ocean's dominance on a planetary scale, that its purported provenance—the science fiction writer Arthur C. Clarke—is at times forgotten (Rozwadowski 2010: 520).

The sea's depths are now increasingly seen as a space for theoretical inspiration and creativity. Whether encompassed under "critical ocean studies" (DeLoughrey 2017), "oceanic studies" (Blum 2013), or the "blue humanities" (Gillis 2013), many of these efforts seek to bring about an appreciation for the three-dimensionality of the oceans, to urge the "oceanic turn" to go beyond a historical preoccupation with surface to examine human "encounters" with its "turbulent materiality" (DeLoughrey 2017; Steinberg 2013; Steinberg and Peters 2015: 248). Not simply the *site* of new inquiry, the oceans now figure as a "methodological model for nonlinear or nonplanar thought" (Blum 2013: 151). Steinberg emphasizes the oceans as a historical body and "a space of society," which has demanded greater attention from geographers over recent decades, contributing in part to the development of the subdiscipline of marine geography (1999: 367; 2001: 9). Steinberg employs "ocean-space" to signal its encompassing "the sea"—that is, the global oceans— and to denote "the fluidity between the study of landward and seaward domains, as both are socially and physically constructed through linked dynamics" (1999: 367–368). It is worth noting that the now self-evident terminology of oceanic demarcation, and the very notion of a globally connected ocean, has emerged over time. For instance, the modern geographical conceptualizing and naming of oceans as separate bodies of water is different from some sixteenth-century cartographic classifications, which saw parts of seas as "segments of water situated off an eponymous area of land" (Lewis 1999: 199; Rozwadowski 2018).

Sensory, aesthetic, and affective explorations of submergence are also appearing (e.g., Ingersoll 2016). The anthropologist Stefan Helmreich (2010), in investigating the soundscapes of the deep ocean, notes that scientists understand the oceans as intensely auditory places; they "no longer think the deep is a quiet, meditative space, a silent world" (2007: 625). Perhaps this is because we are also paying greater attention to the destructive impacts of human-generated sound—better described here as noise—on marine life. In 2018, representatives of the nineteenth meeting of the United Nations Open-ended Informal Consultative Process on Oceans and the Law of the Sea—established in 1999 to "facilitate the annual review . . . of developments in ocean affairs" (UNGA 2000)—gathered to pay special attention to the issue of "anthropogenic underwater noise."

The conceptual and theoretical relationship between the oceans and history is evolving, and vital for enriching emerging technological engagements with oceanic spaces. The historicization of the oceans—particularly seeing history in, rather than just on the seas—signaled a movement toward expanding scholarly encounters with the oceans (Dening 2012; Gillis 2013; Lewis 1999). The work of the historian Helen Rozwadowski has been an essential part of re-routing what she calls the "overall benign neglect of the sea" by historians (2010: 520). This article is much indebted to Rozwadowski's attention to ocean depths and technological mediation, which affords it a critical historical perspective and a necessary grounding in oceanic imaginings. It also seeks to extend and shift some of this thinking toward an examination of new forms of imagining the oceans, which echo in some ways the ideas and visions of earlier technologies while altering or diverging from them in others. Elizabeth DeLoughrey has suggested that, in the turn toward the sea, "the ocean became a space for theorizing the materiality of history, yet it rarely figured as a material in itself" (2017: 33). Hester Blum gives emphasis to the sea's materiality, suggesting that oceanic studies offers "capacious possibilities for new forms of relationality through attention to the sea's properties, conditions, and shaping or eroding forces" (2013: 152). Yet the foundational work of scholars in the oceanic turn and the emergent work of others in this latest marine moment notwithstanding—social science engagements with the oceans are still often, quite literally, surface level.

One reason for a close investigation of the scientific and engineering literature on oceanic explorative technology lies precisely in the comparative lack of social science engagement with submarine worlds, with submergence, and with "human-sea relationships" that extend beyond the coast (Cardwell 2015: 157). Some of this comes from the materiality of the oceans—anthropologists, in particular, face challenges to engaging in submerged "fieldwork" in deep and high seas (Helmreich 2009: 220). If we are to examine human involvement with deeper ocean spaces, work in the domain of the "hard" sciences represents some of the significant ways that human relationships with the sea are evolving.

Technology has mediated human understanding of the oceans since at least the mid-nineteenth century, when deep-sea "hydrographers" from the United States engaged in a variety of exploratory and metrological efforts leading to the creation of the first bathymetric chart, measuring the depth of the ocean floor (Rozwadowski 2001: 225).

Particularly for the deep sea, machines must mediate human understanding because its material qualities make it inaccessible (219). Stretching back further, William Hasty and Kimberley Peters consider the ship itself a mediating technology of oceanic exploration that for many centuries was "a means of extending the 'vision'" of the discipline of geography: "The history of the production of knowledge is one in which the figure of the ship looms large." Because of its "stability" as a material living space and its mobility as a vessel, it is both a "site of thought and accumulation of thought" (2012: 661–662). From the beginning, exploration of the deep oceans was profoundly intertwined with economic interests. Deep-sea soundings enabled the laying of the first submarine telegraph cables and revealed faster shipping routes. It was in part through these labors that scientists began to nurture the "human relationship with the deep sea" (Rozwadowski 2001: 218).

From this foundation, marine information today is becoming still more space-based as geospatial technologies come to feature prominently in approaches to managing marine resources. The application of these technologies aims, in part, to make the oceans visible (St. Martin and Hall-Arber 2008: 779). Their use also derives from a greater appreciation for the vulnerability of marine resources and places, a recognition that the ocean is not endlessly regenerative but requires nuanced approaches that are sensitive to spatial and ecological concerns. At the same time, the relationship of more recent marine, particularly deep-sea, exploration with the economic and political appeal of unfamiliar and "uncontrolled" places should not be ignored.

A final point about the scope of this analysis: data sets derived from different sources are often used in combination with each other, as integration allows for new insights and a certain degree of data triangulation. This is particularly true for GIS, where combining layers of different data is fundamental to its utility (St. Martin and Hall-Arber 2008: 780). I do not suggest scholars see digital and remote observation as the only means through which to understand the oceans. Rozwadowski perceived that sounding technology of the nineteenth century "was not just gear but rather a constantly shifting set of work practices and tools embedded in the social context of the mid-century maritime workplace" (2001: 232). Similarly, the purpose of this article is not to cover absolutely the different applications of remote and digital technologies but rather to draw out some of the ideas, values, and expectations—with an evident focus on those rooted in Euro-American contexts— that ocean spaces are made to embody, as scholars, explorers, and the public become drawn into these different digital and technoscientific practices.

Extending Human Reach through Nonhuman Means

The application of remote modes of envisioning the oceans continues to encourage the ever-expanding sphere of human influence over oceanic mega-spaces. This vastness is not limited to square area covered by water but, most crucially for the sea, is also found vertically, in that more neglected dimension: depth (Phillips 2018). Through an investigation of these mediating technologies and their histories, I seek to show how these are autonomous and obfuscatory technologies that offer a particular understanding of human presence, specifically, and life, more generally, in the sea. This understanding suggests humans can perform a digital and disembodied emplacement in the oceans.

This is not to imply there is nothing human in remote technologies or to deny the many researchers encountering a spectrum of marine conditions and challenges to be present in their study of the oceans. Undersea robots often require that their developers accompany them "to sea, sometimes working in rough weather or in the middle of icebound oceans" (Bellingham and Rajan 2007: 1099–1100). Here, we might locate the human in these technologies (albeit above the surface). Similarly, important counter-examples to views that reinforce the notion of an empty, open ocean exist. Laura Kracker (1999) suggests underwater remote sensing is important precisely for understanding the "biological distribution" of the oceans through spatial data, especially for fisheries. In this way, technology can fill what historically would appear as a void to the human perceiver. Satellite-based remote sensing, GIS, remotely operated vehicles, autonomous underwater vehicles (AUVs), robotics, and artificial intelligence are among the technologies that have been mediating human understanding of the oceans in recent years (Wynn et al. 2014). Connecting these approaches is a world of digital information that is now a primary mode through which people study large ocean spaces. The study of marine microbes, particularly as genetic data become a more significant focus of deep-sea investigations and interstate deliberations, likewise reflects this: "These days, the genre of information that concerns many marine biologists is digital, bioinformatic" (Helmreich 2009: 208).

Many of these technologies aim to expand spatial understandings. Maps have historically been a precursor to ownership: "a tool for recording and controlling space" and one that "colonizes space" (Fox 1998: 1; De Certeau 1984: 121). More recently, different mapping methodologies have emerged with the aim to deliver a wider variety of processes and purposes. Participatory mapping, for example, has long been concerned with involving indigenous or local community members in the documentation of land and sea ownership, resources, and activities, with the idea that it can make rights legitimate or help defend claims against governmental or private interests. As a means of integrating socio-spatial information with biophysical, some similarly see collaborative mapping and participatory GIS as having the potential to "empower" indigenous communities around the identification, demarcation, and systemization of information on oceanic and terrestrial territories, when local and indigenous participation might otherwise be overlooked (De Freitas and Tagliani 2009; Ferse et al. 2010; Levine and Feinholz 2015; McCall and Minang 2005; Thornton and Scheer 2012). The perceived legitimacy and effectiveness of mapping in cases that set formal tenure systems against the informal is suggestive of why spatial projections and understandings of the oceans are so valued: they are a tool of authority (Fox 1998: 2).

Mapping extends human and capital influence as spatial knowledge and commercial exploration frequently go hand in hand. As chart making grew more sophisticated, motivated by the needs of commercial interests, it in turn enabled the intensification of deep-sea activities (Rozwadowski 2001: 221). Deep-sea sounding allowed hydrographers to clear erroneous "shoals and rocks off charts," which "boosted commerce by opening new, often faster, and more direct routes previously dismissed as too dangerous" (223). Yet, while the growing use of ever more sophisticated technologies suggests a correspondingly enhanced understanding of marine places, Rozwadowski cautions against seeing a linear trajectory of increased insight into the oceans. Her work instead intends to "[complicate] that picture by pointing out that each new sounding device or method was designed to answer a particular set of questions about the seafloor" (242). Henri Lefebvre argued more generally that "representations of space . . . also play a part in social and political practice" ([1974] 1991: 41). In this way, we might consider what answers are being sought in the various applications of remote and digital technologies, and what partial views are emerging.

Entangled in the use of digital platforms for the collection and analysis of data is the material element of mediating technologies that involve direct oceanic encounters. Submersibles allow humans to visit the seafloor, but the financial cost of this access is high. Thus, the field of robotics has long promised, and realized, an extended reach that circumvents the limitations of human physiology, "allowing a much more pervasive presence in the ocean" (Bellingham and Rajan 2007: 1098). The scientific use of autonomous marine robots began in the 1960s and is now increasingly widespread (Brito et al. 2010; Wright

1999). In an analysis in 1999 of deep-sea geographic techniques, Wright (1999: 432) noted AUVs were still "largely developmental" but held great potential for mapping since they can move untethered from a larger vessel, unlike remotely operated vehicles which are limited in speed, mobility, and range because of their tethers (Eriksen et al. 2001; Wynn et al. 2014: 452). Soon after, by the early 2000s, an expanding array of actors, including military and oil and gas, were using AUVs and underwater robotics, and an increasing number of commercial companies were involved in their production (Bellingham and Rajan 2007: 1100; Yuh 2000).

Many scientists view technological "autonomy" as especially relevant to ocean exploration given the communication and physical challenges posed by the environment. This is where artificial intelligence has potential. Exploratory robots must be able to respond to random disturbances by "sens[ing] their surroundings and act[ing] to avoid problems or improve performance" (Bellingham and Rajan 2007: 1098). James Bellingham and Kanna Rajan also propose that autonomous operations reflect a "necessary convergence between the fields of autonomy, machine learning, and robotics to tackle real-world problems of scientific interest in detecting and tracking episodic events" (2007: 1099). In this, the authors reflect their conviction in the potential of technology more generally, and belief in robotics and artificial intelligence more specifically, for being able translators of the marine environment and, ultimately, for solving "real-world" challenges. Yet translations are particular interpretations of information. As Rozwadowski notes, for early explorative technologies, hydrographers' use of machines to understand the qualities of the seafloor meant their "conception of this environment did not, however, represent a clear translation from technology" (2001: 219).

How do autonomous machines get us "closer" to ocean spaces through mediated knowledge, through separation? What does it mean to mimic the sensation of being underwater, and what things are lost from the knowledge that emerges from that physical experience? The use of remote and mediating technologies suggests humans can encounter the oceans and still be absent from them. These technologies and methodologies allow people to "see" large oceanic spaces without being in them. Some efforts to make the oceans visible draw on water-associated acts, calling for users to "dive" into digitized marine information and "swim" to virtual ocean hotspots (Henderson 2017; NOAA 2017). Helmreich observes that "immersion as a kind of communion"—not simply being in an oceanic place but experiencing a connection with it—has historical roots in eighteenth-century romanticism, when immersing oneself suggested the potential for "achiev[ing] a sublime union with the sea" (2009: 219). One can imagine that new efforts to allow for digital immersion have shades of this, seeking not only a scientific or educational but also an aesthetic and transcendent experience.

Moreover, because we are only "seeing," our extended presence can be imagined as barely detectable. For example, subaqueous sounds, which humans require "technical and cultural translation" to hear, Helmreich notes, are already perceptible to marine animals. The translations we must employ to comprehend these sounds in turn affect the soundscapes themselves, "likely altered by such sounds as *Alvin's* transponder pitter-patter, to say nothing of the racket created by large-scale sonar surveys" (2007: 624–625). As a result, the soundscapes relied on by marine life are distorted by the mediated act of human auditory perception. When humans are digitally emplaced—present to perceive, but not to be perceived—this distortion is still less evident. Despite being a comparative aside for Helmreich (2007), this attention to the question of human presence in perceiving the acoustic elements of oceanic space is perhaps a meaningful precursor to Helmreich's consideration, elsewhere in his work, of the absence of marine life in Google Ocean's digital representation of the sea: "This is not the dark deep, but a clear fishbowl—though with no fish; sea life does not swim in this space. It is also difficult to grasp scale here;

understanding the size and location of the body one would have to inhabit to access these views is unclear" (2011: 1226). Here, this absence is of life generally. Yet it similarly suggests the perception of disembodied presence—that we can see without being present or noticeable and therefore without impacting the marine environment. It also recalls the notion of the ocean as empty and ready for human exploration and use.

Helmreich (2011) points to the confusion of scale when he observes the difficulty in envisioning the size of a human body in comparison to these vast spaces projected by Google Earth/Oceans. The sea often challenges scalar understandings because it is materially dynamic. What is "local" in a landscape can be marked, both physically and conceptually, through more permanent means than in the oceans. Legal scales and spatialities are complicated in the marine context because the ocean is a "fluid, motionful, space" on which lines of legal territories are harder to keep stable (Hasty and Peters 2012: 663). DeLoughrey suggests that, distinct from terrestrial spaces, "the perpetual circulation of ocean currents means that the sea dissolves phenomenological experience and diffracts the accumulation of narrative" (2017: 33). Oceans are sometimes seen as inherently connected, in "perpetual circulation," and therefore one space, existing at a scale that is difficult to comprehend, much less envision. The use of "the sea" as a singular term is indicative of this. This very scale—the oft-repeated statement that the oceans cover 70 percent of the earth's surface—is habitually employed to substantiate the importance of the ocean. David Lambert and colleagues write that, in the "imaginative geography of the oceans . . . perhaps the most pervasive vision, is of the sheer vastness of the sea" (2006: 483). This vastness may be part of the geographic imagination, but there is a materiality to the scale of oceanic mega-spaces that demands recognition yet is difficult to convey in a digital view.

There are important connections between digital methodologies that continue to portray large, empty spaces, and the well-established concern of scholars that legal regimes of ocean management are ignoring the "local" in the sea. Sea rights and ocean meanings have historically been overlooked with respect to indigenous, native, or local systems. Steinberg contends, "The sea plays an important role not only in modern political geography but also in the cultural geography of identity and representation," and "by turning their attention to the sea, cultural geographers can gain appreciation for the role of ocean-space in indigenous peoples' sense of place; these insights can then be used to design marine tenure systems that transcend the Western perspective of the ocean as 'empty'" (1999: 369, citing Jackson 1995).

It remains to be fully seen whether virtual oceans can help us move beyond notions of oceanic emptiness to allow for a greater inclusion of a diversity of epistemological and ontological approaches to the sea, yet current forms suggest some cautiousness is warranted. For example, the digitization of marine genetic information means interested companies "can bioprospect in databases, in the biomedia of cyberspace, in the uploaded ocean, leaving local places behind" (Helmreich 2009: 142). This obfuscation of context or geographic specificity stands in contrast to the aim of generating precise and geographically specific information within large, fluid spaces (e.g., bathymetric or GIS data). Anna Tsing argues the ability to "scale up" is now "a hallmark of modern knowledge." She defines this scalability as the ability to be relevant to increasing scales without requiring a fundamental change in approach or framework. It allows "project elements [to] be oblivious to the indeterminacies of encounter . . . banish[ing] meaningful diversity, that is, diversity that might change things" (2015: 38). The ability to zoom in and out, to pinpoint the local and jump to the global, might be a sought-after feature of the "uploaded ocean," but Tsing warns of what might be lost in making these scale jumps possible.

Frontier Futurisms: Imagining the Sea as a Site of Possibilities

Much legal and policy scholarship has explored the legacy of a "mare liberum" or "freedom of the seas" approach to marine governance (Ardron et al. 2008; Brown 1983; Grotius [1609] 2009; Orbach 2003), particularly as international deliberations continue around the conservation and sustainable use of the high seas—spaces that represent some the largest common resources (Merrie et al. 2014: 21). Comparatively under-plumbed is what ideas emerge as technological, and more specifically digital and Internet-based, methodologies aim to bring about a new understanding and use of ocean spaces. This is a task that may be especially well suited to historical and anthropological approaches. Rozwadowski suggests, "The humanities are uniquely positioned to grapple with an important characteristic of the ocean: it is a place known through imagination as well as through direct experience" (2012: 583; see also Cardwell and Thornton 2015: 162).

Ocean imaginaries are closely intertwined with frontier fictions. They are inheritors of a collection of historically rooted ideas that hinge on the sea as a place of abundance and wildness, oscillating between a narrative centered on oceanic bounty and a rhetoric of risk. In this conception, the high seas and deep oceans are resource-rich spaces, yet open for unfettered extraction: a "blue ocean of frontier promise" (Helmreich 2009: 125). Steinberg argues the perspective of scholarly work on the oceans is usually "that of the ocean as a space of resources. The ocean is perceived as akin to other resource-rich spaces, and its management is characterized by similar dilemmas" (2001: 11). From early on, the oceans were captured by commercial interests and reflected the imperial nature of exploration: "While nationalism often undergirded oceanic investigation, the more immediate motive for government funding usually related to the commercial importance of the sea" (Rozwadowski 2001: 221). In this era, the oceans were spaces of fishing, whaling, shipping, and later telegraphy.

In the 1960s, scholars, scientists, and others established the discursive links between the oceans and outer space, and through this, the depths of the sea became the counterpart to the loftiness of space (Rozwadowski 2012: 581), something that continues today in statements like the following: "the marine environment and the space environment provide a common motivation to endow robotic platforms with greater onboard autonomy" (Bellingham and Rajan 2007: 1098; Yuh 2000). The geographers Dawn Wright and Michael Goodchild supported their call for greater applications of GIS to marine spaces by noting that more information existed on the topography of Venus than that of Earth's ocean floor (1994: 523–524). Others have asserted, "we know less about Neptune's realm than we do about the planet Neptune" (Turner 2005:6, citing Blidberg et al. 1991). Lambert et al. echo this in contrasting knowledge of the moon's surface to the comparatively unfamiliar ocean floor—a lunar-oceanic association that brings to mind tidal forces (2006: 483–84). DeLoughrey (2014) also finds this relationship in the space shuttle *Endeavour*, named for the ship helmed by James Cook, a British naval captain most known for his cartographic expeditions in the Pacific and for marking the beginning of Western incursions into the worlds of the islands of Oceania. DeLoughrey contends these "vessels symbolize an empire's use of narratives of technological progress to expand toward the 'ends of the earth' in ways that naturalize dominance over the global commons such as the high seas and outer space" (2014: 258). Here, she points to an important point of connection that draws together researchers across marine and outer spaces: the status of these as legal "commons" through state and planetary extraterritoriality. As commons, these spaces purportedly belong to all and, at the same time, are distanced from what is considered internal or national territory. The anthropologists Valerie Olson and Lisa Messeri (2015: 39) also see Helmreich's (2009) use of "alien" in his study of the marine microbial world as an "epistemological heuristic, connecting Earth's deep sea with the potential watery mysteries of Jupiter's moon, Europa." The 2018 discovery of an underground, liquid water lake on Mars by the Italian Space Agency surely underscores the association of water as the foundation for life and of the "ocean as origin" (Lambert et al. 2006: 484).

This comparison suggests some equivalence between seafloor surveys and outer space exploration—something that of course fails to reflect the reality of geography and scale. Rozwadowski suggests that when, in the postwar mid-twentieth century, the oceans came to be seen through the lens of the frontier, outer space also took up this "powerful metaphor" (2012: 579). She tracks the elaboration of the sea as a frontier space through this postwar period, where the promise of the seafloor as a place for fish cultivation, extractive industries, and human habitation inspired new imaginings about technology-enabled submarine futures that would follow a supposedly inevitable, ever-upward trajectory from hunting to farming to industry (580, 591). Rozwadowski also links this rhetoric with past notions surrounding the American West, locating traces of the "western frontier" in ideas about whale ranching, wealth creation, and the potential of the "spiritual sustenance" of the oceans (580–581).

That people should see the oceans a site of possibility, where inscrutability and mystery allow for a range of future imaginings, also has roots in a prior moment of the industrial West: "Pristine nature, now in short supply in industrialized heartlands, found refuge in the oceans, while the mystery once associated with terra incognita relocated to the deeps," and "people began to come back to the sea in search for a quality they felt to be missing in the new industrial environment, that something called wilderness" (Gillis 2013). Andrew Merrie and colleagues highlight the positioning of the high seas as the "last frontier of exploitation" and "a figurative final 'Wild West'" (2014: 19). Here, oceanic "gold-rush dynamics" targeted at resources such as deep-sea fisheries, mining, and marine genetic resources are likely to threaten deep sea and open ocean ecosystems before science and regulatory caution can "react" in time to impose limits (26). Ideas about the "wildness" and perils of the sea undergird the oceanic frontier. A rhetoric of risk is noticeable in recent work about the application of robots to the oceans and figures as powerful validation for it. Robotic platforms are able to "survive" the dangers of the deep or high seas, these "distant," "hostile," and "hazardous" places that people are compelled to pursue (Bellingham and Rajan 2007: 1098; Brito et al. 2010: 1771; Orbach 2003: 21; Yuh 2000: 7).

What is remarkable about oceanic "frontiers" is their near endless ability to shift and replace (West 2016). In her history of mid-nineteenth-century deep-sea explorations, Rozwadowski notes some of the first versions of deep-sea sampling techniques, designed only to grab material for the sake of assessing the suitability of the seafloor for telegraphic cables, were ultimately improved upon by biologists and zoologists more interested in recovering seafloor organisms: "They considered the sea not as territory which had been conquered through hydrography and telegraphy, but as a new frontier opening for exploration" (2001: 243). No longer unknown for the purposes of navigation and communication, the frontier shifted to zoological concerns. In a similar, if more microscopic, way, Helmreich finds that recent discussions of the plight of the oceans are still often balanced by excitement for the "unexplored biotic variety—a biodiversity that might contain resources for sustaining the planet and its resident humans" (2009: 9). In this view, the current oceanic frontier rests with the marine genetic diversity of deep places. Contrary to Rozwadowski's suggestion that the spiritual and cultural possibilities of a limitless outer space eventually meant it surpassed the comparatively finite oceans as the ultimately "better" frontier, contemporary explorative technologies draw on ideas of wild encounter, possibility, and futurity that reflect the enduring power of the oceanic frontier (2012: 596).

There is an obvious material contradiction to the frontier imaginary. Ocean spaces already contain the material evidence of technology and extraction, and they are the "medium for movement" of much of the material—the goods that people produce, transport, and consume by way of transoceanic shipping—that makes up contemporary life (West 2016: 42–43). For example, the cables that enable almost all "transoceanic digital communication" lie under the sea (Starosielski 2015). These submarine fiber optic cables, following in the footsteps of telegraphy and telephony since the 1980s, are responsible for sending vast amounts of data around the world and are expected to increase as global demand for Internet bandwidth continues to mushroom (Coffen-Smout and Herbert 2000: 442; Merrie et al. 2014: 24). In 2009, the oceans contained more than a million kilometers of fiber optic cables, which have displaced satellites as the primary instrument of international telecommunications (Carter et al. 2009: 16; Coffen-Smout and Herbert 2000: 441). Yet Nicole Starosielski (2015) argues this vast infrastructure of undersea cables is largely "invisible," following Susan Leigh Star (1999), to those who use it.

The oceanic aspect of the Internet draws attention to the physical infrastructure of these digital perspectives. Web-based communication and information may connect increasing numbers of people in disparate places, across oceans and around the planet, but physical cables connect us as well. Increased fluidity is reliant on these "extensive systems of immobility" (Sheller and Urry 2006). Decisions about the physical infrastructure of the Internet can also be political, historically situated, and contentious. "Route selection" must take into account marine geopolitical boundaries, since permitting and maintenance processes may prove trickier in some contexts than others and because submarine fiber optic cables must "eventually come ashore" (Carter et al. 2009: 8, 21). Starosielski (2015), whose work on undersea cables highlights the "contentious spatial politics" of this submarine network and "the physicality of the virtual," finds that, in Hawai'i, some saw the cables and their landings as "part of a colonial legacy." The oceans are the literal foundation for a great deal of the Internet, which suggests a strangeness to the effort to "see" the oceans through sea-based, Internet-enabled digital data. The sea enables the movement of the Internet, while the Internet turns to the sea as an object of its vision. The digital age draws our eyes to "the cloud," but this suggests we might also look down into the sea (Peterson 2015; Starosielski 2015).

Why, then, do the oceans continue to be seen as a "frontier" space? It derives in part from the perceived lack of detectable human presence in the oceans and the opaque materiality of water, which means human impacts remain somewhat invisible. These qualities provoke the use of the oceans as a "blank slate" suitable for experimentation and invite people to envision futures in and on the oceans, drawing additionally from the idea that, in the depths of the ocean, there is a "unique world" waiting for scientists (Kracker 1999: 441). This frontier-futurist thinking is also made possible by technology. It is not just that the sea invites visions of the future: it is a particular (better), technology-enabled oceanic future. Bellingham and Rajan, for example, propose, "Vehicles that seem like science fiction, capable of simple self-repair and dealing with the complexities of the hazardous environment around them, may well provide a more permanent and pervasive presence in the distant reaches of our planet's oceans as well as in the solar system in the coming decades" (2007: 1102). The authors collapse the space between science and science fiction, invoking a future time in which humans are more "permanently" situated in both outer and marine space frontiers.

Peter Neill (2017a) of the World Ocean Observatory asks, "How do we transform the ocean into the ultimate operating system for the successful, sustainable future of our ocean planet?" He suggests "the role of digital platforms and algorithmic utility will expand exponentially" for the oceans in the future. In another piece, Neill (2017b) reviews recent work published in conjunction with the World Ocean Observatory, in which the authors "address the best examples of revolutionary tools and financial models that could unleash vast new opportunities to sustain the ocean as nurturer and protector of human survival in the 21st century." The discursive positioning of the ocean-as-salvation is present in such statements, where the ocean is the "nurturer and protector" of humanity. Finally, in a piece for the World Economic Forum, Nishan Degnarain of the National Ocean Council of Mauritius and the marine scientist Douglas McCauley (2016) report on a variety of technological developments that represent a convergence of life and nonlife: "The field of ocean robotics has begun borrowing blue prints from the world's best engineering firm: Mother Nature. Robo-tuna cruise the ocean on surveillance missions; sea snake-inspired marine robots inspect pipes on offshore oil rigs; 1,400 pound robotic crabs collect new data on the seafloor; and robo-jellyfish are under development to carry out environmental monitoring." Other biomimetic efforts include creating robots with more autonomy through emulating the compensatory behaviors of animals when injured—that is, to parallel the innate trial-and-error actions that allow animals to adapt to new conditions (Cully et al. 2015). In these instances, nature is an "engineering firm" from which inspiration for futuristic marine tools can be drawn, to better serve human needs. Importantly, though, Degnarain and McCauley (2016) include a note of caution, suggesting titularly that these and similar technologies might "make (or break)" the oceans.

The Promise of Observation and Exploration

Frontier ideas about the oceans that derive implicitly from the history of the American West reflect an assumption that these spaces should be similarly a source for the accumulation of capital (Rozwadowski 2012; West 2016). This assumption becomes especially important when we consider what exploration of the oceans promises. This final section discusses the discursive representations of the promise that remote and digital marine technologies hold for sustainability-oriented and environmentally minded scientific objectives on the one hand and extractive purposes on the other. Drawing from social science literature, this section engages in a critical examination of what observation and exploration might mean for how we understand large ocean spaces—particularly when they are purported to hold the potential for divergent ends.

The emphasis on the visual is detectable in many forms, for example, in "the creation of ocean observing systems composed of diverse assemblies of underwater robots" (Bellingham and Rajan 2007: 1101). Some suggest the oceans have been some of the "least-well-observed portions of the planet," thus demonstrating the importance of the continued push to see these spaces (1098). The bathymetric action, to sound, also comes to us not through sound as noise but rather through the geographical sound—a body of water. Likewise, "sonar" may evoke sound, yet it is fundamentally visual, as Helmreich (2007) also notes: its ultimate purpose to create a graphic representation of space. Additionally, Helmreich suggests the "three-dimensional soundscape" in which one is embedded when traveling to the seafloor in a submersible is empirically different from the "largely visual experience" produced when employing a remotely operated vehicle (2009: 219). Given the overwhelming focus on using remote and autonomous vehicles, engagement with the oceans will likely continue to favor visual over other sensory experiences, particularly as DeLoughrey claims, "Because extraterritorial spaces cannot be fully inhabited, we rely on their visual, specifically photographic representations by satellite and other vessels" (2014: 260). This is tied to the staying power of the notion of "exploration" as it relates to the sea—an assumption that such visual voyaging can illuminate new insights into the oceans and allow for ever greater access to its depths. A 2019 exhibition by the American Museum of Natural History entitled *Unseen Oceans* takes up these potent visual narratives: "A marvelous, alien world lies hidden beneath the sunlit surface. With the use of twenty-first-century technologies like robotics, satellite monitoring, and more, scientists are revealing the unseen habitats of the oceans' most mysterious animals and mapping remote, inhospitable areas in unprecedented detail" (AMNH 2019).

What does it mean to "see" a hidden world through these technologies? Much of the literature seeking to explicate the application of autonomous or semiautonomous digital technologies for the oceans focuses primarily on observation and exploration, as if any logical step from observation to action can remain unstated, or as if the moves within that logic can remain unexamined. Underwater mapping with AUVs can aid in collecting data on physical, chemical, and biological changes in the marine environment (Hernández et al. 2016). They have the potential to help advance science around some of "the great challenges facing scientists and policy makers involved in coastal ocean management, defining marine protected areas, and regulating sustainable fisheries" (Ryan et al. 2010: 394). The sea's role in regulating the climate also offers greater "imperatives for marine robots" (Bellingham and Rajan 2007: 1098; Brito et al. 2010). Ocean observation and exploration comprise diverging aspirations that are occasionally articulated not just as different possible objectives but also alongside each other. These statements, which are seemingly simple and self-evident assertions to the significance of this work, deserve attention precisely because they appear as such. We see this in assertions about the ways in which remote and autonomous explorative technologies "can help us better understand marine and other environmental issues, protect the ocean resources of the earth from pollution, and efficiently utilize them for human welfare" (Yuh 2000: 7; Yuh and West 2001), as well in statements about their increasing "applications in the defence, industry and policy sectors, such as geohazard assessment associated with oil and gas infrastructure" and as "a potentially attractive proposition to organisations responsible for large-scale and cost-effective marine data collection programmes" (Wynn et al. 2014: 451).

If to see is to make real, it suggests an underlying belief that digital visualization can make ocean spaces real in a way that other mediating practices cannot, with observation as a kind of conduit to truth. This has the potential, then, to summon long-standing concerns about assumptions of the ascendancy of the "penetrating human gaze" or the "facticity of first-hand experience" (Comaroff and Comaroff 1992: 8). Such a view also suggests a particular understanding of the role of science generally: "Science generates knowledge generates care generates stewardship in a feedback loop that tunes the social order into the holistic complexity revealed by science" (Helmreich 2009: 240). Sebastian Vincent Grevsmühl (2016: 3) suggests there are two interlinked functions of the visual for science: images and icons of the global environment are always both "objects and instruments of knowledge and imagination." In other words, they are both produced by knowledge and "participate actively in the construction" of ideas.

Technologies that have enabled an expansion of knowledge about the oceanic world—for example, to understand fish stocks—have also allowed for the greater exploitation of marine resources (Kracker 1999: 441). Donna Haraway (1988: 582) has said such technological mediations belong to an "ideology of direct, devouring, generative, and unrestricted vision." Additionally, efforts to alter the oceans, such as using iron fertilization to enrich the sea with nutrients, "[fall] within what Gísli Pálsson calls the 'regime of the aquarium,' the treatment of the sea as a manageable, measurable space" (Helmreich 2009: 133). Many biologists are justifiably skeptical of this type of tampering. Yet, is the goal of "seeing" to create a fully transparent ocean—an aquarium to measure and manage? Such narratives suggest caution in embracing the pure promise of digital data and remote technologies. Haraway, writing presciently three decades ago, warned that (post)modern "instruments of visualization" have intensified the sense of "disembodiment" in seeing. By this "endless enhancement" of human vision, Haraway was particularly affected, cautioning, "[v]ision in this technological feast becomes unregulated gluttony" (1988: 581). The work that has been done to challenge the notion of space as self-evident (Lefebvre [1974]

1991) and to explore visual spaces as "contingent, historically situated spaces, profoundly marked by the material, socio-cultural, political and institutional settings from which they emerge" (Grevsmühl 2016: 6)—evoking Haraway's (1988) "situated knowledges"— suggests observation should not be so easily accepted as teleological but rather be seen as a critical part of the process of imagining the oceans.

Conclusion

The application of remote technologies follows in the legacy of older explorations of seaspace, where the images we create of the oceans reflect not only increasing technical sophistication but also an unstable assemblage of human needs and values. They are not simply the product of observation. Efforts to see oceanic mega-spaces through remote and digital technologies tend to present a specific understanding of the sea, where life, futures, and potential can be imagined in particular ways. Acknowledgment of the material aspects of seas—the materiality of scale of ocean spaces, of nonhuman life, of the physical infrastructure of digital systems through which we seek to envision and understand oceanic spaces—is a productive reminder to consider the many different and complicated things that "fill up" a historically "empty" and vast ocean.

This article has sought to uncover some key issues and questions that emerge through the application of remote and digital modes of envisioning and imagining the oceans. While these modes extend the reach of humans over vast oceanic spaces, it is the specific understanding of this reach—a type of disembodied presence—that raises questions about how notions of oceanic emptiness and openness remain salient even within the use of novel technologies and methodologies. Moreover, the frontier imaginary, sustained by ideas of extraterritoriality and wildness, continues to shape our visions of the sea, as well as our aspirations to envision it. Finally, this emphasis on observation through mediating technologies is bound up in wider assumptions of what "seeing" means and allows. That the visual makes available particular oceanic worlds to ever more people is a notion worthy of examination. Moreover, it cannot be understood as relating to the purpose of "seeing" alone. Advancing traffic within submarine spaces will allow certain trajectories of extraction, conservation, and governance. These trajectories relate to very real material opportunities and challenges that are sometimes blurred in narratives of seeing and exploring, in which their objectives are either unstated or uncontested. For an increasingly dominant mode of mediation, recalling "the embodied nature of all vision" can aid in the work of recognizing how these technologies seem to "signify a leap out of the marked body and into a conquering gaze from nowhere" (Haraway 1988: 581). I have suggested remote and autonomous applications of observing and imagining the sea bypass the need for human presence and allow a particular extended reach over vast and deep oceanic spaces. I have also proposed these ways of seeing oceanic vastness are entangled in future imaginings, visions of the wild, and the perilous possibilities of a frontier. Both have the potential to occlude prior and present indigenous and other modes of envisioning the oceans and create different conditions of possibility for their futures (Diaz 2011; Diaz and Kauanui 2001; Hau'ofa 1994, 1998; Ingersoll 2016; Kauanui 2015). What space will different forms of knowledge have for places that exist in scales and depths that are largely beyond, at least for now, the potential for human encounter?

Steinberg diagnoses an "undertheoriz[ing]" of the sea within ocean region studies influenced by political economy, and an "overtheoriz[ing]" of the sea by those that lean toward poststructuralist critical theory (2013: 158). I end with this because there is a way in which the dream of wild encounter with and within the sea is reflected in emergent social science and humanist moves toward it. In this, there may be no less risk of fetishizing oceanic spaces and liquid engagements than there is in the efforts to lay claim to the deep for scientific and, even potentially, resource-oriented purposes. That is to say, social scientists can be susceptible to the thrill of the frontier—scholarly or otherwise—and, in recognizing this, may be better positioned to engage in critical and constructive reflection on oceanic scholarship that goes beyond attention to its function as mere theoretical metaphor.

◼ ACKNOWLEDGEMENTS

Sincere thanks to the journal editors and anonymous reviewers for their thoughtful and helpful comments for improving this article. I am also grateful to Paige West for her insightful review and to the Yale Fox International Fellowship program for their support of this work.

◼ **STEPHANIE RATTÉ** is a PhD student in the Department of Anthropology at Columbia University. Her research interests include the entanglement of climate change, oceanscapes, and placemaking in the Pacific, the politics of space and scale, and the temporal dimensions and uncertainties of climate change futures.
Email: stephanie.ratte@columbia.edu

◼ REFERENCES

American Museum of Natural History (AMNH). 2019. "Unseen Oceans." 12 March 2018–18 August 2019. https://www.amnh.org/exhibitions/unseen-oceans.

Ardron, Jeff, Kristina Gjerde, Sian Pullen, and Virginie Tilot. 2008. "Marine Spatial Planning in the High Seas." *Marine Policy* 32 (5): 832–839.

Bellingham, James, and Kanna Rajan. 2007. "Robotics in Remote and Hostile Environments." *Science* 318 (5853): 1098–1102.

Blidberg, D. Richard, Roy M. Turner, and Steven G. Chappell. 1991. "Autonomous Underwater Vehicles: Current Activities and Research Opportunities." *Robotics and Autonomous Systems* 7 (2–3): 139–150.

Blum, Hester. 2013. "Introduction: Oceanic Studies." *Atlantic Studies* 10 (2): 151–155.

Brito, Mario Paulo, Gwyn Griffiths, and Peter Challenor. 2010. "Risk Analysis for Autonomous Underwater Vehicle Operations in Extreme Environments." *Risk Analysis* 30 (12): 1771–1788.

Brown, E. D. 1983. "Freedom of the High Seas Versus the Common Heritage of Mankind: Fundamental Principles in Conflict." *San Diego Law Review* 20 (3): 521–560.

Comaroff, John, and Jean Comaroff. 1992. *Ethnography and the Historical Imagination.* Boulder, CO: Westview Press.

Cardwell, Emma, and Thomas F. Thornton. 2015. "The Fisherly Imagination: The Promise of Geographical Approaches to Marine Management." *Geoforum* 64: 157–167.

Carter, Lionel, Douglas Burnett, Stephen Drew, Graham Marle, Lonnie Hagadorn, Deborah Bartlett-McNeil, and Nigel Irvine. 2009. "Submarine Cables and the Oceans: Connecting the World." UNEP-WCMC Biodiversity Series no. 31.

Coffen-Smout, Scott, and Glen J. Herbert. 2000. "Submarine Cables: A Challenge for Ocean Management." *Marine Policy* 24 (6): 441–448.

Cully, Antoine, Jeff Clune, Danesh Tarapore, and Jean-Baptiste Mouret. 2015. "Robots That Can Adapt Like Animals." *Nature* 521 (7553): 503–507.

De Certeau, Michel. 1984. *The Practice of Everyday Life.* Berkeley: University of California Press.

De Freitas, Débora M., and Paulo Roberto A. Tagliani. 2009. "The Use of GIS for the Integration of Traditional and Scientific Knowledge in Supporting Artisanal Fisheries Management in Southern Brazil." *Journal of Environmental Management* 90 (6): 2071–2080.

Degnarain, Nishan, and Douglas McCauley. 2016. "12 Robots That Could Make (or Break) the Oceans." World Economic Forum, 16 September. https://www.weforum.org/agenda/2016/09/12-cutting-edge-technologies-that-could-save-our-oceans.

DeLoughrey, Elizabeth. 2014. "Satellite Planetarity and the Ends of the Earth." *Public Culture* 26 (2): 257–280.

DeLoughrey, Elizabeth. 2017. "Submarine Futures of the Anthropocene." *Comparative Literature* 69 (1): 32–44.

Dening, Greg. 2012. "Deep Times, Deep Spaces: Civilizing the Sea." In *Sea Changes: Historicizing the Ocean*, ed. Bernhard Klein and Gesa Mackenthum, 13–35. London: Taylor & Francis.

Diaz, Vicente M. 2011. "Voyaging for Anti-Colonial Recovery: Austronesian Seafaring, Archipelagic Rethinking, and the Re-mapping of Indigeneity." *Pacific Asia Inquiry* 2 (1): 21–32.

Diaz, Vicente M., and J. Kēhaulani Kauanui. 2001. "Native Pacific Cultural Studies on the Edge." *Contemporary Pacific* 13 (2): 315–342.

Eriksen, Charles C., T. James Osse, Russell D. Light, Timothy Wen, Thomas W. Lehman, Peter L. Sabin, John W. Ballard, and Andrew M. Chiodi. 2001. "Seaglider: A Long-Range Autonomous Underwater Vehicle for Oceanographic Research." *IEEE Journal of Oceanic Engineering* 26 (4): 424–436.

Ferse, Sebastian C.A., María Máñez Costa, Kathleen Schwerdtner Máñez, Dedi S. Adhuri, and Marion Glaser. 2010. "Allies, Not Aliens: Increasing the Role of Local Communities in Marine Protected Area Implementation." *Environmental Conservation* 37 (1): 23–34.

Fox, Jeff. 1998. "Mapping the Commons: The Social Context of Spatial Information Technologies." *Common Property Resource Digest* 45: 1–4.

Gibbs, Leah Maree and Andrew Warren. 2014. "Killing Sharks: Cultures and Politics of Encounter and the Sea." *Australian Geographer* 45 (2): 101–107.

Gillis, John R. 2013. "The Blue Humanities: In Studying the Sea, We Are Returning to Our Beginnings." *Humanities* 34 (3). https://www.neh.gov/humanities/2013/mayjune/feature/the-blue-humanities.

Grevsmühl, Sebastian Vincent. 2016. "Images, Imagination and the Global Environment: Towards an Interdisciplinary Research Agenda on Global Environmental Images." *Geo: Geography and Environment* 3 (2): 1–14.

Grotius, Hugo. (1609) 2009. *Hugo Grotius Mare Liberum 1609–2009*. Ed. Robert Feenstra. Leiden: Brill.

Haraway, Donna. 1988. "Situated Knowledges: The Science Question in Feminism and the Privilege of a Partial Perspective." *Feminist Studies* 14 (3): 575–599.

Hasty, William, and Kimberley Peters. 2012. "The Ship in Geography and the Geographies of Ships." *Geography Compass* 6 (11): 660–676.

Hau'ofa, Epeli. 1994. "Our Sea of Islands." *Contemporary Pacific* 6 (1): 147–161.

Hau'ofa, Epeli. 1998. "The Ocean in Us." *Contemporary Pacific* 10 (2): 392–410.

Henderson, Emily. 2017. "Dive into World Oceans Day with Google Earth and Maps." *The Keyword*, 8 June. https://blog.google/products/earth/dive-into-world-oceans-day-google-earth-and-maps.

Helmreich, Stefan. 2007. "An anthropologist underwater: Immersive soundscapes, submarine cyborgs, and transductive ethnography." *American Ethnologist* 34 (4): 621–641.

Helmreich, Stefan. 2009. *Alien Ocean: Anthropological Voyages in Microbial Seas*. Berkeley: University of California Press.

Helmreich, Stefan. 2010. "Listening against Soundscapes." *Anthropology News*, 10 December.

Helmreich, Stefan. 2011. "From Spaceship Earth to Google Ocean: Planetary Icons, Indexes, and Infrastructures." *Social Research* 78 (4): 1211–1242.

Hernández, Juan David, Klemen Istenič, Nuno Gracias, Narcís Palomeras, Ricard Campos, Eduard Vidal, Rafael García and Marc Carreras. 2016. "Autonomous Underwater Navigation and Optical Mapping in Unknown Natural Environments." *Sensors* 16 (1174): 1–27.

Ingersoll, Karin Amimoto. 2016. *Waves of Knowing: A Seascape Epistemology*. Durham, NC: Duke University Press.

Jackson, S. E. 1995. "The Water Is Not Empty: Cross-Cultural Issues in Conceptualising Sea Space." *Australian Geographer* 26 (1): 87–96.

Kauanui, J. Kēhaulani. 2015. "Imperial Ocean: The Pacific as a Critical Site for American Studies." *American Quarterly* 67 (3): 625–636.

Kracker, Laura M. 1999. "The Geography of Fish: The Use of Remote Sensing and Spatial Analysis Tools in Fisheries Research." *Professional Geographer* 51 (3): 440–450.

Lambert, David, Luciana Martins, and Miles Ogborn. 2006. "Currents, Visions and Voyages: Historical Geographies of the Sea." *Journal of Historical Geography* 32 (3): 479–493.

Lefebvre, Henri. (1974) 1991. *The Production of Space*. Trans. Donald Nicholson-Smith. Oxford: Blackwell.

Levine, Arielle Sarah, and Christine Loftus Feinholz. 2015. "Participatory GIS to Inform Coral Reef Ecosystem Management: Mapping Human Coastal and Ocean Uses in Hawaii." *Applied Geography* 59: 60–69.

Lewis, Martin W. 1999. "Dividing the Ocean Sea." *Geographical Review* 89 (2): 188–214.

McCall, Michael K., and Peter A. Minang. 2005. "Assessing Participatory GIS for Community-Based Natural Resource Management: Claiming Community Forests in Cameroon." *Geographical Journal* 171 (4): 340–356.

Merrie, Andrew, Daniel C. Dunn, Marc Metian, Andrew M. Boustany, Yoshinobu Takei, Alex Oude Elferink, Yoshitaka Ota, et al. 2014. "An Ocean of Surprises: Trends in Human Use, Unexpected Dynamics and Governance Challenges in Areas beyond National Jurisdiction." *Global Environmental Change* 27: 19–31.

Neill, Peter. 2017a. "Artificial Intelligence and the Ocean." *Medium*, 29 November.

Neill, Peter. 2017b. "Soul of the Sea In the Age of the Algorithm: How Tech Startups Can Heal Our Oceans." *Medium*, 29 November.

NOAA (National Oceanic and Atmospheric Administration). 2017. "Take a Dive: Ocean in Google Earth." 6 July. https://oceanservice.noaa.gov/news/weeklynews/feb09/googleocean.html.

Olson, Valerie, and Lisa Messeri. 2015. "Beyond the Anthropocene: Un-earthing and Epoch." *Environment and Society: Advances in Research* 6: 28–47.

Orbach, Michael. 2003. "Beyond the Freedom of the Seas: Ocean Policy for the Third Millennium." *Oceanography* 16 (1): 20–29.

Peterson, Andrea. 2015. "Everything You Need to Know about the Undersea Cables That Power Your Internet—and Why They're at Risk of Breaking." *The Independent* 27 October. https://www.independent.co.uk/life-style/gadgets-and-tech/everything-you-need-to-know-about-the-undersea-cables-that-power-your-internet-and-why-theyre-at-a6710581.html.

Phillips, Jon. 2018. "Order and the Offshore: The Territories of Deep-Water Oil Production." In *Territory Beyond Terra*, ed. Kimberley Peters, Philip Steinberg, and Elaine Stratford, 51–67. London: Rowman & Littlefield.

Rozwadowski, Helen M. 2001. "Technology and Ocean-scape: Defining the Deep Sea in Mid-nineteenth Century." *History and Technology* 17 (3): 217–247.

Rozwadowski, Helen M. 2010. "Ocean's Depths." *Environmental History* 15 (3): 520–525.

Rozwadowski, Helen M. 2012. "Arthur C. Clarke and the Limitations of the Ocean as a Frontier." *Environmental History* 17 (3): 578–602.

Rozwadowski, Helen M. 2018. *Vast Expanses: A History of the Oceans*. London: Reaktion Books.

Ryan, J. P., S. B. Johnson, A. Sherman, K. Rajan, F. Py, H. Thomas, J. B. J. Harvey, et al. 2010. "Mobile Autonomous Process Sampling within Coastal Ocean Observing Systems." *Liminology and Oceanography: Methods* 8 (8): 394–402.

Sheller, Mimi, and John Urry. 2006. "The New Mobilities Paradigm." *Environment and Planning A* 38 (2): 207–226.

Star, Susan Leigh. 1999. "The Ethnography of Infrastructure." *American Behavioral Scientist* 43 (3): 377–391.

Starosielski, Nicole. 2015. *The Undersea Network*. Durham, NC: Duke University Press.

Steinberg, Philip E. 1999. "Navigating to Multiple Horizons: Toward a Geography of Ocean-Space." *Professional Geographer* 51 (3): 366–375.

Steinberg, Philip E. 2001. *The Social Construction of the Ocean*. Cambridge: Cambridge University Press.

Steinberg, Philip E. 2013. "Of Other Seas: Metaphors and Materialities in Maritime Regions." *Atlantic Studies* 10 (2): 156–169.

Steinberg, Philip, and Kimberly Peters. 2015. "Wet Ontologies, Fluid Spaces: Giving Depth to Volume through Oceanic Thinking." *Environment and Planning D: Society and Space* 33 (2): 247–264.

St. Martin, Kevin, and Madeleine Hall-Arber. 2008. "The Missing Layer: Geo-technologies, Communities, and Implications for Marine Spatial Planning." *Marine Policy* 32 (5): 779–786.

Thornton, Thomas F., and Adela Maciejewski Scheer. 2012. "Collaborative Engagement of Local and Traditional Knowledge and Science in Marine Environments: A Review." *Ecology and Society* 17 (3). http://dx.doi.org/10.5751/ES-04714-170308.

Tsing, Anna. 2015. *The Mushroom at the End of the World: On the Possibility of Life in Capitalist Ruins*. Princeton, NJ: Princeton University Press.

Turner, Roy M. 2005. "Intelligent Mission Planning and Control of Autonomous Underwater Vehicles." Paper presented at the International Conference on Automated Planning and Scheduling, Monterey, CA, 5–10 June.

UNGA (United Nations General Assembly). 2000. "Resolution 54/33: Results of the Review by the Commission on Sustainable Development of the Sectoral Theme of "Oceans and Seas": International Coordination and Cooperation. A/RES/54/33, 18 January. https://undocs.org/en/A/RES/54/33.

West, Paige. 2016. *Dispossession and the Environment: Rhetoric and Inequality in Papua New Guinea*. New York: Columbia University Press.

Wright, Dawn J. 1999. "Getting to the Bottom of It: Tools, Techniques, and Discoveries of Deep Ocean Geography." *Professional Geographer* 51 (3): 426–439.

Wright, Dawn J., and Michael F. Goodchild. 1997. "Data from the Deep: Implications for the GIS Community." *International Journal of Geographic Information Science* 11 (6): 523–528.

Wynn, Russell B., Veerle A. I. Huvenne, Timothy P. Le Bas, Bramley J. Murton, Douglas P. Connelly, Brian J. Bett, Henry A. Ruhl, et al. 2014. "Autonomous Underwater Vehicles (AUVs): Their Past, Present and Future Contributions to the Advancement of Marine Geoscience." *Marine Geology* 352: 451–468.

Yuh, J. 2000. "Design and Control of Autonomous Underwater Robots: A Survey." *Autonomous Robots* 8 (1): 7–24.

Yuh, J., and M. West. 2001. "Underwater Robotics." *Advanced Robotics* 15 (5): 609–639.

CHAPTER 9

Home and Away

The Politics of Life after Earth

Micha Rahder

Outer space imaginaries are booming. Reborn from Cold War projects into the post-9/11 securitized era, imaginaries of expanding life—human and otherwise—beyond the surface of the planet Earth are proliferating, creating new material impacts and new politics of expansion, exploration, and exclusion. Motivated by fears of looming environmental or sociopolitical disaster, including the Anthropocene, many extraterrestrial imaginaries rework earthly fantasies of technoscientific progress and human mastery over nature. Space programs are increasingly privatized, with tech entrepreneurs leading the way to extraterrestrial futures. I refer to these projects, often framed as a necessary step in human social and evolutionary history, as in search of Earth 2.0—a new and improved human future enabled by Silicon Valley innovation.

Other narratives about extraterrestrial futures, which I call eco-centric, displace human uniqueness, stretching beyond human timescales to the longer evolutionary history of life on Earth. These share with Earth 2.0 the assumption that our planet is defined by its living systems, but mark the Anthropocene as only the latest biological revolution to reshape Earth's surface. In this frame, humans are not unique in our planetary impact; whether we are unique in our potential to take life beyond Earth's surface is an open question. Eco-centric extraterrestrial imaginaries present alternatives based not on mastery, innovation, or human exceptionalism, but on unruly evolutionary ecologies that displace intention from life's expansion. Earth 2.0 and eco-centric imaginaries offer different understandings of the human, life, time, space, and the relations between these categories.

This article traces these two imaginaries for the future of life after Earth, both of which are flexible and internally varied. The word "imaginaries" builds on the definition of sociotechnical imaginaries, or ways in which "science and technology become enmeshed in performing and producing diverse visions of the collective good, at expanding scales of governance from communities to nation-states to the planet" (Jasanoff and Kim 2015: 11)—and now beyond. I mobilize "imaginaries" to encompass the range of effects and entanglements between language, cultural production, scientific research, technological innovation, politics, temporal frameworks, and more-than-human evolutionary ecological trajectories. If (or when) life moves beyond Earth, humans will likely be instrumental, but not necessarily in control. As attention to the political and environmental geographies of outer space proliferates (Olson 2018), this article instead turns its gaze back "inward" toward Earth, exploring the current and potential terrestrial impacts of extraterrestrial expansionary megaprojects.

Displacing the Earth

"Displacements" describe how imagined extraterrestrial futures work to rearrange human/life relations in the earthly present. As multiple possible futures materialize in research programs, policy proposals, social movements, and private investments, they bring displacements of ontological, epistemological, and temporal orders into the present—with both oppressive and liberatory possibilities (Valentine 2017). Displacements describe scalar reconfigurations such that phenomena that might be incomprehensible or beyond human sensorial reach are brought into the scales of human experience (Messeri 2016). Extraterrestrial displacements work through analytical double movement: making extraterrestrial environments familiar by incorporating them into earthly epistemic and aesthetic frameworks, and making terrestrial environments strange by way of new perspectives (Markley 2005; Messeri 2017a, 2017b; Olson 2018; Praet and Salazar 2017). These two directions work together to co-constitute terrestrial presents with extraterrestrial futures.

Rather than a straightforward outward gaze, space expansion imaginaries always involve seeing Earth from a new perspective (Lepselter 1997). These visions range from the widespread use of "Spaceship Earth" metaphors in twentieth-century US environmental movements (Fuller 1969), to Carl Sagan's (1994) "pale blue dot" emphasizing Earth life's uniqueness in the universe, to the politically unifying "overview effect" proposed by Frank White (1987). Early space programs coproduced the emergence and coherence of the global scale, which has come to dominate political and environmental ideologies (Jasanoff 2004; Lazier 2011). Scientific understandings of life on Earth are increasingly framed with reference to the presence or absence of other life in the universe, and how we might recognize it if it is there (Helmreich et al. 2016).

Extraterrestrial displacements are temporal as well as spatial. Imaginaries of futures displace linear time such that their potentialities can be materialized in the present (Denning 2013; Mathews and Barnes 2016). Space expansion imaginaries reinstantiate what many argue is the dominant temporal framework of the early twenty-first century, anticipation: "a moral economy in which the future sets the conditions of possibility for action in the present, in which the future is inhabited in the present" (Adams et al. 2009: 249). Critical scholars can be fearful of the "dangers of prognostication" (Valentine et al. 2012) but increasingly attend to how prognostication figures as a key political and material practice for creating new worlds. In this case, these new worlds may be brought into existence on or off Earth.

Leaving Earth—Fact or Fiction?

There is a huge range of extraterrestrial research and development projects around the world, both public and private. In this article, I focus on those that work toward the expansion of life (human and otherwise) beyond Earth in a more or less "permanent" fashion. The boundary drawn for this article mirrors trends in public interest and political rhetoric that prioritize human expansion over other investigations of the universe (Messeri 2017b; Wright and Oman-Reagan 2017). These projects and imaginaries share significant overlap with others, such as new capitalist resource frontiers (Genovese 2017a; Valentine 2012) or the search for extraterrestrial intelligence, known as SETI (Battaglia 2006; Denning 2001a, 2011b, 2011c; Vakoch 2013). More than 70 countries have national space programs, including many that train humans for spaceflight, but only the United States, Russia (and the former Soviet Union), and China have successfully launched humans into space. This article has a bias toward US-based projects, both public and private, as these are most prolific and have generated the most media attention and academic analyses to date. In addition, most national programs, especially in the Global South, focus on satellite systems, launch facilities, and vehicle manufacture, with private companies extending these ventures toward resource extraction and potential tourism. Yet NASA, the European Space Agency, Russia's Roscosmos, the UAE Space Agency, China's National Space Administration, and private SpaceX have all declared intentions to send humans to Mars in the next few decades, moving toward expansion.

The charisma of expansion imaginaries can displace attention from the more substantial material investment in other extraterrestrial infrastructures. For example, Ted Cruz, Republican Chairman of US Senate Commerce Subcommittee on Space, Science, and Competitiveness, has claimed that NASA is not (and should not be) a scientific institution but rather one focused on exploration—a strong contrast to the agency's present and historical activities (Showstack 2017). While the bulk of space programming is not expansion-oriented, expansionist imaginaries are on the rise as the international publics of Mars rover adventures, Silicon Valley cultures, and climate catastrophe narratives intersect. As a result of the mismatch between material investments and circulating space narratives, expansionist imaginaries are political as well as material megaprojects: most humans on Earth doubt or dismiss the possibility of life beyond the planet, so making these narratives salient enough to mobilize resources is a megaproject in itself, one that works to reshape the relations between humans, other life, and Earth itself.

Outer space has long served as a canvas for sociopolitical imaginations, calling up the worlds of science fiction and fantasy long relegated to the "genre" peripheries of literature and considered irrelevant to "serious" scholarly work (Dickens and Ormrod 2007; Haqq-Misra 2016; Markley 2005). This division is breaking down as the accelerating pace of interconnected technological, geopolitical, and environmental change leaves many with the sense that they are already living in the sci-fi future (Collins 2003, 2005). The Anthropocene has itself been called an academic science-fiction imaginary (Swanson et al. 2015), and scholars across fields are drawing attention to how science fiction has long influenced technological and scientific developments, particularly in extraterrestrial projects (Cheston 1986; Haraway 1991, 2016; McCurdy 2011; Praet and Salazar 2017). As Peter Redfield notes, "fictions provided space exploration with a recognizable future, and thus helped engender fantastic practices. These dreams found engineers, eager to materialize them" (2002: 799). Dreams finding engineers (not the reverse) describes how imaginaries reshape sociotechnical worlds.

Whether metaphor becomes material or vice versa, language is central to exchanges between fictional and factual extraterrestrial worlds. It matters whether Mars is to be "settled" or "colonized" (Wright and Oman-Reagan 2017), whether space is "discovered" or "conquered" by the scientific gaze (Redfield 2002). Language can shape the materiality of space projects and draw lines of exclusion around who might participate in them. Reflecting this, I use "humans" instead of "humanity" to retain a sense of multiplicity and difference as opposed to a unified singularity. Similarly, I use "expansion" to collect diverse extraterrestrial imaginaries that might elsewhere be described under terms like settlement, colonization, or terraformation.

While imperfect, these choices follow this article's concern with the categories of the human, life, and the relations between the two on Earth. Life, as distinguished from nonlife (rather than death), is a grounding metaphysics of modern colonial ontologies (Povinelli 2016). While biological and philosophical debates over the definition of the category are as lively as ever (Helmreich et al. 2016), I follow theorizations that define life as more verb than noun: life is an energetic process that characterizes certain material things on the planet Earth (Margulis and Sagan 1995; Mautner 2009). "Expansion" captures a facet of life's evolutionary histories that imaginaries of technological progress into space do not: "Life may not progress, but it expands" (Sagan and Margulis 1997: 235).

What this imagined future expansion might mean—at home or away—is being shaped in the earthly present. Following a brief history of human projects oriented toward life's expansion beyond Earth, I examine Earth 2.0 and eco-centric extraterrestrial imaginaries in detail. I then turn to the implications of both imaginaries for humans and life on Earth in the present, exploring the social and ecological politics of competing expansionist visions. This focus on the earthly now excludes many works that examine the extension of human environmental ideas, impacts, and management into space itself (as in rich debates over "space junk" or "planetary protection"). This choice follows the framework of displacements to turn our gaze collectively back inward, examining space projects as not only shaping possible futures but also as reconfiguring environmental and political worlds here and now.

Space and Environment: From Cold War to Anthropocene

"Things that happen in Silicon Valley and also the Soviet Union: . . . promises of colonizing the solar system while you toil in drudgery day in, day out"
—Anton Troynikov (@atroyn), Twitter, 5 July 2018

Narratives projecting human expansion into space have been present since at least the late nineteenth century but proliferated in response to the military-technological developments of the Cold War (Andrews and Siddiqi 2011; McCurdy 2011). The threat of nuclear warfare was enmeshed with narratives of modernist scientific progress, resulting in the satellite infrastructures we now take for granted for navigation, communication, weather forecasting, and so on. Twentieth-century extraterrestrial military research and infrastructures developed in close relation with terrestrial sciences and environmental movements, both through collaborations and oppositions (DeLoughrey 2014; Olson 2018). Terrestrial and extraterrestrial science programs shared funding streams, codeveloped cybernetic systems theories, and led to concepts that have become fundamental to environmental management on Earth, such as carrying capacity, island ecology, or the dominance of engineering approaches to ecological problems (Anker 2005). These "one Earth" environmental sciences and politics emerged in and from the cultures of colonialism, reinforcing ideologies of militarized surveillance and rational management of more-than-human worlds (DeLoughrey 2014). Through linked terrestrial and extraterrestrial technosciences, "one Earth" imaginaries grew deeper entrenched even as the projects of colonialism and development were unraveling into irrevocably damaged socioenvironmental orders.

Despite space's centrality to the ecological sciences, mainstream environmental movements in the United States and Europe have often been opposed to space expansion programs. Opponents argue that resources would be better spent attending to Earth's problems rather than imagining others we might one day escape to (Cockell 2006). Narratives of new capitalist frontiers led many environmentalists to view space exploration as a "jingoistic boondoggle," fearing it will lead to ideologies of a disposable planet (Hartmann 1986). Yet expansion imaginaries took on new significance in the 1970s and 1980s in relation to globalized debates about the human population limit of Earth (Dickens and Ormrod 2007). Space has alternately figured as a solution or distraction from earthly environmental problems, a shared point of reference for a global humanity.

The end of the Cold War brought a short lull in expansionist space imaginaries, with extraterrestrial colonization set aside in favor of earthly applications of satellite technology. But while government funding of space programs has declined since the early 1990s, entrepreneurial capitalists—or NewSpace—have now stepped in to fill this gap, collectively investing billions of dollars into extraterrestrial technologies, projects, and futures. Anton Troynikov, a writer and robotics researcher, noted the displacement of this techno-fantasy in his humorous series of tweets from 2018 comparing life in Silicon Valley to the Soviet Union. NewSpace extends far beyond Central California, however: the growing accessibility of computing and other technologies has led to space programs beyond the former superpowers or colonial centers (these are mostly satellite focused, though Nigeria plans to launch humans into space by 2030). Public interest in space expansion is on the rise again, most often articulated in connection to global environmental change. Before his death in 2018, Steven Hawking projected that the human species will last no more than one hundred years unless we expand into space.

In the NewSpace era, the push for expansion beyond Earth is no longer defined by competing capitalist and communist superpowers but by the divisions (and collaborations) between public and private entities. A sense of impending apocalypse remains, though this has shifted from sudden nuclear annihilation to the slow violence of a warming atmosphere, rising seas, and other environmental devastation (Ahmann 2018; Nixon 2011). Though understood as new or different, Cold War space science was instrumental in transforming the "threat" of nuclear annihilation into that of climate crisis (DeLoughrey 2014; Masco 2010, 2012). Space infrastructures enabled not only new futures but also the possibility that there might be an "end of ends" negating futurities altogether (Masco 2012). These contradictory possibilities are co-constituted such that the end of Earth becomes the inevitability of extraterrestrial expansion, and vice versa. As Anthropocene discourses mix with NewSpace futures, human ecological relations with other living matter are entering extraterrestrial imaginaries in a new way. These sometimes amplify urgency and reinscribe humans as "saviors" of Earth, and other times challenge conventional thinking about managerial control. This contradictory Anthropocene sets the stage for the emergence of Earth 2.0 and eco-centric imaginaries for life after Earth.

Earth 2.0

Dominating current efforts to expand human life beyond Earth are public-private partnerships, mostly based in the United States, Europe, and the United Arab Emirates. Participants in NewSpace worlds are dominated by older white men from the United States, though are still surprisingly diverse in political and demographic makeup (Valentine 2012). With names like the Lifeboat Foundation, the Space Frontier Foundation, or the Alliance to Rescue Civilization, motivations for these projects range from imperialist nationalisms to profits to new utopian social orders, often mixed together in unexpected configurations. Yet these Earth 2.0 visions are resolutely united by one thing: the centering of the human *species* as the ontological basis and scale for extraterrestrial futures.

In the United States, amid the inflammatory rhetoric of his presidency, Donald Trump's proclamations on outer space as the "next great American frontier" have largely been met with derision or relative disregard. He signed executive orders in 2017 and 2018 to reformulate US space policy, including new directives to build public-private partnerships to return to the moon, followed by a Mars mission. In early 2019, he established new extra-terrestrial branch of the US military known as the Space Force. Despite relative inattention to these policies in contrast to other executive actions, the 45th president has done much to enliven public attention to space futures in the country, causing what seem to many observers to be uncomfortable or strategic alliances with his bombastic rhetoric (e.g., gleeful circulation of Buzz Aldrin's pained facial expressions in memes after a joint press conference with the president). While easily dismissed in the face of his violently right-wing proclamations and policy decisions, Trump's space dreams reinforce the power of his America First doctrine. Although figures like Aldrin proclaim more universalist narratives of international cooperation in space, they continue to line up in support of Trump's space programming. Rather than an exception in globalist visions of unified humanity, Trump's (and Trump-like) racisms have been at the heart of liberal democratic projects all along—preelection events like viral video footage of police shootings of African Ameri-cans or Native American protests against the Dakota Access Pipeline reveal how liberal sovereignty rests on the violent exclusion of racialized others (Rosa and Bonilla 2017).

Military and nationalist narratives are easily imported into privatized realms. The tech entrepreneur Elon Musk is a prominent figure in NewSpace, alternately characterized in the press as a techno-futurist hero or a supervillain. Musk's SpaceX holds launch contracts with NASA and other national space programs and is a leader in the development of space tourism. Musk's visions for settling Mars are immensely popular and filled with super-lative exaggeration, such as referring to his planned technology as the BFR (big fucking rocket) (Pope 2018). Musk (2018) plans to send the first cargo missions to Mars in 2022, with crew missions following two years later, establishing a base from which humans can become a multi-planetary species. Robert Zubrin (2002, 2012, 2019) is another popular leader who has published numerous books advocating for human expansion to Mars. The founder of the Mars Society, Zubrin is a former Lockheed Martin engineer, and a vocal proponent of privatized space futures.

Many private space organizations replicate the worst aspects of late capitalism: secu-ritized property regimes, essentialized identities, and competitive extraction (Genovese 2017a). Language describing space as a "frontier" is common, particularly American "manifest destiny" and Mars as the new US American West (Grinspoon 2004; Wright and Oman-Reagan 2017). Indeed, space has become a resource frontier in the sense defined by Anna Tsing (2003): neither place nor process, but a capitalist imaginary that shapes both. Frontier imaginaries transform the ontological status of extraterrestrial materials into "resources," whether for capitalist or scientific exploitation. The existence of extrater-restrial resources is then used as justification for expansion: they are out there; therefore, we should use them (e.g., Cockell 2006). Peter Dickens and James Ormrod (2007) thus extend David Harvey's analysis of capitalism's expansionist frontiers as a "spatial fix" to an "outer spatial fix," though endless extraction is rarely the goal in itself.

Instead, through utopias or through the protection of distance, space expansion is widely framed in Earth 2.0 imaginaries as a kind of pressure release for Earth-bound human problems. Among NewSpace proponents, even within the most profit-motivated arenas, most people express unexpected or contradictory utopian visions of new social and political relations enabled by extraterrestrial futures. NewSpace representatives like Musk celebrate an extreme version of neoliberal entrepreneurialism and libertarian socioeconomic ethics, projecting these as necessary steps in the directed evolutionary development of the human species. Rather than short-term profit motivations leading to unpredictable long-term futures, as most critiques of NewSpace would have it, short-term R&D projects are more commonly motivated by long-term visions of extraterrestrial sociality not yet in existence (Valentine 2012). NewSpace utopian visions resonate with, but cannot be explained away by, expansionary profit seeking.

The coexistence of these contradictory visions was established in US cultural narratives through early Apollo mission photographs, which were rooted in the mastering gaze of US military imperialism yet projected an environmentally and politically united Earth (Cosgrove 2003). The unification of a divided humanity is often figured as the result of shared intrinsic values that define the species: curiosity, innovation, and exploration. Zubrin's Mars Society (1998) argues that space expansion will not just reduce conflict but *replace* it as a driving force behind innovation:

> Civilizations, like people, thrive on challenge and decay without it. The time is past for human societies to use war as a driving stress for technological progress. As the world moves towards unity, we must join together, not in mutual passivity, but in common enterprise, facing outward to embrace a greater and nobler challenge than that which we previously posed to each other. Pioneering Mars will provide such a challenge.

A collective leap into space is seen as fulfilling the broken promises of capitalist modernity: equality, liberty, and progress.

These utopian visions are still grounded by earthly concerns. Jacob Haqq-Misra argues for "liberating Mars," basing future settlement not on an extension of earthly sociopolitics (whether organized in terms of nation-states or corporations) but instead by establishing a new Martian planetary citizenship to create a "test bed for new ideas that could lead to unforeseen epistemic transformations of our values and preferences" (2016: 66). Yet his argument compares this "transformative experience" to a "trust fund child" gaining new values from a wilderness trip (65). "Nature"—whether earthly wilderness or Martian extremity—is called upon as a resource for human cultural transformation, reimagining a modernist dichotomy as the basis for a planetary move beyond modernism.

These narratives frame the search for a new Earth 2.0 as a *necessary* project for collective human and environmental survival. Deflecting critiques that space programs divert too many resources from earthly problems, Cameron Smith and Evan Davies (2012) claim that "all worthwhile things" (among which they list boats and wedding rings) are worth large expense. Space expansion, framed as a form of long-term insurance for the human species, is moved from the question "Can we afford to go?" to "Can we afford not to?" (Hartmann 1986). This powerful mixture of apocalyptic narratives, new resource frontiers, and utopian schemes combine to create a sense of space expansion as not just inevitable, but a present in which we are *behind* rather than working toward something yet to come. As Musk argued in a speech at the International Astronautical Congress: "It's 2017 . . . We should have a lunar base by now."

This present, beholden to the future, makes strange work of history. Earth 2.0 imaginaries offer the opportunity to start anew; these narratives erase collective responsibility for harms done by colonial projects and seem to "cleanse" history (Redfield 2002: 797). Alternately, history is turned into an "objective" knowledge resource for avoiding repeated mistakes (e.g., Haqq-Misra 2016). Most striking is the frequent collapse of timescales, with recent historical and deep evolutionary time brought into new resonances (Codignola et al. 2009). Space expansion is commonly figured as an inevitable step in a conjoined evolutionary-colonial history: "We wriggled onto dry land, ventured out of the African savannah as apes, set sail for new worlds—how could we not expect, someday, to live in colonies on Titan or starships cruising through deep space?" (Austen 2011). This vision places white, Western, masculine techno-capitalist humanity at the pinnacle of evolutionary scales.

The future Earth left behind in Earth 2.0 imaginaries tends to fall into two categories. By far, the most common are visions of an Earth destroyed, uninhabitable to humans if not to all carbon-based life. Other narratives project that we might get off Earth in time to "save" it from ourselves, leaving behind a global park of purified nature (Austen 2011). Both versions resonate with environmentalisms that take an anti-humanist turn, as in visions of humanity as a global pollution or disease, out of balance, or otherwise in need of reduction or eradication (Anker 2005; Dumit 2005). Projections of natural purity resonate in multiple directions, into pasts and futures, and both on and away from Earth. Lisa Messeri (2017a), working with scientists searching for potentially habitable exoplanets, notes that "earthlike" planets are imagined as a kind of new Eden, representing a purification of human industrial histories by way of long-term futures. These futures of Earth 2.0 proliferate both at home and away—a rebooted humanity offered a chance to "do nature better," to recapture Eden.

Life for Humans, or Humans for Life?

In Earth 2.0 imaginaries, which other life-forms travel with humans? The selection of living others for these extraterrestrial futures is centered on human needs and desires: food species, oxygen producers, waste recyclers, and so on. Occasionally, companion animals or aesthetically preferred species are imagined off world, though in short-term scenarios, they are excluded from the engineered calculus of necessity. Microbes play an increasingly prominent role, especially as functional parts of encapsulated life support systems or as potential terraformers. Above all, nonhuman life is reduced to utilitarian function for the maintenance and reproduction of humans. In the same move, human difference is absorbed into *species*, defined by biological needs. Yet, strangely, many Earth 2.0 imaginaries turn from humans to life in their furthest displacements. Musk, for example, has made multiple statements about his space projects as motivated not by human expansion but by the evolutionary history of planetary life. At once instrumentalized and made the basis for a new intergalactic ethics, *life itself* is a grounding concern on which space projects can be built. NewSpace expansionary visions are again framed as necessary, or as unassailably good—to spread life is a moral endeavor, full stop.

This places humans in a particular frame: a species united to *life* by evolutionary history (and not divided by lived difference) but distinguished from all other species by the uniqueness of our extraterrestrial technological capabilities. Some of these narratives begin to open to the agencies of nonhuman life beyond technocentric control narratives, as in Grinspoon's (2004) suggestion for sciences of "cultivation" or "animation" of Mars rather than colonization or settlement. As human exceptionalism becomes less and less possible to justify bioscientifically, this twist of extraterritoriality reunites humans with Nature while dividing them once again as special: "Alone of the creatures of the Earth, we have the ability to continue the work of creation by bringing life to Mars, and Mars to life. In doing so, we shall make a profound statement as to the precious worth of the human race and every member of it" (Mars Society 1998). This account of the human-as-species unites moralized historical teleologies with the otherwise a-human perspectives of evolutionary time.

Earth 2.0 imaginaries are entangled with proposals for "life-centered ethics," "pan-biotic ethics," or an "ethics of life," in which the role of humans in sustaining life itself is brought into relation with discourses of more-than-human intergenerational justice (Ketcham 2016; Kramer 2011; Mautner 2004, 2009, 2014). In these formulations, life's tendency to self-propagation and expansion is read as an indicator of *purpose* and therefore of the good (Mautner 2009). Some proposals, with linked astroecological research projects and experiments, have nothing to do with expansion of *human* life, even as they are offered as a way to give "human endeavors a cosmic purpose" through the seeding of microbial, plant, or other nonhuman life into nearby solar systems (Mautner 2014). These versions of more-than-human ethics, in which "What is best for *life*?" serves as a central guiding question, continue to enforce singularity of a "best" answer, and rely on ontologically singular definitions of humanity, species, life, and so on.

Full Seed Ahead

Earth 2.0 imaginaries and their partial connections to life-centered ethics hinge on placing the human within the larger category of life while continuing to mark humans as exceptional. Another reading of the same evolutionary histories, found in eco-centric space expansion narratives, marks this hubris as displaced, with questions of intention or moral purpose tossed aside. Lynn Margulis and Dorion Sagan write: "Will we humans, godlike, wave our wand? Do we really think, in our naiveté, that strewing our scientific instrumentation over the red surface of Mars via robots in a geological wink of an eye will produce a New Blue Earth? Far more probably, Mars will be colonized slowly and gradually, and not by humanity but through humanity, facilitated by robots" (1995: 230).

Contrary to apocalyptic environmental discourses that reinstantiate human exceptionalism, earthly life has repeatedly overhauled the planet's geophysical and chemical realities. Every stage of evolution on Earth, beginning with the first microbial fermenters in the primordial soup, has been characterized by a novel approach to resource use, leading to rapid proliferation and thus to a shortage of resources and accumulation of dangerous "pollution" that threatens those very life-forms that proliferated so wildly. The advent of the oxygenated atmosphere by photosynthesizing bacteria vastly overshadows our carbon contributions. Inevitably, new life-forms arise that harness that "pollution" as a new resource, and the cycle begins again (Margulis and Sagan 1995). Taken in this long view, humans are only the latest, and not the most impactful, in a history of life reshaping the surface of Earth.

Patiently waiting to digest Earth 2.0 imaginaries into their own purposes are eco-centric alternatives that center this long view in post-earthly futures. Work at the intersections of microbial biology, science studies, and evolutionary theory has begun to challenge the species-centric theories of Darwinian evolution, particularly their emphasis on modes of selection acting on individual organisms (Haraway 2008; Helmreich et al. 2016; Hird 2009; Hustak and Myers 2012). Remixing evolutionary narratives with feminist social theory reworks understandings of ecological relations in ways that decenter not only human exceptionalism but also the ontological category of species altogether. Margulis, the biologist most known for her work on the role of symbiosis in evolution, is a central figure in eco-centric space imaginaries. With her biological theories and social beliefs causing controversy throughout her life (Glorfeld 2018; Mann 1991; Teresi 2011), Margulis was deeply critical of dominant space expansion imaginaries yet a prolific proponent of her own versions.

Margulis and others, in contrast to Earth 2.0 imaginaries, argue that space (especially Martian) colonization by way of terraformation is simply unrealistic given our current technological and epistemic limitations. She distinguished "ecopoiesis," or the creation of ecosystems, from terraformation: the former is about extending life, the latter about replicating Earth. Eco-centric imaginaries of ecopoeitic extraterrestrial futures not only displace human desires, moralities, or futures but also may be explicitly distasteful to humans: "Ecopoiesis would not make Mars into an extraterrestrial paradise, so much as it would transform it into a global cesspool" (Margulis and West 1997: 229). Similarly, these narratives assert that it is *life*'s drive to expand that will move it beyond Earth; human vectors may not be necessary: "Given time to evolve in the absence of people, the descendants of raccoons—clever, nocturnal mammals with good manual coordination—could start their own space program" (Sagan and Margulis 1997: 237).

Microbes in particular move to the center of these imaginaries. Earth 2.0 visions are met with what Myra Hird (2010) calls "bacterial indifference" to human-centric schemes, material or conceptual, of environmental change or globality. Hird decenters the human in earthly globality by attending to the far more consequential actions of microbiota—including the radical asymmetry in which we depend wholly on microbes for survival and "self," but not vice versa. Microbial futures—the forms and effects of microbial evolution yet to come—have only recently begun to enter realms of human speculation (Crosby 2009; Helmreich 2009), but attention to these questions is proliferating rapidly. Microbial research, particularly on "extremophiles" in relation to both entrepreneurial bioprospecting futures and post-earthly astrobiology imaginaries, is booming (Salazar 2017).

Eco-centric extraterrestrial imaginaries build on Gaia theory, to which Margulis was a major contributor. Plagued by frequent misrepresentations as "new agey" or even antiscience, Gaia theory frames Earth not as a living organism (because it recycles its own waste) but rather as a living system, the components of which are organisms (Lovelock and Volk 2003; Margulis and West 1997). While the historical development of James Lovelock and Margulis's Gaia hypothesis began with "Spaceship Earth" discourses, their Gaia differed significantly from many of these earthly visions. Gaia emphasizes the whole of life, rather than technoscientifically capable humans, as maintaining the "capsule ecology" of the planet. Gaia theory thus enfolds extraterrestrial narratives into a broader understanding of life as an expanding planetary phenomenon, which could reproduce through "budding" or "seeding" (Margulis and Guerrero 1995).

Humans still appear in eco-centric imaginaries, but in a way that absorbs their behaviors and technologies within the larger category of life without marking exceptionalism (Margulis and West 1997). Strangely, this move already occurs in many concrete extraterrestrial practices, as evidenced by public fascination with the "taboo" necessities of human bodies in space, such as defecation, sex, menstruation, and so on (Genovese 2017b). Bodily needs and desires seem out of place in the technocentric capsules of space because they make us of a kind with other (animal) life, decentering exceptionalism and bringing our reliance on (living and machine) others into the foreground. The practical realities of making human bodies work in space requires a radical reworking of the analytical idea of "context," as things taken for granted on Earth—like the ability to breathe air—are suddenly called into the center of attention (Valentine 2016).

Normative understandings of human bodies shift in space. Valerie Olson (2010) finds that space medicine reconceptualizes the human body from biological to ecological models, emphasizing co-relation and dependence. Similarly, Leah Aronowsky's (2017) work writes embodied human relations with living and nonliving others back into the techno-progressivist history of US space exploration. Early attempts to ensure human survival in space called upon the ecological sciences, particularly the work of the Odum brothers, in a way that *could have* led to sciences of interdependency and multispecies extraterrestrial environmental imaginaries, rather than reinstantiations of human-technological control. That the latter path now seems "inevitable" is evidence of the power of dominant sociotechnical imaginaries to set epistemic limits on the proper relations between humans, technologies, and other life on and off the planet Earth.

The role of humans in extraterrestrial eco-centric futures is transformed from Earth 2.0's *when* or *how* to a more open *if*. This *if* calls for new ecological ethics, distinguished from life-centered ethics by a move from species to relation as the key to ethical practice, and a corresponding move away from a unitary morality (Gaard 2013; Sagan and Margulis 1997). Relations between human and nonhuman life are transformed into an open political question, and are typically anti-capitalist—Margulis and Sagan (1995), for example, remind their readers that all human "wealth" is ultimately derived from plant-based photosynthesis and will return to Earth. Inklings of these relations already appear in extraterrestrial worlds, as in discourses and practices of mutual care in unequal plant-human relations aboard the International Space Station (Oman-Reagan 2015).

These questions are explored in Octavia Butler's unfinished black feminist science-fiction *Earthseed* series, which echoes with the final line of Margulis and Sagan's (1995: 197) book *What Is Life?* as the latter projects extraterrestrial futures: "Earth is going to seed." The fictional Earthseed religion, which now has real followers,[1] states: "The Destiny of Earthseed is to take root among the stars." Reading the two side by side, Butler's fictional religion and Margulis and Sagan's theoretical biologies share uncanny resonances. Both books take for granted the inevitability of life expanding into space, but by centering change, process, and ecological relations over the presumed stability of identities and political economic systems of the present human moment, the politics of these imaginaries are vastly different from those of Earth 2.0.

In a final displacement of human mastery narratives, the possibility of humans *accidentally* spreading life through the universe haunts Earth 2.0 schemes. Despite protocols in space programs to prevent the transport of microbes onto pristine extraterrestrial Edens, known as "planetary protection" measures (McKay 2009; Siefert 2012), this is perhaps one of the most likely scenarios for post-earthly expansion, given historical failures at human attempts to enforce purity through techno-control. Eco-centric imaginaries easily absorb, even celebrate, this possibility (Margulis and West 1997). Ironically, microbial extraterrestriality is figured as the eco-centric future of life *even if* it is the capitalist extractionists who take us there. Eco-centric imaginaries suggest that it is far more likely that our intricate, fragile, and slow-to-reproduce species will die of unforeseen effects in attempting long-term space colonization, but our relatively simpler, more robust, and much more quickly evolving microbial companions will find ways to go on.

Unequal Earths

Eco-centric imaginaries, in some ways, absorb those of Earth 2.0. But both require material efforts directed toward making these futures come to pass—with uneven distributions of resources, energies, and impacts across lived worlds on Earth. This final section explores these political and ecological effects in the present with respect to both imaginaries. While extraterrestrial imaginaries may project a singular humanity, or even a post-human, life-filled universe, they are differently supported or opposed by particular humans in the present. Similarly, even if the environmental impacts of space launches are relatively small in the global scheme of carbon emissions and industrial pollution, there *are* impacts, including large bursts of emissions required for launch, burning or waste impacts at launch sites, and so on. Launch points and research sites might also offer local jobs or scientific training opportunities, strongly desired in many places. When and where these potential benefits and harms are distributed are intensely political questions.

Humans versus Humanity

"Black girl magic, y'all can't stand it
Y'all can't ban it, made out like a bandit
They been trying hard just to make us all vanish
I suggest they put a flag on a whole 'nother planet

. . .

We gave you life, we gave you birth
We gave you God, we gave you Earth
We fem the future, don't make it worse
You want the world? Well, what's it worth?"
—Janelle Monáe, "Django Jane" (2018)

Both Earth 2.0 and eco-centric imaginaries tend to erase human difference, reducing humans (and other life) to species type. The question is always about *human*-other relationships, rarely Haudenosaunee-extraterrestrial, Dutch-algal, or Igbo-bacterial relations. But as Jason Wright and Michael Oman-Reagan note, "the universality in Carl Sagan's vision of Earth as the cradle of humanity is because his Pale Blue Dot is home not just to 'everyone you ever heard of' . . . but also everyone you've never heard of—the marginalized, oppressed, erased, and forgotten" (2017: 15). The scales of post-earthly imaginaries are incommensurable with those of earthly difference in the now, yet we must somehow contend with both. From calls to "decolonize Mars" (Decolonizing Mars 2019) to Janelle Monáe's lyrical suggestion that "they put a flag on a whole 'nother planet" and leave life on Earth to a "fem" future built on "black girl magic," the singularity of humanity in space expansion imaginaries is increasingly challenged. In this section, I follow Redfield's (2002) call to provincialize outer space, that is, to attend to the multiplicity of spatial and temporal frames embedded in these imaginaries and their intersections with uneven relations of human difference.

William Kramer (2011), in one of the few eco-centric arguments to mention human cultural difference, addresses it as a subcategory to broader ethical considerations: how do we account for cultural values when framing more-than-human ethics? The overall silence in both narratives reflects broader ecological scientific frameworks, which are historically blind to questions of race or cultural difference—particularly after the growth of cybernetic theories in the twentieth century (Rusert 2010). In *Environment, Power and Society*, the foundational ecologist Howard Odum (1971) "did not use the space capsule as a vague analogy or metaphor, but as an ontological claim about the world. His methodological reductionism of all biological life (including human behavior) to charts of energy circuits became the justification for proposals to manage human society scientifically" (Anker 2005: 246). Despite their commitments to entrepreneurial techno-capitalisms, Earth 2.0 imaginaries are more likely to address human difference, though largely through oversimplified imaginaries of "solutions" to conflict.

Despite universalizing rhetoric about humans' place in the universe, space cultures have grown from European and North American histories and are dominated by white men. But the mid-twentieth century saw a proliferation of space development in many places, with China now emerging as a third extraterrestrial power (Erickson 2014). Indonesia's achievement of the first satellite system by a "developing" country solidified political discourses of national unity and progress during the authoritarian regime of Suharto (Barker 2005), and at least 10 African countries have or are developing space programs (Hopkins 2013; Matthews 2016). Yet these programs' focus on satellite systems for Earth applications reveals that expansion imaginaries in particular remain grounded in the former centers of colonial power.

Afrofuturism, indigenous science fiction, and other counter-narratives can help decolonize terrestrial and extraterrestrial futures (Lempert 2014). Israeli kibbutzes have been proposed as sociological models for extraterrestrial communities, a counter to the implicitly suburban visions of US cultural imaginaries (Ashkenazi 1992). Indigenous futures draw on rich stores of knowledge regarding adaptation not just to changing environments but also to the violence and oppression of colonial capitalist projects (Whyte 2017). Native American critiques of the NASA space program in the 1980s countered imaginaries of a new frontier with their long-held intimate relationships with Father Sky, the Sun, moon, stars, and their inhabitants (Young 1987). More recently, a science-fiction episode of *Futurestates*, "The 6th World" (2012), showed a dying technocratic mission to Mars rescued by the financial resources, human-maize intimacies, and ceremonial practices of the Navajo Nation (Becker 2012).

Amid these growing counter-hegemonic futures, both the pasts and presents of space projects are shifting. Emerging recognition of the role of marginalized people in the space industry, such as the hugely successful film *Hidden Figures* (2016) or the popularity of the astrophysicist Neil deGrasse Tyson, can reinforce logics of anticipation that space will fix the broken social contract of modernity. Yet political support for space research in the United States is strongly divided along racial and gendered lines, reflecting the continued overwhelming whiteness and maleness of NASA space programs (McCurdy 2011). Shifting away from the US context reveals similarly complex socio-temporal politics. In French Guiana, Redfield (2002) traces the temporal conflicts over launch facilities, particularly whether these should be framed through abstracted, European-universalist futures or through racist, colonial exploitative pasts.

Efforts to diversify today's astronauts will similarly have major impacts on future space developments, especially as the question of who will serve as foundational extraterrestrial settlers approaches (Wright and Oman-Reagan 2017). Yet, in Earth 2.0 imaginaries, foundational human settlers are increasingly framed not in terms of earthly categories of race, gender, class, or culture but by their emergent biotechnological genomes engineered for space travel. Genomic editing, microbiome and/or epigenome therapies, and borrowing or transgenically implanting useful genes from other species (ranging from elephants to tardigrades) offer synthetic evolutionary futures for an extraterrestrial humanity. These futures are being materialized in the earthly now, as in the research of George Church, a geneticist and synthetic biologist who has begun working on human genome modification for long-term space flight or settlement.[2] Like many versions of transhumanism, eugenic ideals are resuscitated and sanitized as "technological progress" with little attention to social consequences—as in a recent argument that extraterrestrial eugenics are not a problem because nobody would have their reproductive rights taken away in the creation of an altered genetic "race" of astronauts (Pontin 2018). While the synthetic biological alteration of microbes, plants, and other earthly life for space travel is often doubly justified in terms of "solving some of the main agricultural and industrial challenges here on Earth," (Llorente et al. 2018), the racist ideologies underpinning human genetic modification schemes are carefully excluded from this multidirectional calculus.

Human differences of gender or sexuality are also erased in both imaginaries, which reduce these to a technical question of biological reproduction. Post-earthly human imaginaries rarely include reference to gender as an aspect of reproduction, or to race, except perhaps as a "resource" for maximizing genetic diversity (e.g., Birdsell 1985). But reproduction is always entangled with complex cultural formations of technology, gender, and sexuality. Instead of addressing these issues head-on, most space futures reinscribe heteronormative understandings on (particularly female) astronaut bodies (Casper and Moore 1995). If queerness can be understood as a negation of reproductionist futurity (Edelman 2004), then there appears to be no space for queers in space whatsoever.

Political Ecology of Space on Earth

Finally, the siting of launch points and experiments in extraterrestrial living distributes political and environmental impacts unevenly across Earth. Remote and uninhabited (by humans) locations are preferred for these sites, particularly those that involve launches or potential explosions: "When one is seeking to leave the globe, wasteland becomes valuable, and underdevelopment can appear a virtue" (Redfield 2000: 125). Experimental facilities for living in isolation have been or will be built in the deserts in the United States and the UAE, on a Hawaiian volcano, in a Moscow suburb, and in Antarctica. The "humanization" of extreme environments like the deep oceans, volcanoes, or Arctic or Antarctic research stations serves as proxy for extraterrestrial futures; these involve novel geopolitical experiments and arrangements, often hinged on the presumed universality of modernist techno-science (Helmreich 2009; O'Reilly 2017). These sites, chosen because they were previously beyond direct human interventions, are now slowly but radically re-shaped in the name of extraterrestrial futures: they are subjected to a kind of terraforming (DeLoughrey 2014; Salazar 2017).

In some places, local political action can resist the reshaping of Earth in the name of space futures. Resistance to the construction of a Thirty Meter Telescope on Mauna Kea, considered sacred land by Native Hawaiians and as ecologically fragile by allied environmentalists, built on long battles over Hawaiian sovereignty and conflict with the US settler colonial state (Naylor 2017). After years of successful resistance, however, the Supreme Court of Hawaii ruled in late 2018 to allow construction to proceed on the volcano. Neighboring Mauna Loa volcano is home to the Hawaii Space Exploration Analog and Simulation, one of the most prominent Mars simulation training programs. In Brazil, resistance similarly failed to halt the construction of a satellite launch facility in one of the poorest regions of the country, but the futuristic transformative promises of the site were undermined by the displacement of thousands of Afro-Brazilians and intersections with the politics of race and inequality in the country (Mitchell 2017). Finally, in an ironic twist of extraterrestrial alliances in the United States, SpaceX property marked for launch site development in the US-Mexico borderlands poses a barrier to Trump's border wall plans, setting up a clash between Musk and Trump, two of the most prominent Earth 2.0 figures (Nixon and Ferman 2018).

Finally, though frequently dismissed as "minor" relative to other human activities, rocket launches can lead to air, water, or soil pollution, disturbances to local (human and nonhuman) life, and acoustic or vibrational effects with unknown impacts on living and nonliving environments. These impacts will vary, depending on whether launch sites are sited next to wetlands, tropical forests, or deserts—all locations favored for their "re-moteness." Ultimately, little is known about impacts, as environmental impact assessment protocols are designed for minimal disturbance to technoscientific goals. Downplaying impacts is routine, as in reports surrounding the plans for Spaceport America (2019), the world's first commercial launch site currently under construction in the New Mexico desert. The project website highlights the planned Leadership in Energy and Environ-mental Design certification of the facilities, and describes impacts on local ecosystems in a passive and deemphasized manner: "The rural nature of the site reduced the project's ability to earn a few Sustainable Site credits." The accompanying technical report neglects ecological aspects of site selection altogether, beyond a lack of locally available water for a project whose water use is anticipated to be "roughly analogous to that of a modern airport" (Jefts and Paz 2019: 7). Notably, the same report's site history begins with Spanish conquistadors' encounters with the area, excluding any mention of indigenous presence (before or after).

As a result of technical approaches like these, questions of siting, increased human presence and activity in previously remote areas, and the more extreme impacts of occasional disasters have not been systematically accounted for. Launches have contributed an estimated 1 percent of human-caused ozone depletion, though this proportion is expected to increase as banned chlorofluorocarbons are reduced in the upper atmosphere and as the number of launches increases in coming years (Ross et al. 2009). Though single launches do not produce an exceptional amount of carbon emissions, if private and public ventures follow through on stated plans to start launching more often, and as public and private space programs proliferate around the globe, these impacts could quickly add up. These impacts are primarily coming from the material installations of Earth 2.0 imaginaries, but while eco-centric imaginaries might displace humans in extraterrestrial futures, they continue to move with and through these unaccounted for practices in the present.

Conclusion: As Below, So Above

Earth 2.0 imaginaries motivate investments and downplay impacts in the short term through longer-term visions of evolutionary progress or purpose. Overall, this is the most prominent imaginary in the present and is leading the way into space. Some people, mostly rich white men in or from the United States and Europe, will make exorbitant profits in the short term, no doubt, and others will be tossed aside. But those with the financial and political power to pursue their imaginaries aggressively in the present will likely lose control of their projects as soon as they start coming into reality. Indeed, a Spanish space scientist recently suggested that human activities on Mars might make the Anthropocene the first "first multiplanetary geological period" (Fairén 2019), an indication that the displacements of space science might further rework earthly time and space.

To imagine that humans as a species could engineer our own political, economic, and biological stability while abandoning the life and nonlife on Earth with which we evolved is a dangerous claim. It is true that new social, ecological, and political norms already emerge within the much shorter-term enclosures of space crews and on-Earth experiments in capsule living, so the idea of larger shifts engendered by longer journeys is not entirely far-fetched. The practical but radical rehabituation to space environments (such as living without an up/down reference point of Earth's gravity, or without reliable atmosphere) may entirely shift definitions of colonialism, humanness, or difference in as yet unanticipated ways (Valentine 2017). But openness to the radically unpredictable changes brought by extraterrestriality is a poor fit with the broader anticipatory temporal regimes of Earth 2.0 imaginaries, as they work in the present through uneven distributions of harms and benefits.

In contrast, an eco-centric Earth going to seed might use humans and our technological ingenuity, but we are made a small part of the bigger living picture. Rather than trying to reassert control or domination, allowing relation, mutuality, and change back into our futuristic imaginations expands the possibilities for life on Earth, and beyond it. Eco-centric imaginaries respond that the outcome of Earth 2.0 projects, if rushed, are "likely to be highly unpredictable—possibly even tragic" (Margulis and West 1997: 230). But their displacements of human exceptionalism can also do away with questions of justice, politics, or difference, lost in the timescales of life on Earth. Ultimately, both imaginaries must do better to address their distributions of harms and benefits, "staying with the trouble," as Donna Haraway (2016) suggests in studies of life, humanity, science, and earthly politics. Evolutionary ecological changes, like colonial technocratic projects, can and do involve violence, suffering, and death. As both projects work toward their imagined futures in the present, these questions—who or what suffers, when, how much, with what meaning—should remain central rather than dismissing harms as a necessary evil, minor collateral damage in the race toward progress.

▪ ACKNOWLEDGMENTS

The Department of Geography and Anthropology at Louisiana State University provided support for this research. I also thank Lisa Messeri, David Valentine, Michael Oman-Reagan, and Willi Lempert for their generous sharing of resources.

MICHA RAHDER is an independent scholar based out of North Carolina. Her research centers on the intersection of science and social justice in environmental thought and practice, from Central American forest conservation to outer space colonization. Email: micha.rahder@gmail.com

▪ NOTES

1. See https://godischange.org.
2. For this and related extraterrestrial human synthetic biology projects, see http://arep.med.harvard.edu (last updated 4 January 2019).

▪ REFERENCES

Adams, Vincanne, Michelle Murphy, and Adele E. Clarke. 2009. "Anticipation: Technoscience, Life, Affect, Temporality." *Subjectivity* 28 (1): 246–265. https://doi.org/10.1057/sub.2009.18.

Ahmann, Chloe. 2018. "'It's Exhausting to Create an Event out of Nothing': Slow Violence and the Manipulation of Time." *Cultural Anthropology* 33 (1): 142–171.

Andrews, James T., and Asif A. Siddiqi. 2011. *Into the Cosmos: Space Exploration and Soviet Culture*. Pittsburgh, PA: University of Pittsburgh Press.

Anker, Peder. 2005. "The Ecological Colonization of Space." *Environmental History* 10 (2): 239–268.

Aronowsky, Leah V. 2017. "Of Astronauts and Algae: NASA and the Dream of Multispecies Space-flight." *Environmental Humanities* 9 (2): 359–377.

Ashkenazi, Michael. 1992. "Some Alternatives in the Sociology of Space Colonization: The Kibbutz as a Space Colony." *Acta Astronautica* 26 (5): 367–375. https://doi.org/10.1016/0094-5765(92)90082-T.

Austen, Ben. 2011. "After Earth: Why, Where, How, and When We Might Leave Our Home Planet." *Popular Science*, 16 March. https://www.popsci.com/science/article/2011-02/after-earth-why-where-how-and-when-we-might-leave-our-home-planet.

Barker, Joshua. 2005. "Engineers and Political Dreams: Indonesia in the Satellite Age." *Current Anthropology* 46 (5): 703–727. https://doi.org/10.1086/432652.

Battaglia, Debbora. 2006. *E.T. Culture: Anthropology in Outerspaces*. Durham, NC: Duke University Press.

Becker, Nanobah. 2012. *The 6th World*. San Francisco: Independent Television Service.

Birdsell, Joseph B. 1985. "Biological Dimensions of Small, Human Founding Populations." In *Interstellar Migration and the Human Experience*, ed. Ben R Finney and Eric M. Jones, 110–119. Berkeley: University of California Press.

Casper, Monica J., and Lisa Jean Moore. 1995. "Inscribing Bodies, Inscribing the Future: Gender, Sex, and Reproduction in Outer Space." *Sociological Perspectives* 38 (2): 311–333.

Cheston, T. Stephen. 1986. "Space and Society." In *Beyond Spaceship Earth: Environmental Ethics and the Solar System*, ed. Eugene C. Hargrove, 20–44. San Francisco: Sierra Club Books.

Cockell, Charles S. 2006. *Space on Earth: Saving Our World by Seeking Others*. London: Palgrave Macmillan.

Codignola, Luca, Kai-Uwe Schrogl, Agnieszka Lukaszczyk, and Nicolas Peter. 2009. *Humans in Outer Space Interdisciplinary Odysseys*. New York: Springer.

Collins, Samuel Gerald. 2003. "Sail On! Sail On! Anthropology, Science Fiction, and the Enticing Future." *Science Fiction Studies* 30 (2): 180–198.

Collins, Samuel Gerald. 2005. "'No Anthropologist Aboard the Enterprise': Science Fiction and Anthropological Futures." *Anthropology & Education Quarterly* 36 (2): 182–188.

Cosgrove, Denis. 2003. *Apollo's Eye: A Cartographic Genealogy of the Earth in the Western Imagination*. Baltimore: Johns Hopkins University Press.

Crosby, Alfred W. 2009. "Micro-Organisms and Extraterrestrial Travel." In *Humans in Outer Space: Interdisciplinary Odysseys*, 6–13. Vienna: Springer.

Decolonizing Mars. 2019. "Decolonizing Mars." Accessed 5 June. https://www.decolonizemars.org.

DeLoughrey, Elizabeth. 2014. "Satellite Planetarity and the Ends of the Earth." *Public Culture* 26 (2): 257–280. https://doi.org/10.1215/08992363-2392057.

Denning, Kathryn. 2011a. "Being Technological." *Acta Astronautica* 68 (3): 372–380.

Denning, Kathryn. 2011b. "Is Life What We Make of It?" *Philosophical Transactions of the Royal Society A: Mathematical, Physical and Engineering Sciences* 369 (1936): 669–678.

Denning, Kathryn. 2011c. "Ten Thousand Revolutions: Conjectures about Civilizations." *Acta Astronautica* 68 (3-4): 381–388.

Denning, Kathryn. 2013. "Impossible Predictions of the Unprecedented: Analogy, History, and the Work of Prognostication." In Vakoch 2013: 301–312.

Dickens, Peter, and James S. Ormrod. 2007. *Cosmic Society: Towards a Sociology of the Universe*. London: Routledge.

Dumit, Joseph. 2005. "'Come On, People . . . We Are the Aliens. We Seem to Be Suffering from Host-Planet Rejection Syndrome': Liminal Illnesses, Structural Damnation, and Social Creativity." In Battaglia 2005: 201–218.

Edelman, Lee. 2004. *No Future: Queer Theory and the Death Drive*. Durham, NC: Duke University Press.

Erickson, Andrew S. 2014. "China's Space Development History: A Comparison of the Rocket and Satellite Sectors." *Acta Astronautica* 103: 142–67.

Fairén, Alberto G. 2019. "The Mars Anthropocene." *Eos* 100. https://doi.org/10.1029/2019EO111173.

Fuller, R. Buckminster. 1969. *Operating Manual for Spaceship Earth*. Carbondale: Southern Illinois University Press.

Gaard, Greta Claire. 2013. "Animals in (New) Space: Chimponauts, Cosmodogs, and Biosphere II." *Feminismo/s* 22: 113–145.

Genovese, Taylor R. 2017a. "The New Right Stuff: Social Imaginaries of Outer Space and the Capitalist Accumulation of the Cosmos." PhD diss., Northern Arizona University.

Genovese, Taylor R. 2017b. "Shitting in Space: Engagements with Cosmic Taboo." *Savage Minds*, 13 July. https://savageminds.org/2017/07/13/shitting-in-space-engagements-with-cosmic-taboo.

Glorfeld, Jeff. 2018. "Science History: Lynn Margulis, Contrarian to the End." *Cosmos Magazine*, 23 November. https://cosmosmagazine.com/biology/science-history-lynn-margulis-contrarian-to-the-end.

Grinspoon, David H. 2004. "The Logistics and Ethics of Colonizing the Red Planet." *Slate*, 7 January. http://www.slate.com/articles/health_and_science/science/2004/01/is_mars_ours.html.

Haqq-Misra, Jacob. 2016. "The Transformative Value of Liberating Mars." *New Space* 4 (2): 64–67.

Haraway, Donna. 1991. *Simians, Cyborgs and Women: The Reinvention of Nature*. New York: Routledge.

Haraway, Donna. 2008. *When Species Meet*. Minneapolis: University of Minnesota Press.

Haraway, Donna. 2016. *Staying with the Trouble: Making Kin in the Chthulucene*. Durham, NC: Duke University Press.

Hartmann, William K. 1986. "Space Exploration and Environmental Issues." In *Beyond Spaceship Earth: Environmental Ethics and the Solar System*, ed. Eugene C. Hargrove, 119–139. San Francisco: Sierra Club Books.

Helmreich, Stefan. 2009. *Alien Ocean: Anthropological Voyages in Microbial Seas*. Berkeley: University of California Press.

Helmreich, Stefan, Sophia Roosth, and Michele Ilana Friedner. 2016. *Sounding the Limits of Life: Essays in the Anthropology of Biology and Beyond*. Princeton, NJ: Princeton University Press.

Hird, Myra J. 2009. *The Origins of Sociable Life: Evolution after Science Studies*. New York: Palgrave Macmillan.

Hird, Myra J. 2010. "Indifferent Globality." *Theory, Culture & Society* 27 (2–3): 54–72. https://doi.org/10.1177/0263276409355998.

Hopkins, Curt. 2013. "African Space Programs Aren't Science Fiction." *OkayAfrica*, 20 May. http://www.okayafrica.com/african-space-programs-arent-science-fiction.

Hustak, Carla, and Natasha Myers. 2012. "Involutionary Momentum: Affective Ecologies and the Sciences of Plant/Insect Encounters." *Differences* 23 (3): 74–118.

Jasanoff, Sheila. 2004. "Heaven and Earth: The Politics of Environmental Images." In *Earthly Politics: Local and Global in Environmental Governance*, ed. Sheila Jasanoff and Marybeth Long Martello, 31–52. Cambridge, MA: MIT Press.

Jasanoff, Sheila, and Sang-Hyun Kim, eds. 2015. *Dreamscapes of Modernity: Sociotechnical Imaginaries and the Fabrication of Power*. Chicago: University of Chicago Press.

Jefts, Alan R., and Jerry Paz. 2019. "Spaceport America Sustainable Design and Construction in the Desert." Spaceport America, accessed 5 June. https://spaceportamerica.com/wp-content/uploads/2012/07/SPACEPORT-AMERICA-SUSTAINABLE-DESIGN-AND-CONSTRUCTION-IN-THE-DESERT_Rev-3.pdf.

Ketcham, Christopher. 2016. "Towards an Ethics of Life." *Space Policy* 38: 48–56. https://doi.org/10.1016/j.spacepol.2016.05.009.

Kramer, William R. 2011. "Colonizing Mars: An Opportunity for Reconsidering Bioethical Standards and Obligations to Future Generations." *Futures* 43 (5): 545–551. https://doi.org/10.1016/j.futures.2011.02.006.

Lazier, Benjamin. 2011. "Earthrise; Or, the Globalization of the World Picture." *American Historical Review* 116 (3): 602–630.

Lempert, William. 2014. "Decolonizing Encounters of the Third Kind: Alternative Futuring in Native Science Fiction Film." *Visual Anthropology Review* 30 (2): 164–176.

Lepselter, Susan. 1997. "From the Earth Native's Point of View: The Earth, the Extraterrestrial, and the Natural Ground of Home." *Public Culture* 9 (2): 197–208.

Llorente, Briardo, Thomas C. Williams, and Hugh D. Goold. 2018. "The Multiplanetary Future of Plant Synthetic Biology." *Genes* 9 (7). https://doi.org/10.3390/genes9070348.

Lovelock, James E., and Tyler Volk. 2003. "Gaia and Emergence; Seeing Deeper into Gaia Theory; Discussion and Reply." *Climatic Change* 57 (1–2): 1–3, 5–7.

Mann, Charles. 1991. "Lynn Margulis: Science's Unruly Earth Mother." *Science* 252 (5004): 378–382.

Margulis, Lynn, and Ricardo Guerrero. 1995. "Life as a Planetary Phenomenon: The Colonization of Mars." *Microbiologia (Madrid, Spain)* 11: 173–84.

Margulis, Lynn, and Dorion Sagan. 1995. *What Is Life?* Berkeley: University of California Press.

Margulis, Lynn, and Oona West. 1997. "Gaia and the Colonization of Mars." In *Slanted Truths: Essays on Gaia, Symbiosis, and Evolution*, ed. Lynn Margulis and Dorion Sagan, 221–234. New York: Springer.

Markley, Robert. 2005. *Dying Planet: Mars in Science and the Imagination*. Durham, NC: Duke University Press.

Mars Society. 1998. "Founding Declaration." 16 August. http://www.marssociety.org/home/about/founding-declaration.

Masco, Joseph. 2010. "Bad Weather: On Planetary Crisis." *Social Studies of Science* 40 (1): 7–40.

Masco, Joseph. 2012. "The End of Ends." *Anthropological Quarterly* 85 (4): 1107–1024. https://doi.org/10.1353/anq.2012.0061.

Mathews, Andrew S., and Jessica Barnes. 2016. "Prognosis: Visions of Environmental Futures." *Journal of the Royal Anthropological Institute* 22 (S1): 9–26.

Matthews, Chris. 2016. "Why Ghana Started a Space Program." *Motherboard*, 5 January. https://motherboard.vice.com/en_us/article/nz7bnq/why-ghana-started-a-space-program.

Mautner, Michael N. 2004. *Seeding the Universe with Life: Securing Our Cosmological Future*. Weston, FL: Legacy Books.

Mautner, Michael N. 2009. "Life-Centered Ethics, and the Human Future in Space." *Bioethics* 23 (8): 433–440. https://doi.org/10.1111/j.1467-8519.2008.00688.x.

Mautner, Michael N. 2014. "Astroecology, Cosmo-Ecology, and the Future of Life." *Acta Societatis Botanicorum Poloniae* 83 (4): 449–464. https://doi.org/10.5586/asbp.2014.036.

McCurdy, Howard E. 2011. *Space and the American Imagination*. Baltimore: Johns Hopkins University Press.

McKay, Christopher P. 2009. "Biologically Reversible Exploration." *Science* 323 (5915): 718. https://doi.org/10.1126/science.1167987.

Messeri, Lisa. 2016. *Placing Outer Space: An Earthly Ethnography of Other Worlds.* Durham, NC: Duke University Press.

Messeri, Lisa. 2017a. "Gestures of Cosmic Relation and the Search for Another Earth." *Environmental Humanities* 9 (2): 325–40.

Messeri, Lisa. 2017b. "Resonant Worlds: Cultivating Proximal Encounters in Planetary Science." *American Ethnologist* 44 (1): 131–42.

Mitchell, Sean T. 2017. *Constellations of Inequality: Space, Race, and Utopia in Brazil.* Chicago: University of Chicago Press.

Musk, Elon. 2018. "Making Life Multi-planetary." *New Space* 6 (1): 2–11. https://doi.org/10.1089/space.2018.29013.emu.

Naylor, Emerald. 2017. "Mauna Kea: Construction Site or Sacred Land? A Look at the Long-Lasting Effects of the Hawaiian Annexation." *Waterloo Historical Review* 9. http://dx.doi.org/10.15353/whr.v9.147.

Nixon, Rob. 2011. *Slow Violence and the Environmentalism of the Poor.* Cambridge, MA: Harvard University Press.

Nixon, Ron, and Mitchell Ferman. 2018. "SpaceX May Be New Barrier for Trump's Border Wall." *New York Times*, 12 December. https://www.nytimes.com/2018/12/12/us/politics/trump-texas-border-wall-.html.

Odum, Howard T. 1971. *Environment, Power and Society.* Malden, MA: Wiley-Interscience.

Olson, Valerie A. 2010. "The Ecobiopolitics of Space Biomedicine." *Medical Anthropology* 29 (2): 170–193. https://doi.org/10.1080/01459741003715409.

Olson, Valerie A. 2018. *Into the Extreme: U.S. Environmental Systems and Politics beyond Earth.* Minneapolis: University of Minnesota Press.

Oman-Reagan, Michael P. 2015. "The Social Lives of Plants, in Space." *Astrosociological Insights* 4 (2): 4–8.

O'Reilly, Jessica. 2017. *The Technocratic Antarctic: An Ethnography of Scientific Expertise and Environmental Governance.* Ithaca, NY: Cornell University Press.

Pontin, Jason. 2018. "The Genetics (and Ethics) of Making Humans Fit for Mars." *Wired*, 7 August. https://www.wired.com/story/ideas-jason-pontin-genetic-engineering-for-mars.

Pope, Nick. 2018. "Elon Musk and SpaceX Want to Send You to the Moon on a 'Big F**king Rocket.'" *Esquire*, 14 September. https://www.esquire.com/uk/latest-news/a23125518/elon-musk-and-spacex-want-to-send-you-to-the-moon-on-a-big-fking-rocket.

Povinelli, Elizabeth A. 2016. *Geontologies: A Requiem to Late Liberalism.* Durham, NC: Duke University Press.

Praet, Istvan, and Juan Francisco Salazar. 2017. "Introduction: Familiarizing the Extraterrestrial—Making Our Planet Alien." *Environmental Humanities* 9 (2): 309–324. https://doi.org/10.1215/22011919-4215315.

Redfield, Peter. 2000. *Space in the Tropics: From Convicts to Rockets in French Guiana.* Berkeley: University of California Press.

Redfield, Peter. 2002. "The Half-Life of Empire in Outer Space." *Social Studies of Science* 32 (5–6): 791–825.

Rosa, Jonathan, and Yarimar Bonilla. 2017. "Deprovincializing Trump, Decolonizing Diversity, and Unsettling Anthropology." *American Ethnologist* 44 (2): 201–208. https://doi.org/10.1111/amet.12468.

Ross, Martin, Darin Toohey, Manfred Peinemann, and Patrick Ross. 2009. "Limits on the Space Launch Market Related to Stratospheric Ozone Depletion." *Astropolitics* 7 (1): 50–82. https://doi.org/10.1080/14777620902768867.

Rusert, Britt M. 2010. "Black Nature: The Question of Race in the Age of Ecology." *Polygraph: An International Journal of Culture & Politics* 22: 149–166.

Sagan, Carl. 1994. *Pale Blue Dot: A Vision of the Human Future in Space.* New York: Random House.

Sagan, Dorion, and Lynn Margulis. 1997. "Gaia and the Colonization of Mars." In *Slanted Truths: Essays on Gaia, Symbiosis, and Evolution*, ed. Lynn Margulis and Dorion Sagan, 235–246. New York: Springer.

Salazar, Juan Francisco. 2017. "Microbial Geographies at the Extremes of Life." *Environmental Humanities* 9 (2): 398–417. https://doi.org/10.1215/22011919-4215361.

Showstack, Randy. 2017. "Scientists, Policy Makers Push for Mars Exploration." *EOS* 98. https://doi.org/10.1029/2017EO074107.

Siefert, Janet L. 2012. "Man and His Spaceships." *Mobile Genetic Elements* 2 (6): 272–278. https://doi.org/10.4161/mge.23238.

Smith, Cameron McPherson, and Evan Tyler Suliëman Davies. 2012. *Emigrating beyond Earth: Human Adaptation and Space Colonization*. New York: Springer.

Spaceport America. 2019. "About Us > Sustainability." Accessed 5 June. https://spaceportamerica.com.

Swanson, Heather Anne, Nils Bubandt, and Anna Tsing. 2015. "Less Than One But More Than Many: Anthropocene as Science Fiction and Scholarship-in-the-Making." *Environment and Society: Advances in Research* 6: 149–166. https://doi.org/10.3167/ares.2015.060109.

Teresi, Dick. 2011. "Discover Interview: Lynn Margulis Says She's Not Controversial, She's Right." *Discover*.

Tsing, Anna Lowenhaupt. 2003. "Natural Resources and Capitalist Frontiers." *Economic and Political Weekly* 29 (48): 5100–5106.

Vakoch, Douglas A, ed. 2013. *Astrobiology, History, and Society: Life beyond Earth and the Impact of Discovery*. New York: Springer.

Valentine, David. 2012. "Exit Strategy: Profit, Cosmology, and the Future of Humans in Space." *Anthropological Quarterly* 85 (4): 1045–1067. https://doi.org/10.1353/anq.2012.0073.

Valentine, David. 2016. "Atmosphere: Context, Detachment, and the View from above Earth." *American Ethnologist* 43 (3): 511–24.

Valentine, David. 2017. "Gravity Fixes: Habituating to the Human on Mars and Island Three." *HAU: Journal of Ethnographic Theory* 7 (3): 185–209. https://doi.org/10.14318/hau7.3.012.

Valentine, David, Valerie A. Olson, and Debbora Battaglia. 2012. "Extreme: Limits and Horizons in the Once and Future Cosmos." *Anthropological Quarterly* 85 (4): 1007–1026. https://doi.org/10.1353/anq.2012.0066.

White, Frank. 1987. *The Overview Effect: Space Exploration and Human Evolution*. Boston: Houghton Mifflin.

Whyte, Kyle Powys. 2017. "Indigenous Climate Change Studies: Indigenizing Futures, Decolonizing the Anthropocene." *English Language Notes* 55 (1–2): 153–162.

Wright, Jason T., and Michael P. Oman-Reagan. 2017. "Visions of Human Futures in Space and SETI." *International Journal of Astrobiology* 17 (2): 177–188. https://doi.org/10.1017/S1473550417000222.

Young, M. Jane. 1987. "'Pity the Indians of Outer Space': Native American Views of the Space Program." *Western Folklore* 46 (4): 269–279.

Zubrin, Robert. 2002. *Entering Space: Creating a Spacefaring Civilization*. New York: Jeremy P. Tarcher.

Zubrin, Robert. 2012. *The Case for Mars*. New York: Simon & Schuster.

Zubrin, Robert. 2019. *The Case for Space: How the Revolution in Spaceflight Opens Up a Future of Limitless Possibility*. New York: Prometheus Books.

Index

CPSIA information can be obtained
at www.ICGtesting.com
Printed in the USA
JSHW030820070821
17659JS00006B/63